AF355497

Positive Impact

Positive Impact

The Purpose Launchpad mindset and the framework
to improve your startup, your organization,
and the world

FRANCISCO PALAO

bubok
EDITORIAL

*For my sources of infinite love: my daughters,
Mar and Luna, and my wife, Andrea,
the star that lights my way*

Index

Foreword

Humans are a fascinating species. Always pursuing new achievements.

Exploring.

Innovating.

Evolving . . .

According to the latest data, *Homo sapiens* appeared on Earth about 300,000 years ago. We were nomads at first, wandering from here to there as we hunted, fished, and gathered everything we needed to survive. We improved our mastery of hunting and fishing techniques and were consequently able to survive for thousands and thousands of years throughout what we call the Paleolithic Age.

But it was not enough. About 10,000 years ago, our eagerness to innovate and improve led us to become farmers and raise livestock. With the discovery of new skills and techniques, we were able to settle down and produce our own food and ensure our sustenance, laying down the foundations of our current civilization. Thus began a period we know as the Neolithic Age.

That was not the end of it. Improving our quality of life and safety as a species made us refuse to conform. Soon we acquired new knowledge about working with metals like copper, bronze, and iron, which allowed us to leap forward as a civilization. We developed new tools and continued to learn about the universe, about life, and about ourselves.

In recent centuries, evolution has been spectacular. Discoveries and advances in medicine have enabled us to double our average life expectancy from approximately thirty-five years in the Middle Ages to over seventy years today. We discovered that the Earth is round and that we live on a planet within a solar system in a galaxy we named the Milky Way. We invented the combustion engine, which led to the Industrial Revolution and radically changed the way we travel and move goods from one place to another. We discovered electricity and learned to control it to produce energy, light, and heat and provide our homes with endless possibilities. We created systems for exchanging value, inventing the concept of money and creating a space for economies, markets, and businesses and a long "et cetera" that could fill the entire book. Humans, with our continuous purpose of improving our own existence, have the amazing ability to imagine something that does not yet exist and make it happen.

Information and communication technologies, especially the Internet, have now provided us with new ways of living and interacting with the world. They have also brought about a new paradigm in the business world with the emergence of start-ups and the era of digital innovation. During the last few years, we have seen a new generation of innovative companies with a strong tech component emerge, completely disrupting the status quo and leading to the disappearance of entire industries and large organizations.

This new environment has given rise to new techniques for business management and the development of innovative products and services. Until recently, when a company wanted to develop a new product, they drew up a detailed plan and put it to work. Known as the waterfall model, this works when we know the problem we want to solve and are clear about the right solution. But, in a changing context full of uncertainty, fixed plans no longer make sense. Customers' needs and solutions that the market demands are constantly changing, requiring us to implement techniques that allow for continuous adjustments.

This need for new approaches to product and service development led to the birth of "agile" techniques supported by the *Agility Manifesto* and solidified by frameworks such as Scrum. Nevertheless, focusing exclusively on agile product development turned out not to be enough. In constantly changing, highly uncertain environments, it seemed more logical to first discover who the customers really are and who they are not—that is, to focus on the problem rather than on developing the solution. An initial approach to this came from Steve Blank, who created a new methodology called Customer Development, which makes it possible to develop the customer before the product and create a solution to a real market problem.

A few years later, Eric Ries strengthened the use of agile principles and customer development by creating Lean Startup, one of the most widespread methodologies in the world of entrepreneurship and innovation, which teaches us to implement a continuous cycle, gathering customer input to improve our product using three simple but powerful steps: build, measure, and learn.

Business models were forced to adapt to this new situation. To facilitate that adaptation, Alex Osterwalder developed the Business Model Canvas, a simple tool that lets us easily define and communicate business models. Subsequently, many new canvases were designed for different tasks using the same approach. Salim Ismail then described the exponential organizations concept, a new phenomenon centered on organizations with a business model that lets them grow exponentially by connecting with abundance and managing it.

I feel profound admiration for humanity and for those who have brought us here. I feel a special gratitude toward the entrepreneurs and innovators who did not limit themselves to developing a project but dedicated much of their lives and energy to sharing their knowledge so that others could leverage it and avoid the mistakes they had made. Some of them, like those I have mentioned—Steve Blank, Eric Ries, Alex Osterwalder, and Salim Ismail—shared a series of techniques based on their experience and knowledge so that we could take our ventures to the next level. However, as throughout human history, new scenarios force us to develop new techniques and new ways of interacting with the world. This book and the framework I describe, Purpose Launchpad, are part of this evolution and the beginning of a new era of Positive Impact.

I am absolutely convinced that the time has come to start acting as a species and not as individuals, taking our purpose beyond improving our own existence and focusing on improving the world we live in. Today, we face significant economic, social, and environmental challenges that are generating unprecedented global awareness. More than ever before in our history, we need to respond to global problems. It is imperative that we act.

It is no longer enough to innovate and generate new products and services that create value for our customers; it is now necessary to create innovations that improve the world. It is no longer enough to be sustainable; it is now necessary to regenerate the resources we have consumed and the assets we have eliminated.

We are moving from the innovation and sustainability era to the era of Positive Impact.

In March 2022, a group of more than 100 impact-oriented innovators, entrepreneurs, activists, and investors from across the globe gathered to create the *Purpose Manifesto* (which you will find at the end of the book), sending a crucial message out to the world: It is no longer enough to do things the right way (as the *Agile Manifesto* announced to us all 20 years ago); it is also necessary to do the right things. The good news is that we can do this. We can do the right things correctly, generating value for our projects and for the world.

Innovation techniques like agile, Customer Development, Lean Startup, or exponential organizations (among many others) continue to be completely valid; just as in many environments, waterfall models are still the right choice. However, we needed to integrate all these innovation techniques and create something that went a step further. Purpose Launchpad was born from that need—a new, completely open framework that combines innovation methodologies, integrating and sorting them so that entrepreneurs and organizations can create a positive impact on the world and on their own projects.

Purpose Launchpad's main contributions, which I will describe in detail in the book, are as follows:

1. **Integrating innovation methodologies to activate our purpose and turn it into positive impact.** The global challenges facing humanity, many of which we have caused ourselves, demand immediate action. Many of these challenges represent enormous business opportunities that must be implemented using innovation techniques to minimize risk. However, it is not enough to do things the right way; we must also do the right things. It is time to move from the innovation era to the impact era. Purpose Launchpad brings us the best of existing innovation techniques, integrating and sorting them to activate our purpose and turn it into positive impact on the world and on our projects.

2. **An approach based on eight axes: Purpose, People, Customers, Sustainability, Abundance, Processes, Product, and Metrics.** Every innovative project is a set of hypotheses that must be evaluated. These hypotheses refer not only to the customer and the product, as many

of the existing innovation methods indicate, but also to every aspect of the endeavor. Purpose Launchpad introduces eight axes addressed in an agile manner and in parallel to develop our projects comprehensively. It also integrates the various innovation techniques and methodologies into each axis, including (among others) Customer Development for the Customer axis, Lean Startup for the Product and Customer axes, exponential organizations for the Abundance axis, and so on. In addition, any other tool or methodology linked to innovation or impact can be incorporated into Purpose Launchpad's open, common framework.

3. **Three action modes for each project's three phases: Exploration, Evaluation, and Impact.** In an innovative initiative's early stages of development, we cannot know what we do not know, so, rather than focusing on evaluating hypotheses, we'll have to discover new ones. And, when we find a market opportunity, it must be validated with the first customers (and with actual sales) before the product is developed and sent to the mass market. Purpose Launchpad helps us adapt how we act and think in each of the three basic phases: Exploration, Evaluation, and Impact.

4. **A regenerative growth model.** Exponential growth is not sustainable, and our planet is warning us of this. Similarly, no industry can support continued exponential growth, for the very size of the market has a limit. It is possible, however, to have unlimited growth by generating a massive positive impact around a purpose. Purpose Launchpad shows us how pioneering organizations are moving from single-industry models to purpose-based ecosystems. This generates a wealth of opportunities that enable unlimited growth sustainably while creating a positive impact.

5. **A framework for both startups and established organizations.** Established organizations and businesses are focused on operating to maximize their bottom line. Startups, on the other hand, are focused on exploring new markets and business models. Purpose Launchpad makes it easy for both to interact within a common framework, leveraging the best of each world and maximizing their synergies.

6. **A new mindset.** The key to success does not lie exclusively in using the latest technology or even in implementing the right innovation methodologies. The key to launching successful initiatives and evolving organizations towards new models is a new mindset. Purpose Launchpad incorporates a series of principles and elements specially designed to help people evolve the way they think and see the world while they implement it. It is not merely a new framework but a new mindset as well.

As a species, humans are guided by their curiosity. We are explorers searching for new knowledge and new techniques to improve our lives and the world around us. We cannot remain anchored in the techniques and tools of the past but must integrate them and take them a step further, developing new models that are more suitable for the environment we inhabit. Thus, I invite you to do just that: go one step further.

Welcome to the era of Positive Impact!

FRANCISCO PALAO
Granada, June 24, 2022

Introduction

I will never forget that Sunday afternoon when I received a very special message from someone in Mexico: "Thank you so much for creating this website! Thanks to you I met the woman who is now my wife. We just married and are very happy. You've changed our lives!" It was 2002. I was 20 years old and had never been to Mexico, but I was generating a positive impact on the people living there through BuscarAmigos.com, the web platform my friends Rafa, Raul, and I had created the year before. Rafa was a very talented graphic artist who loved technology, which led him to quickly learn to use different digital graphic design applications, and he created the graphics and the interface. Raul and I were studying computer engineering, and, as the university was not teaching webpage design at that time (it was too "new"), we decided to learn about web development on our own by searching for information on the Internet, a source that was starting to offer abundant resources. We did it all without any previous skills—and, of course, without any experience—but we had the most important element: the right mindset. We knew we could create something new by leveraging the possibilities offered by technology, especially the Internet, and felt we literally held the power in our own hands. So, while most of our friends and peers focused on other activities, we developed the platform in our free time. We worked from each of our bedrooms in our parents' homes, our parents unaware that, from their homes, their sons were changing the lives of thousands of people.

Three years later, when the platform already had thousands of users around the world, we sold it to a larger company, receiving the offer at a time when we didn't have enough funds to continue. Plus, we were quite busy studying our respective college courses. None of us thought of looking for funding for the project; it wasn't something in our mental frameworks, as, among other reasons, nobody had ever spoken to us about that possibility. At the time, in 2002, there was barely any entrepreneurial culture in Spain, and the word startup, so widely used around the world today, was practically unknown. Therefore, when we got the offer, we simply thought it was a good option to make a little money and move on to the next chapter of our lives.

If I could go back, I would probably not have sold Buscar-Amigos.com, because the growth and positive impact margins were still huge; the Internet was starting to take off just at that time. Nevertheless, I learned from that experience that we all currently have the possibility of accessing knowledge and technologies that allow us to change the world and our lives. So, after finishing college and obtaining a doctorate in artificial intelligence, I focused on launching new projects. Some were very successful, like Nativoo, a smart system for customizing tourist visits, later acquired by the Brazilian company SBTUR, or like LeanMonitor, a platform to help entrepreneurs and organizations implement Lean Startup methodologies, eventually bought by Gust.com.

Besides my activity as an entrepreneur, I've had the opportunity to collaborate with companies around the world regarding innovation and disruption, helping them shift towards new, more scalable models with greater impact. I am currently dedicated to promoting a global community called Purpose Alliance, focused on empowering extraordinary people and organizations to create a better world.

This entire experience has led me to develop the Purpose Launchpad framework, which is the basis for this book and is something I would certainly have loved to have when I started out in entrepreneurship twenty years ago. Since then, technology's potential for creating a positive impact in the world has multiplied. The amount of knowledge we can find on the internet has grown exponentially, as has the number of technologies we can access to create new things or improve existing ones, regardless of where we live, our age, and even our education. That said, neither technology nor innovation methodologies are as important as your mindset. I'd like this idea to be clear from the start, and I will continue to insist on the concept throughout the book.

What will you find here? I'll summarize it so you can optimize your reading time.

The book's first part ("You Change the World") focuses on what I consider the most important starting point: you and your purpose. We all have superpowers for changing the world in a positive way, but we must be aware of them and have the will to do so. I'd like to begin by helping you find (or refine) your purpose and learn about the elements that will boost your projects, evolve your startup, or transform your organization while you create a positive impact on the world in alignment with your essence.

In the second part, I will introduce you to the Purpose Launchpad mindset and framework, which I've developed based on my own experience and that of numerous organizations (which I will also talk about). The goal is to help entrepreneurs and organizations properly develop their projects while creating a positive impact on the world. Here I'll talk about some of the core principles of the Purpose Launchpad that will be applied further on. You might find this part of the book somewhat more conceptual, but it is important for you to learn the foundation of the Purpose Launchpad to get the maximum leverage from it.

In the third part, I'll talk about how to properly evolve a startup or a new product to reduce risk and maximize its positive impact, both for your own project and for the world. You'll learn how to apply the eight axes of Purpose Launchpad (Purpose, People, Customer, Sustainability, Abundance, Processes, Product, and Metrics) to a startup throughout the three phases of the framework: Exploration, Evaluation, and Impact. If you are an entrepreneur, intrapreneur, or launching a new product, you can't miss this part. This content will also interest you if you work for an established organization or company, since companies increasingly need to launch their own startups or innovative products as part of their transformation strategy.

I'll address precisely the more important challenges traditional organizations face upon transforming and evolving in the fourth part of the book. Whenever we try to innovate in an established organization, the "internal immune system" goes on the attack. The main challenge is changing the mindset. We'll analyze the most effective ways to evolve established businesses while creating a positive impact in the world. In fact, we'll see that the best path for evolving an organization and maximizing its outcomes is not directly and exclusively seeking its own benefit but rather by generating a positive change in the world.

Keep reading to discover all these subjects in detail and incorporate them gradually using the activities I propose. My value proposition is simple and clear: as you absorb and apply the Purpose Launchpad mindset and framework, you will be able to develop startups and new products and maximize their chances of success, as well as transform established businesses so that they remain relevant in a changing environment—and all this while positively impacting the world. Will you come with me?

Part One

You Change the World

1
Evolution

It all started with a single point of energy. It all began with the Big Bang.

Look around you for a moment and realize that everything you see is the product of that primordial explosion, which occurred about 14 billion years ago. Since then, the universe has never stopped expanding. We don't know if there is any meaning to existence; all we know is that the universe evolves constantly and relentlessly.

The Big Bang transformed energy into matter, resulting in hydrogen atoms composed of a proton, an electron, and a neutron. These atoms gradually clustered into cosmic clouds that attracted more and more hydrogen due to gravity, and that gave rise to the first stars.

The changes didn't stop there. In the nucleus of those starts, the hydrogen atoms began to come together, giving rise to new, more complex atoms with more properties. For example, they created the iron atom, composed of twenty-six protons, twenty-eight neutrons, and twenty-six electrons, thus originating a metal with new properties, since iron, unlike hydrogen, is malleable, tough, and magnetic. We have called this phenomenon "emergence," meaning that the elements resulting from the sum of simpler elements not only exhibit greater atomic and structural complexity but also new properties. In other words, the result is greater than the sum of its parts.

Let's continue with the evolution of the universe. Molecules emerged from the different atoms, including the one for water, which was created by joining two hydrogen atoms with one of oxygen. Continuing with the phenomenon of emergence, having greater atomic complexity, water offered new properties and was fundamental to life. Consequently, at some point about 3.5 billion years ago, the first unicellular organisms were generated on Earth, some with properties as incredible as the ability to reproduce. It seems normal to us today, but, if you think about it for a moment, it is surprising that, at one given moment, the universe evolved so that some of its elements were able to reproduce themselves.

As part of the universe, life continued to evolve and gave rise to multicellular beings: bacteria, fungi, plants, animals ... These beings were increasingly complex and had increasing capabilities, including humans, whose brains are the most complex atomic and molecular structure known in the entire universe. It has astonishing properties, some of which we don't even fully understand, such as consciousness, which allows us to perceive our own existence, unlike hydrogen, iron, single-celled beings, or plants.

Consciousness is precisely what now allows you and me to stop and think about all of this and understand that we are part of the universe. We not only see it when we look up at the stars but also when we look in the mirror, because we are each of us a tiny piece of the universe. Each of our atoms has been created in the core of a star or in the explosion that happens when a star dies. We are, as they say, "stardust."

The universe, at least as far as we know, continues to evolve and will continue to do so forever. And, as part of it, humans will too. In addition to consciousness, we can imagine things that do not exist—and, best of all, create them! We can create art; we can create technology; we can create whatever is needed to fill the space between reality and our desires. If we want to run faster, we create shoes for our feet. If we want to fly, we create airplanes and other devices in order to travel through the air. We constantly create things that did not exist before, and, in doing so, we continue to push the boundaries of what is known and of the universe itself.

We are all here to create something that did not exist before we were born. We are all cosmic elements and, as such, actors in the evolution of the universe. We are all here to change the world, and we do it with our actions every day.

Key Points

- The universe has not stopped evolving since the primordial Big Bang.
- Humans have consciousness and the ability to imagine things that do not exist and to create them.
- As part of the universe, we are also active agents of change.

Activity

As I mentioned at the beginning of this book, I'm going to suggest a series of activities so you can put the different key concepts from each chapter into practice. Here's the first one!

Think of something you have done or created—anything—that contributed to the world being different. It could be a project of great scope, like a book or a new company, but it could also be something simpler, like a poem you've written for someone or a positive action you had towards someone. Describe it briefly below:

....
....
....
....
....
....

This exercise will help you understand two things:

- That you have changed the world on numerous occasions.
- That you constantly change the world with your actions.

2
Discover Your Purpose

When I was little, someone told me, "If you have health, money, and love, you'll be happy." Over time, I have discovered that, despite being very popular, this belief is not true. I have been able to verify that there are people who enjoy good health, have enough money to live on, and people close to them who love them, and yet they do not feel fulfilled. They spend a lot of time doing all sorts of activities, but they do them because, in their own words, "it's what there is," "it's my job," or "it provides me an income."

They appear to have it all, but they feel empty inside; they feel that their lives have no meaning. And meaning is precisely what their lives lack.

We all need for what we do to have a purpose, to have sense. As the Roman philosopher Seneca said, "If a man knows not to which port he sails, no wind is favorable." Purpose is the North Star that helps us stay the course, even in times of vital storms. It is the fourth leg that the popular recipe is missing: health, money, love, and … purpose.

I recall the day I wrote my purpose down on paper. I felt I had something inside me and needed to express it, to take it out and let it do its job. I sat at my desk, pen in hand, and began writing. I connected with it very quickly and wrote it down succinctly: "To help humanity evolve." Everything fell into place: I understood the type of projects I wanted to dedicate my life to, which kind of people I wanted to share them with, and how I could help make a better world. Since then, everything I've done has been focused in that direction.

It was also clear to me from the beginning that I wanted to do it through technology. A while back, I had spoken with Eudald Carbonell, co-director of the archeological dig at Atapuerca (Burgos, Spain), a conversation that had a profound effect on me. He explained to me that, were it not for technology's contribution to social advancement, humans would not live beyond an average age of thirty-five. I perfectly remember what he said: "Technology is what makes human beings evolve." At that moment, I felt that I wanted to be a part of that, to contribute to the advancement of humanity as others had done before.

This book is a fundamental part of my purpose, for my desire is that it inspire many people to create projects that have a positive impact on the world. Nothing would make me happier than to encourage you to think differently, to evolve your mindset, thus contributing to the evolution of humanity. So, the first thing I want to do is to help you discover, remember, or redefine your purpose—or at least get you a little closer to it. To do that, I will share below a simple and very effective method consisting of three steps: connect with your essence, express your purpose with words, and share it with others.

Step 1: Connect with Your Essence

It is not easy to connect with our true essence, as it is often hidden under many layers of culture and education. To find your purpose, it is imperative that you delve into your true essence. To do this, I propose that you ask yourself three questions, one about the past, one about the present, and one about the future (do not answer them yet; you will do so at the end of the chapter):

- *Past*: When you were a child, what did you want to be when you grew up? Connect with your inner child and try to remember not only what you wanted to be but why. In my case, I remember it perfectly: I wanted to be an inventor, an athlete, and a hermit.
- *Present*: We lose track of time while doing certain activities. Which ones are they for you? You can find a very important clue there for identifying your purpose. In my case, I love reading about science, psychology, philosophy, and astronomy. I love learning more and more about the universe in general and about humanity's role in it.
- *Future*: What would you dedicate your life to if you won 100 million euros or dollars through the lottery? The first thing you will probably think of is traveling to places you've never been to or buying things that you can't afford now, but try to take it further and imagine what you would do after that to make sense of your minutes, hours, and days. In my case, if I had unlimited resources, I would

probably still be doing the same thing I do today. If this is your answer, you are surely already very close to your purpose and only need to express or remember it to give more strength and direction to everything you do.

The combination of these three answers will help you connect with your essence and purpose. This is the first step: to identify it and feel it. Answering these questions and reflecting on them is often a very emotional process. You may feel frustration, sadness, joy, anger ... Whatever it is, it's okay. Feel it and then find the way to align yourself with your purpose—or, if you already have it, to strengthen it.

Step 2: Express Your Purpose with Words

Writing down your purpose will help you remember it and share it. To do so effectively, I recommend you follow this guideline:

- Make sure it describes the impact you want to achieve, the vision you'd like to turn into reality—for example, "access to quality education for everyone" or "eradicate poverty from the world." It could also have a more local scope of action—for example, "making my city safer."
- The second rule is that the change must be a positive one—that is, it must contribute to improving society and the world in general. The examples above are valid in that sense, since they each would improve the world we know today.
- Lastly, the wording must be inspiring. It should inspire you first and then others. It should be like a mantra we can remember whenever needed, especially when we lose our way or things get complicated. It will not only help to remind us where we're going but will also fill us with energy.

By the way, do not do this yet; wait for the exercise that you will find at the end of the chapter.

Step 3: Share Your Purpose

The third and final step is to share your purpose with others. I initially recommend sharing it with people who know you well and who you trust enough to share something so intimate. This will help you validate your essence, since those who really know you will be able to tell you if those magic words are part of you or not. Stay away from purposes with a merely commercial focus and go to the essence of who you really are. Once you have shared your purpose with people close to you (and possibly fine-tuned it based on their feedback), you will have to continue sharing it with others you might not necessarily know but who may have an affinity to it. This will help you continue validating it and connect with people who may eventually become your partners in a future project or customers of a potential company focused on your purpose.

In short, it's about finding a phrase connected to your essence that, as I pointed out earlier, inspires you and others to have a positive impact on the world—a simple phrase that, together with health, money, and love, will lead you to a full life.

Key Points

- To lead a full life, it's not enough to have health, money, and love. We also need a purpose.
- To discover your purpose, you can follow a simple three-step method:
  - Connect with your essence.
  - Express your purpose with words.
  - Share your purpose.
- Defining your purpose will help you find like-minded people with whom to share experiences and even projects.

Activity

Now, connect with your essence and answer these three questions:

- When you were a child, what did you want to be when you grew up?
- We lose track of time while doing certain activities. Which ones are they for you?
- What would you do if you won 100 million euros or dollars through the lottery?

Try to express your purpose with words to describe the positive change you would like to make in the world. Make sure they're inspiring.

....

....

....

....

....

....

If you have achieved it, remember to share it to evaluate and continue to improve it, both with people who know you well and whom you trust and with people aligned with your purpose.

If, for any reason, you feel that you haven't figured out your purpose or can't express it, that's okay. Below is a link to an open program that proposes a series of much more complete exercises and to *"Massive Transformative Purpose,"* a book I wrote a few years ago. I hope you find these resources helpful. The important thing is that you reflect on these things, because, in doing so, you will discover very relevant information about yourself that will give more meaning to your actions.

Resources

- "Discover your Personal Purpose" Open Program: *www.purposealliance.org/academy/personal-purpose-discovery-open-program*
- "Massive Transformative Purpose" book: *www.purposealliance.org/books/massive-transformative-purpose*

3
You Are Your First Company

I don't know what your current work situation is; maybe you are self-employed, a freelancer, or run your own business, or maybe you are an employee, part of a private organization, or in public service. It's also possible that, for whatever reason, you are not working right now, or perhaps you're studying. Whichever your current situation, the truth is that you are an entrepreneur. That's right. You are the entrepreneur of your own life.

Just like a company has income and expenses, in order to live, every person needs resources obtained sustainably. Just like a company must have a strategic plan, everyone must plan their lives to some extent. And, even in the same way that a company has a team of people and external collaborators, we all need other people to carry out our lives.

We usually spend our time working for the organization that employs us or for our own company, and we forget to think about our personal plans. I don't mean plans for the weekend or for your next vacation; I mean the vital plans for the short, medium, and long term. It's something that companies do. They have strategic plans, annual plans, marketing plans, and all other sorts of documents that help them sort out their ideas and communicate their goals to the team and to potential customers and investors. But people don't usually do this.

What about you? Do you have any kind of document to visualize and plan your life? Do you at least have clear ideas in your head to neatly communicate your life plans for the short, medium, and long term? If the answer is yes, great—reading this chapter can help you continue developing them. If the answer is no, that's OK. I will explain how below and give you some guidelines so that your personal plan is consistent with your purpose.

You have surely already taken the first step of defining your purpose or at least reflecting on it. It all starts there. This is your reason for being and what will shed light on the rest of the elements that we will define below. The first of these is vision, which consists of visualizing how you would like to see yourself in the long term. It is one of the strategic components also used by companies, and I will define it on an individual level.

Formally speaking, your vision is a phrase that describes how you would like to see yourself in the future using your purpose as the starting point. As we saw, our purpose is focused on positively impacting the world. If, for example, my starting point is "eradicating poverty from the world," my vision could be "to become a world leader in the fight against poverty" or "to live a life in which my contribution helps create a world without poverty."

The next step is to define your mission, which will describe the path you will travel to achieve your vision. If I take as a starting point the vision "to become a world leader in the fight against poverty," I could define my mission as "to promote high-impact projects to eradicate poverty worldwide, as well as to share my experience through conferences and books to inspire others and encourage them to join this cause." Your mission is a first step in grounding your purpose and vision, which are more abstract, and in beginning to express them more tangibly.

Phases

Dreaming and writing good intentions on paper is relatively easy, but making them a reality is often tricky. Therefore, just as companies do, we must consider a strategy with different phases.

You may not have the right job, the financial resources, or life circumstances at this time to pursue your purpose and try to fulfill your vision. Nothing, however, prevents you from thinking about the steps that will lead you to it. For example, if you currently work for an organization that has no link to your purpose or vision, you can think about maintaining this situation for a time while creating the circumstances that will allow you to change jobs. Or you can even keep the job and work towards your vision in your free time. It's important not to be maximalist—that is, remember that you do not necessarily have to dedicate your entire life to your purpose. The important thing is to keep it in mind and dedicate some time and energy to making your life full.

My advice is to dream big and start small—or, as my wife Andrea always says, "dream, but keep your feet on the ground." Let's take, for example, the mission suggested above: "to promote high-impact projects." Let's imagine that I currently have an administrative government job. I could design a plan with three strategic phases:

1. Stay at my job in order to continue having the income I need to survive while connecting with people and communities related to my purpose, volunteering in my free time, and, if necessary, taking courses and training in the subject.
2. Take the leap to a paid position within an organization aligned with my purpose, taking advantage of the fact that I already have some experience in the subject.
3. Lastly, start launching my own initiatives and generate and share content on the subject that might inspire others, both individuals and organizations, to contribute to the purpose, thus achieving a world without poverty.

Circumstances change, so you must adapt your plans to those changes, just like companies do. This requires frequent review, sharing them with others, and staying open to objections and warnings.

In the end, of course, the decisions are yours to make, and you decide the degree of risk you want to assume. I remember that, when I was twenty-four, I decided to leave my position as a researcher and teacher at the university, where I had a promising career ahead of me. Although having a permanent position in a public institution seemed a perfectly respectable option to me, it was not aligned with the vision I had of myself in the future. I wanted to launch my own startup, something consistent with my vision. I shared this decision with my parents, who were not very amused at the time (although they always supported me in all my decisions). It's not that they didn't want me to be happy, but they believed college gave me emotional and financial stability, whereas there was risk involved in starting a company. Over time, they have seen that undertaking projects aligned with my essence, although not an easy path, is what really makes me happy, but they were originally quite influenced by all the "if you have health, money, and love, you will be happy." Therefore, my advice is to share your plans (purpose, vision, mission, and strategic phases) not only with people close to you (family, partner, friends) but also with people related to your purpose, as they can be not only more objective but can also actively help you carry out your plans.

Likewise, before taking a step that commits you fully, it is important to validate that it is the right step by running small tests. For example, before you quit your job to look for one that is more aligned with your purpose, you can volunteer doing something similar. There are always options to try a path before jumping right into it. In my case, before launching my first startup and while I was still in college, I shared the idea of the new project with different people, which resulted in finding two clients before taking the leap. Nothing was easy, but at least I had some initial income. I had a dream but kept my feet on the ground.

It's not imperative to create your own company to drive your purpose. You can also work for an organization aligned with your purpose or achieve it through individual actions (we'll see how to activate your purpose and your projects under different circumstances or contexts later in the book). The important thing is to act and not get stuck with the words. It's the only way you will have a real impact and live a meaningful life. The plans put into action are the ones that really make things happen and move the world. That is precisely why you must plan and manage your life as if it were a company. You are your own company, and it's up to you to have a positive impact that improves the world and your life.

Key Points

- As the entrepreneur of your own life, you need a strategic plan.
- To define it, you must be clear about your vision (how you would like to see yourself in the long-term future) and your mission (the path you will take to fulfill your vision.)
- That path or strategy should consist of several phases. Dream big and start little by little.

Activity

Keeping your purpose in mind, define the following elements:

- Vision (the image of yourself that you'd like to see in the future):

....

....

....

- Mission (how to make this vision a reality):

....

....

....

- Strategic phases (the steps you'll take in the upcoming years to achieve your vision by way of your mission; if it's difficult to lay out a plan with several steps, define at least the first one so you can start walking):

....

....

....

....

....

....

Defining your vision, your mission, and your strategic phases will help you:

- Implement your purpose in life in a practical way.
- Make better decisions in your life, ones that are aligned with your essence.
- Create a true positive impact in alignment with your purpose.

4
Leverage the Democratization of Technology

In 2012, at the very tender age of eight, José Quisocala launched the first bank created by a child: the Students' Bank. The bank currently has over 3,500 clients who receive a bank account, a credit card, and basic financial skills so they can best manage their money.

José Quisocala's story is similar to other extraordinary young people who created businesses that changed the world (Apple,

Microsoft, Facebook, etc.) but with one important difference: the Students' Bank was not created in Silicon Valley (USA) but in Arequipa (Peru). Quisocala had access to knowledge from a very early age through the Internet, which led him to understand how a financial institution works and to new technologies that helped him implement his project. In other words, he leveraged the possibilities offered by technology increasingly available to more people around the world.

Another fascinating story is about Jack Andraka, who, in 2012, at the age of fifteen, created a diagnostic method to detect pancreatic cancer (among others) in five minutes. He earned the Gordon Moore Award at Intel's International Science and Engineering Fair and was invited by US President Barack Obama to attend the 2013 State of the Union Address. Jack had not studied medicine at a university; he learned everything he knows on the internet.

As I am writing this (mid-2022), 60 percent of the world's population has access to the Internet, nearly 4.4 billion people. A privilege of a few only decades ago, today, for most of the world's population, access to technologies, resources, and knowledge is now just one click away. We don't even need a computer; a mobile phone is enough. This small device has computing capabilities millions of times greater than the computer that guided Apollo 11 to the moon over fifty years ago. Don't you think it's incredible that technology has advanced so much in such a short time?

In the last five or six decades, technology has experienced exponential growth, giving rise to artificial intelligence, robotics, biotechnology, etc. Whether we are aware of it or not, they are already part of our daily lives. In 2016, the president and founder of the World Economic Forum, Klaus Schwab, announced the Fourth Industrial Revolution in a book with the same title. This new revolution is based on the intersection of various exponential technologies. According to Schwab, "The Fourth Industrial Revolution is not just about intelligent, connected machines and systems. Its scope is broader. Simultaneously, there are waves of further advances in areas ranging from genetic sequencing to nanotechnology and from renewable energy to quantum computing. It is the fusion of these technologies and their interaction across the physical, digital, and biological domains that makes the Fourth Industrial Revolution fundamentally different from previous ones."

New technologies always arouse fear, even rejection, in some groups, who see them as a threat. One of the most widespread fears today is that artificial intelligence and robotics will take our jobs away. But, in truth, it's not job loss you might fear (especially if it is an activity not aligned with your purpose) but the loss of income from that work, and, to avoid this, we must work on new social models, which I will refer to later. What interests me now is that you clearly understand that technology is not a threat but an opportunity. It does not exist to compete with us but to help us. Those who leverage artificial intelligence will be faster and make fewer mistakes. For example, consider the AI-based GPS app that solves a problem by helping us orient ourselves and reach our destination more efficiently. There are different levels of AI, from very basic and purely reactive systems, such as automatic door openers, to very advanced systems, such as those used for diagnosing diseases. And they are all helpful to us and even necessary.

I recently read a news item that explained, in an alarming tone, that the excessive use of applications and systems to perform certain tasks is causing our brains to lose capabilities. It pointed out, for example, that nobody memorizes phone numbers or addresses anymore. But have we really lost capacity? The answer is no. In the first place, now we have at hand the numbers of many more people and can call them immediately. Technology has become an extension of our bodies and allows us to do much more than we did before. And, secondly, new uses force us to develop new cognitive skills to manage technological devices and applications.

To say that we are now less intelligent due to the use of technology would be like saying that humans are less adaptable to the cold now because we wear warm clothes, which has caused our body hair to decrease and our skin to become less able to withstand low temperatures. The truth is that, thanks to warm clothing, humans are now able to live comfortably in many places that would have been totally inaccessible to us before.

The Technological Revolution

Technology, and the evolution it brings to our lives and our society, is precisely what differentiates us from other animal species. The most important social advances have always gone hand in hand with technological revolutions. We are now in the Fourth Industrial Revolution, accompanied by new technologies, such as AI, 3D printing, genetic engineering, etc. Some even mention a new Fifth Industrial Revolution. In my opinion, we are in a continuous revolution, inspired by constant technological changes.

Where will technological evolution take us in the coming years? It's unpredictable. We can only try to understand the dynamics that exponential technologies are generating and the implications they have on our lives. Peter Diamandis, cofounder of Singularity University with Ray Kurzweil, describes the implications of exponential technologies through the "6 D" process, the different phases that any area goes through when impacted by new technologies. First, everything becomes *digital*. Then the initial results are *deceptive*, and they later exceed our expectations and generate *disruptive* solutions, which usually suffer an effect of *demonetization* and *dematerialization* (of products and services) from the digital effect until, finally, the most powerful effect of all arrives: *democratization*, which gives everyone access to these technological advances.

I would, however, like to go beyond those "6 Ds," as it is not just about democratizing access to technology. There are certainly an enormous number of people in the world who have access to the Internet, to advanced mobile devices, and to many other technologies, but are we really leveraging it? While some young people can learn advanced concepts on their own and develop projects as spectacular as José Quisocala's bank or Jack Andraka's cancer diagnostic method, many people only use technology to play games or to connect to social media. I'm not saying it's wrong to use technology for leisure, but only using it for that is a waste of resources. It's not enough to know that we're holding a supercomputer in our hands; we must be aware that we can do extraordinary things with it. We have the possibility to truly take advantage of the exciting historical times we live in.

Key Points

- Technology has evolved exponentially in recent decades and is increasingly available to more people.
- Although it sometimes generates fear or rejection, technology is not a threat but an opportunity.
- It is important that we ask ourselves if we are leveraging this opportunity.

5
Connect with Abundance

Technological advances offer us increasing access to numerous and varied resources. For example, as I pointed out in the previous chapter, the Internet gives us access to a huge amount of knowledge that was previously only accessible to a few. Until the 20th century, only the noble and privileged classes could access knowledge through teachers or well-guarded books. Things changed during the last century, but, for middle-class families, it was still a great economic effort to acquire an encyclopedia (often even going into debt). Today, practically anyone from any social level with a mobile phone has access to much more knowledge than any of those hefty encyclopedias could ever hold—all for free and constantly updated.

As Peter Diamandis details in his book *Abundance*, the resources at our disposal are becoming increasingly abundant. There are multiple examples. When I was a child, there was already talk of the end of the Oil Age and apocalyptic scenarios that would ensue when it was scarce. It seemed that the world would end when the reserves ran out. However, countries such as the United Arab Emirates, which has the fourth largest oil reserves in the world and the fifth largest for natural gas, are already shifting towards renewable energies, mainly solar, with the aim of reducing carbon emissions. In other words, the Oil Age is ending, not because there is no more oil but rather due to the availability of other, more sustainable sources of energy. Saudi Arabia's Minister of Petroleum and Mineral Resources, Ahmed Zaki Yamani, summed it up this way: "The Stone Age was not over for lack of stones, and the Oil Age will not end for lack of oil."

Earth receives an amount of energy from the sun that is eight thousand times greater than what its inhabitants currently consume. If we can capture it effectively enough, we will have access to an inexhaustible source of energy. My friend José Luis Cordeiro, who headed the energy area at Singularity University, has been stating for years that solar energy has the potential to supply all of humanity. To achieve this, we need to improve energy storage, and, fortunately, we are seeing more and more advances in this regard. Some companies, like Tesla (whose mission is "to accelerate the world's transition to sustainable energy"), are investing billions of dollars to evolve current solar panel and battery technology. Some countries are taking advantage of other energy sources, like El Salvador, the first to adopt bitcoin as their official currency and the first to mine bitcoins by taking advantage of geothermal energy from its volcanoes. They transform the energy of the Earth into digital gold!

Technology, therefore, is a source of abundance and makes more resources available to entrepreneurs than ever before. For example, it enables greater and easier access to funding. Kiva, a platform launched in 2005 that connects investors from all over the planet with entrepreneurs and small businesses from the third world, is one example of this. Kiva, which means "unity" in

Swahili, uses a person-to-person microfinance model that allows anyone to lend money directly to a small business in a developing country. In early 2009, the site had 180,000 entrepreneurial members, who received a weekly total of one million dollars in loans, with a return ratio of over 98 percent (*Time* magazine went so far as to say, "Your money is safer in the hands of the poorest in the world than in a pension fund"). In 2011, loans were funded for almost one billion dollars. People in third-world countries have never been able to access personal loans before to boost their dreams and their economy.

There are multiple *crowdfunding platforms* that allow you to post an initiative and access funding from people around the world. One of the best-known ones is Kickstarter, whose purpose is "to help bring creative projects to life" and which is dedicated to connecting people around the world with innovative projects. Its formula is original: by purchasing products or services in advance, it enables projects to receive funding and have an initial validation of their ideas. Kickstarter was founded in 2008 and has since received more than $5.5 billion from over 19 million people to fund over half a million projects.

Technology is also helping improve access to basic resources that are sometimes scarce, like water. Some companies in recent years, notably Aquovum from the US, have researched water generation by condensing atmospheric humidity through solar irradiation. This technology was initially very rudimentary and needed too much energy, but it has evolved thanks to disruptive advances that will soon make large-scale condensing plants viable. I am convinced that, over time, once the sequence of the "6 Ds" that we saw in the previous chapter has been completed, this technology will be universally accessible and will provide water security to all of humanity.

What I'm trying to convey with all these examples is that generating abundance and connecting with it depends on us, on people. It depends on you. You can look at the world through scarcity glasses, and you will indeed find data and evidence supporting the lack of resources and could possibly get trapped in complaint-filled rhetoric. But you equally have the option of looking at the world through abundance glasses and leverage the technological tools and possibilities available today.

The UAE could remain in the comfortable position of continuing to exploit its limited sources of fossil fuels, but it has decided to evolve towards abundant energy models. Thousands of entrepreneurs could have given up, believing that access to financing was impossible, but they decided to go to crowdfunding platforms and connect with people interested in their creative proposals for their funding. Or the whole of humanity could resign itself to considering water a dwindling resource and limiting its use. Fortunately, there are always pioneers who create new technologies that allow us to generate abundance and distribute it globally. It's what Peter Thum did in 2001 when he partnered with his longtime friend Jonathan Greenblatt to create Ethos Water, a high-end bottled water brand that donated a portion of its profits to projects so that every child in the world had clean water. In 2005, Starbucks bought Ethos Water and offered the bottled water for sale in about seven thousand stores across the US. They diverted five cents from every bottle sold to water-related projects. Since then, they have contributed $10 million to providing water and sanitation to half a million people.

In the current technological paradigm, access to different types of resources (information, energy, financing, etc.) offers you an unprecedented gamut of endless possibilities. Today, more than ever, if you play your cards right, you can live the life you freely choose. However, more freedom also entails more responsibility, a greater awareness of where we are and how the world works. There are no guarantees of a new world that is safer, fairer, happier, or even kinder. Freedom is the space opening up between all those adjectives and many others, a space to choose and grow, to move and create.

Never have people enjoyed more freedom, but with it comes the responsibility of rethinking all the things that make us human and making the best use of our potential. Only those who are aware of this will go from living within the limits of "Stone Age" scarcity to living a new era teeming with an abundance of resources and possibilities.

Key Points

- Although there is a shortage of some resources, we always find ways to connect with new sources of abundance.
- Technology provides the possibility to create abundance and make it available to many people, as evidenced by numerous cases in the fields of information, energy, finance, etc.
- But technology is just a tool; people create abundance. We must look at the world through a lens of abundance and not of scarcity.

Activity

Think of a resource that had been scarce and that is currently abundant or that could be abundant using technology and appropriate actions. Also, think about how to harness that source of abundance within your purpose.

6
Update Your Mindset

During one of her classes, renowned 20th century anthropologist and professor Margaret Mead was asked the following question: What would you consider is the first sign of civilization? Students expected a standard answer: a clay pot, a grinding stone, or some similar utensil. But, to the surprise of her students, Mead replied that the first sign of civilization was a healed femur, explaining that, in the animal world, a broken femur means death: you can't escape predators, you can't walk to the river to drink water, and, of course, you can't forage for food. You can't survive long enough for the bone to heal. Finding a healed femur naturally meant that someone had been taking care of the injured individual. That some individuals helped others indicated the beginning of civilization.

The future of humanity, therefore, was not affected as much by one tool or another as it was by a shift away from thinking only about the individual and towards the common good. Tools allow us to do things that were not previously possible, and they amplify the effect of our actions, but what is truly transformative is the way we see the world and how we behave. The key lies in your mindset.

In fact, what leads us to develop new tools is our trailblazing mindset and our insatiable hunger for progress, which turn dreams that once seemed crazy into reality. Burt Rutan, designer of SpaceShipOne, the first privately owned manned space vehicle, articulated this well: "The day before something is truly a breakthrough, it's just a crazy idea." On October 16, 1903, for example, the idea that humans could fly was simply crazy. The following day, the younger Wright brother completed the first airplane flight and laid the foundations for the development of the aeronautical industry.

People's mindsets change at the pace set by the evolution of society. Until recently, for example, families made great efforts for their children to pursue careers, believing that it guaranteed they would have a stable job and a future. Now, on the other hand, we see that what companies value most is not university degrees but a proactive and entrepreneurial attitude, and what most workers value most is not stability, which is usually synonymous with stagnation and obsolescence, but the possibility of continuing to learn.

Our parents' mindsets were different from ours, and ours is different from what our children will have. They will live a different life and will have to change their mindset to adapt to the changes in society. The only way to ensure a sustainable evolution of our civilization and of each of us as individuals is precisely this: that our mindsets evolve at the same speed as our environment does.

As with technology, if you don't update your mindset, you'll become obsolete. How you react to technology is precisely one of the most important aspects to review with respect to your mindset. The development and continuous improvement of technology is a constant that has survived wars, recessions, and all kinds of social events, and, with each new technological advance, we provide humanity with new possibilities: to live comfortably in situations of cold or heat, cure diseases and prolong our lives, move from one end of the planet to another in a matter of hours, etc. However, most people initially react with suspicion to technological advances and focus on the potential negative consequences rather than on the possibilities they offer. This is particularly prevalent in people over the age of thirty-five, according to Douglas Adams, an author best known for the series *A Hitchhiker's Guide to the Galaxy*. Between the ages of fifteen and thirty-five, on the other hand, we tend to view new technologies that appear in our lives as something exciting that offers new possibilities.

This is because our brain tends to identify the unexpected as dangerous. It goes back to when humans lived at the mercy of potential predators and had to be constantly on alert for suspicious noises or movements. It was essential to pay the utmost attention to any signs of danger in order to survive. That mechanism remains in our brain and is run by the amygdala, which is always alert to any possible threat. This explains, for example, why even today we continue to pay more attention to negative than positive news. Bad news feeds our amygdala!

It's easy to imagine what the first hominids must have felt when they discovered they could light a fire. At first, they surely felt panic. However, when they managed to overcome the panic, they began to see the benefits of their discovery, mainly cooking (thus avoiding multiple diseases) and heating (increasing their resistance to cold).

Technology is actually like a golem, the gigantic mythological being made of mud that faithfully served its master. The golem could be used to build bridges or to tear them down. Similarly, technology can be used for constructive or, on the contrary, destructive purposes. The key, again, is the mindset of those using it. It is in our hands to give the golem the right commands to make the world a better place.

A good way to evolve your mindset towards a positive acceptance of technology is to stop feeding your amygdala with continuous alarm bells that fill you with negativity. I recommend, for example, that you reduce (or even eliminate) the time you spend reading news, like personalities such as Tesla founder Elon Musk do. Among other things, this will help you reflect on how to manage new advances to benefit yourself and society.

We must update our brain mechanisms like we update the software of our mobile phones. The amygdala cannot have the same prominence it had fifty thousand years ago, when we lived in caves and were food for all kinds of predators. We must stop consciously feeding it. Today, more than ever, it is necessary to pay attention to what has brought us here: our ability to imagine and create new possibilities using all the technologies and tools at our disposal.

Challenges

If we want to have a positive impact on the world, we also need to change the way we deal with major social problems. In the past, an effective way to do this was to raise your voice so that the government or other public entities would take care of resolving them, because individuals did not have the necessary tools to do so. But now we have much more power, especially thanks to our access to technology. We all have the capacity to create solutions to solve humanity's great challenges.

Gerald Abila is a good example of that. This young man from Uganda realized while studying law that there was a great gap between the laws applicable to citizens and the true understanding they have of those laws. When a person is detained and in police custody, they do not even know about their rights. Instead of resigning himself or protesting, Gerald created a Facebook page giving legal information to the public. Demand grew incredibly fast, so he improved the system and turned it into the Barefoot-Law platform, which currently provides free legal assistance to more than 450,000 people each month.

We can find another example in blockchain technology and the decentralization of financial power. Major macroeconomic decisions were hitherto in the hands of a few financial institutions, allowing them to abuse their position of power. Today, thanks to new emerging blockchain-based models, we have the possibility of turning to new platforms based on transparent, distributed, and autonomous approaches in which the individual has much more power and independence. If a central bank decides to issue more currency and thus causes a spike in inflation, we can place our savings in cryptocurrencies, which, while presenting their own risks, at least operate transparently with guidance from the community itself. In other words, power goes from being in the hands of a few to being in everyone's hands.

We no longer have an excuse for not being part of the solution to humanity's great problems. So, are you one of those people who focus on problems or on solutions? It's important that you ask yourself this question and that you give an honest answer, because we cannot remain indifferent to problems. If you're not part of the solution, you're part of the problem.

Time is limited, and you choose what you do with it: complain or look for solutions. These are two mindsets and two very different, even opposite, attitudes. We all have the right to feel indignant, but we take it further. We now have a power we didn't before. We can create real solutions; we can generate positive change. More and more of us are going beyond words and taking action; we are those who, once we understand the problem, focus on our improved vision of the world and work to make it happen.

We are living in an exciting time, when having the right mentality means not only raising our voices or declaring how things should be but making things really happen.

Habits

I am aware that changing your mindset is not as simple as downloading and installing a new update of your phone's operating system. Changes in mindset often occur after going through difficult or even painful experiences that forge in us certain attitudes and motivate us to change. But it is also possible to update our mindset without being led to it by any extreme event simply through our own intention, willingness, and inner work.

The best way to consciously change one's mindset is through action and changing our habits. The first step, of course, is accepting that we must identify and change the beliefs and attitudes we wish to adopt. Then we need to put this new way of thinking into practice, even if we occasionally feel we're going against our nature. Those new experiences will positively reinforce the new beliefs, and, with enough time, we'll be able to change our habits and evolve our mindset.

I remember the moment I became an entrepreneur. It wasn't when I created my first company (that happened years later) but when I changed my attitude towards life. During my adolescence,

I understood life as very linear, with all the steps I would take clearly defined. Year after academic year, I studied from Monday to Friday and made plans with my friends on weekends. Things weren't going badly; I just followed the conventional path. I even started to acquire some unhealthy habits like smoking. One day, a book about 3D digital graphic design fell into my hands, and the following weekend, instead of going out with my friends as I normally did, I stayed home reading it and putting into practice some of the exercises it recommended. Over time, I improved my technique and broadened my knowledge—so much so that, before college, I was offered a chance to work on an animated film. Although I never stopped socializing with my friends, dedicating time to what I was passionate about changed the way I viewed the world. I came to understand that I could learn anything on my own and that, with enough perseverance, I could achieve whatever I set out to do, which forged the entrepreneurial attitude I've had all my life. Thanks to that attitude, I have launched all kinds of projects, including several startups. Oh, and I quit smoking.

In short, by changing our habits, we can update our mindset and change the world—you, me, everyone, we can all do this so that, one day, when her students ask her how civilization began, a future Margaret Mead will explain that it happened when, beyond supporting each other through their problems, people began to dream of a better world, and, thanks to a mindset focused on the abundance of resources, they made it a reality.

Key Points

- We must constantly evolve our mindset.
- New technologies offer us more opportunities than threats: focus on opportunities.
- The world's challenges require people to focus on creating solutions.
- We can consciously change a mindset through a change of habits.

Activity

Identify a current technology that you reject or concerns you because of its possible consequences. Think of three positive applications of that technology and list them below:

1. ....
2. ....
3. ....

Identify a current problem in the world (if it's linked to your purpose, all the better) and think about a solution you could provide (either alone or with the help of others). Describe it briefly:

....
....
....
....
....
....

Identify an aspect of your mindset that you think you should change and define one or more actions to begin to change it. Set a timeframe for new actions to become a habit.

Part Two

Purpose Launchpad

7
A Brief History of
Innovation Methodologies

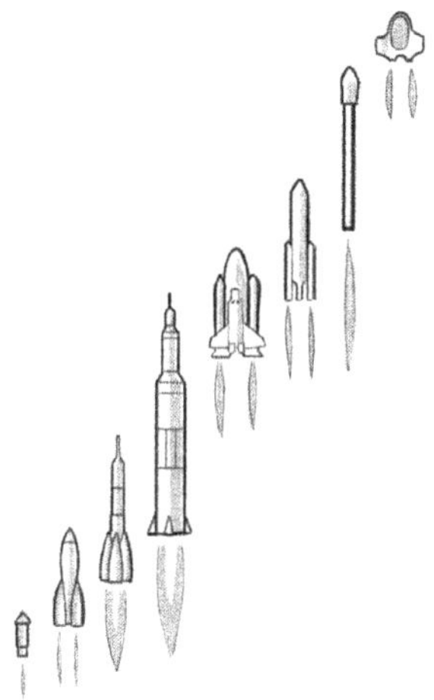

The Purpose Launchpad framework, which I'll describe throughout this second part of the book, did not just pop up out of nowhere. It is the evolution and consequence of other prior innovation methodologies (by the way, I'll tell you the difference between a methodology and a framework in the chapter "Discovering Purpose Launchpad"). It would be difficult to detail the various innovation techniques—there are already books that do so—but, in order to put Purpose Launchpad into context, I'm going to give a brief review of the highlights below, a short historical stroll through innovation methodologies. It goes without saying that, if you're already familiar with them, you can skip this chapter, though it's always good to refresh your knowledge.

The 1950s: Customer-Centered Creativity Techniques (Later Called Design Thinking)

Innovation has existed since humans began to create their first tools, but the concept of innovation as such began to spread after WWII, linked to the desire to generate economic growth in society and a competitive advantage in companies. In the 50s, new design methods were developed based on studies on the psychology of creativity, which later evolved to become what we know today as Design Thinking. It's a non-linear, iterative process that helps us solve problems by placing the customer at the center, empathizing and prioritizing their needs above all else. This allows us to fully understand their true needs as a starting point for designing products and services that provide real value.

Although this process has evolved over time, placing the customer at the center of innovation continues to be the key. Not doing so can trigger dire consequences—believe me, I know. I'll give you the short version of what happened to my partners and me with our company called IActive. In 2004, my two thesis advisors (Luis and Juan), two research project colleagues (Tomás and Oscar), and I launched a company to develop software solutions based on artificial intelligence (AI) technology we had developed beforehand in the Computer Science and Artificial Intelligence Department of the University of Granada. During the first two years, things went well. We focused on developing custom smart solutions for different types of organizations. We grew continuously and gave our customers great value. However, in 2007, we decided to shift from being a service company to creating a product that could escalate exponentially, an advanced tool we later called IActive Intelligent Studio. Our product offered anyone the possibility of developing smart systems without having any skills in this type of technology.

We were excited with the idea, because our tool would simplify the approach of other, similar tools and make access to AI available to everyone. It was going to be awesome! We had one funding round and raised three million euros. That investment allowed us to strengthen our team, not only technically but also with more senior profiles (up to that point, the company's average age was about twenty-eight), people coming from executive positions in important companies in the sector. In addition, as CEO of the company, I decided to pursue an MBA degree at one of the most prestigious business schools in the world, which would complement my technical training with business skills. Before launching the product, we received top awards and recognition for the potential our product represented for the sector. The prestigious consulting firm, Gartner, even named IActive one of the five tech companies with the greatest potential worldwide.

During the next two years, we focused on making our promising vision a reality. We even decided to leave our previous clients in order to fully develop the tool that would enable us to scale our impact and our business. It was a very promising plan, and we had to prepare for the huge growth we were going to experience. We spent those two years practically locked in our offices, bringing about this tool. We finally launched the product in 2010 in a great event that we held in a beautiful venue in Madrid. We never sold a single license. Our plan had failed.

What was our main error? We believed we knew everything the customer would need, but we didn't. Our mistake was in not ever interacting with real customers until after finalizing product development.

The 1980s: Agile Product Development Frameworks (Scrum)

Towards the end of the 20th century, the best way to compete was product innovation. With a perfect understanding of the problem that we want to solve and the right solution for it, we would ideally have an exhaustive design of said solution, create a plan for developing the product, and carry out that plan through its different phases, trying to optimize the use of both financial and time resources. This is called a waterfall approach, which allows you to create the product in the shortest time.

Now, what happens when we don't have complete certainty that the product that we have in mind will work as we imagined? In that case, we shouldn't create a design in detail or focus on developing the product to the end, because it's very possible that, when we're done, we'll discover that it's not what the market really needs. That is precisely why an agile product development framework called Scrum emerged in the mid-80s.

We developed our IActive Intelligent Studio at IActive using the Scrum framework, which let us prioritize and organize the various activities, as well as other agile development techniques such as Kanban. But agile development frameworks alone are useless unless they're combined with a real and constant connection with the market and with real customers. As I said earlier, that was precisely our case. We agilely changed the course of product development but were only guided by our own opinions.

2004: Product Innovation (Blue Ocean Strategy)

One of the most widely used product innovation techniques is the Blue Ocean Strategy, published in 2004 by Chan Kim and Renée Mauborgne in their eponymous book. In this book, highly competitive markets where price wars provoke a violent struggle for potential customers are called "red oceans." The simile refers to the blood that stains the ocean red when many sharks fight for prey. On the bases of this idea, the Blue Ocean Strategy consists of finding a unique differentiating component to define your products, thus distancing them from the competition and giving the company access to new markets, "oceans" yet to be conquered, in whose crystal-clear waters they can navigate and prosper.

The Wii console, released in 2006, is an example of this strategy. At that time, manufacturers were struggling to develop low-price consoles with more features. The competition was so fierce that, eventually, console production costs were greater than their sale price, which generated losses that brands hoped to recover with higher sales margins for video games. In that environment, Nintendo launched a console with a lower production cost and lower graphics quality that included a new component (an accelerometer on the controller) that allowed it to create new types of experiences and offer games that were widely accepted, among adults as well as young people. So, Nintendo not only reduced production costs but found new markets in which it initially had no competition.

2010: Business Model Innovation (Business Model Canvas)

The basic problem when we wanted to scale IActive was that we didn't know what we were; we weren't even fully aware of what we were doing. We thought we were a company with an established business model that aimed to innovate its product in order to increase its sales, but we were actually a startup trying to find a new business model. So, we had to do things differently.

Those approaches we had learned about before, which were very valid for 20th century companies, no longer served the new disruptive businesses emerging in the 90s with the arrival of digital technologies. The startup phenomenon began in that decade, companies like Google or Facebook with tremendous potential for global growth in a very short time. While traditional management methods are about the execution of a plan, which is usually focused on a known market and product or service, the new methods emerging for startups were oriented more on the search for possible paths, on exploring and evaluating whether they really make sense.

After the failed launch of our tool in 2007, I began to search for different innovation methodologies to reorient our activity, because I was convinced that, by doing things differently, we could be very successful. Looking for answers, I moved to Silicon Valley in 2011 for a time. I began attending a program at Singularity University, where I met extraordinary people like Ray Kurzweil and where I learned that, even though technology is key to creating high-impact projects, we should always focus on the problem initially.

My hunger for finding answers made me restless. I remembered that my friend Alfredo Rivela had given me a book in 2010 that had really helped me clarify how were redefining IActive's new business model. The book was *Business Model Generation*, published that same year by Alex Osterwalder, which presented a new tool called Business Model Canvas that made it possible to define a business model graphically and easily. We decided to try it, but it was only a better expression of our business model; it didn't really make it work.

I kept searching for answers and discovered an earlier methodology, so you'll see that the next subsection jumps back a few years to 2005.

2005: Customer Development
(An Evaluation of Customer and Product Hypotheses)

Specifically, I discovered Steve Blank, a prestigious entrepreneur and the author of books such as *The Four Steps to the Epiphany* or *The Startup Owner's Manual*. One of his most well-known phrases impressed me deeply: "No business plan survives first contact with customers." Exactly! That was what we had experienced with our business plan for IActive. After spending years developing it, it did not survive contact with customers.

Steve Blank is known for having developed a method called "Customer Development," which helps you establish the starting hypotheses and perform certain experiments until you understand who your customers are and who they are not, as well as what the value proposition is and the product or service that you should really develop for them. During the years I spent in Silicon Valley, I was fortunate enough to attend a training program at the University of California at Berkeley with Steve Blank, and I began to dive into the innovation methodologies of the 21st century. I then understood that, although the tools I had previously used were very useful and valid, any new idea (or business plan altogether) was nothing more than a hypothesis and should be treated as such. In other words, a business plan is not a document to be executed but a set of hypotheses to be evaluated.

The way we were applying Scrum to IActive when agilely developing the product was not, therefore, correct, since we had defined the product and planned its development under the assumption that our ideas would work instead of thinking of them as hypotheses. This was when I discovered, in fact, the true meaning of the word startup, which Steve Blank himself defines as "a temporary organization designed to search for a repeatable and scalable business model." IActive was a startup, and that's why we had to change the way we did things.

2011: Lean Startup (Build-Measure-Learn and MVP)

In 2011, Eric Ries, a follower of Steve Blank I also had the opportunity to meet, published the well-known book *Lean Startup*, in which he presented a series of advances in innovation that quickly became very popular. Among other things, Ries presented the Build-Measure-Learn cycle, stating that the most important thing when developing a new product or startup was to carry out rapid cycles in which we build something (not perfect), measure the result, and, with the learnings obtained, we build again. In other words, if you have a million euros to build a new product, and that gives you twelve months of financing, you shouldn't spend ten months building your product and two months promoting it to see if it works, because then you only have one chance at it. It's much better to build during the first month, even if it's just a prototype, and quickly present it to potential customers so you can really measure their reactions, learn from it, and make data-driven decisions to improve the product in the next cycle—that is, during the next month. In this way, you'll have twelve opportunities to get it right.

Our mistake with IActive was to play the three million euros on a single card in one two-year cycle. Fortunately, at the end of that period, we still had some capital left, and we were able to give ourselves a new chance. With everything we'd learned, we began launching new products targeted at concrete problems and leveraging our own AI tech. We launched Cognocare, a solution to customize pediatric oncology treatments, which was used by oncologists in different hospitals with very positive results. We also launched Nativoo, an intelligent assistant for customizing tourist visits used by millions of tourists worldwide and acquired in the end by the Brazilian company SBTUR. And, lastly, after all the learning gained on new innovation and entrepreneurship methodologies, we launched LeanMonitor, an agile platform to help innovators and entrepreneurs define and evolve new products and startups. Steve Blank himself showed an interest in LeanMonitor, and it was eventually bought by Gust.com.

2014: Exponential Organizations (ExO)

Innovation methodologies, like anything else, do not stop evolving. After the emergence of the Blue Ocean Strategy (focused on the definition of new products), the Business Model Canvas tool (focused on the definition of new business models), and the Customer Development process and the Lean Startup approach (focused on the evaluation of hypotheses and the evolution of products and new business models) came a new model: the exponential organization. This focuses on a type of organization that connects with abundance, managing it in a way that allows the business to grow exponentially. One example is Airbnb, currently the largest lodging marketplace in the world without owning a single hotel. Their secret is to connect with the abundance of lodging available around the world and manage it through a platform that allows them to grow exponentially.

While at Singularity University, I met Salim Ismail, its founding executive director. One day, while we were having a coffee, he told me about his idea of writing about the phenomenon of exponential organizations, which he called ExO. I thought it was a fabulous idea. Soon afterwards, his book was published and became a bestseller.

In 2015, Salim, who had been my advisor for LeanMonitor, asked me to join him and launch a new business with the ExO model. He wanted us to create a new movement around it and build the "ExO LeanMonitor." My first proposal began defining simple tools to help apply the model—for example, the ExO Canvas. I also designed a ten-week process, which we called ExO Sprint (there's an evolved version for you at the end of this book), to facilitate applying the model in existing companies. It was really the evolution of an earlier process called the Lean Startup Development Program that I had created for Singularity University, with the addition of the ExO model.

We also launched our first business, ExO Works, a consultancy to help large corporations implement the exponential organization model by applying the knowledge acquired at the forefront of innovation methodologies. We had considerable success and were making over three million dollars a year in under two years.

Finally, in 2018, we launched a new project, OpenExO, a community where thousands of people and consultants from all over the world are trained in the ExO methodology, intending to take it to their clients and help them grow exponentially.

They were wonderful years during which I had the opportunity to contribute greatly to the ExO movement. But I felt that I was missing something, that there was some misalignment between OpenExO objectives and my own personal purpose. This led me to leave the team at the end of 2019 to follow a path that aligned with my essence and, at the same time, allowed me to contribute to writing the next chapter in the history of innovation methodologies.

2020: Purpose-Oriented Ecosystems (Purpose Launchpad)

The cover of *Harvard Business Review's* spring 2020 issue announced, "How to Lead with Purpose." It echoed a worldwide trend of increasing numbers of projects and people consciously trying to have a positive impact on the world. In fact, the leaders and organizations achieving the most today are the ones driven by a strong purpose. Elon Musk and Tesla, for example, have the purpose of accelerating the world's transition to sustainable energy. Google's purpose is to make digitized information accessible to the world. TED aims to spread worthwhile ideas. Patagonia's purpose is to save planet Earth. Purpose-oriented organization are not a fad; they are a new generation of businesses that not only seek financial gain but focus on creating a better world aligned with their purpose and, in doing so, generate business. When an organization authentically defines their purpose, not merely as an advertising slogan, an energy is generated that makes the business no longer the center of everything, extending the organization's limits and its impact far beyond what it was originally. Returning to the Tesla example, the current high value of its stock is because it's much more than a company that manufactures and sells cars. In line with its purpose, the company also promotes many other products and services, such as solar roof panels for the home, high-capacity batteries, or its own marketplace of apps used on its devices. But the most interesting thing about the Tesla phenomenon is that, beyond being a business-focused organization, it has become a purpose-oriented ecosystem. The reason for its huge media impact is that many people feel aligned with that purpose and, in one way or another, support the Tesla ecosystem.

Every day, more organizations realize that the best way to create a positive impact while expanding their business is precisely to become an ecosystem. Google, for example, is also an ecosystem made up of a wide variety of products, services, and companies with a community aligned with its purpose: to digitize all information and make it accessible to the world. Even Apple has gone from being a company focused on selling electronic devices to being an ecosystem focused on its purpose of empowering creative exploration and self-expression. Apple used to have customers who bought a computer or a mobile device every two or three years, but now it has users who use its services almost daily.

The concept of industry also becomes obsolete with purpose-oriented ecosystems. Apple itself no longer belongs to a single sector but touches several at the same time. And the same is true for Google, Tesla, and many other smaller organizations, which have ceased to belong to a particular industry to become purpose-focused ecosystems, broadening their positive impact and increasing their business.

There are also communities of self-generated purpose-oriented ecosystems made up of people, startups, and large companies that interact with one another. In this case, there's no formal partnership but rather an interaction to achieve a common purpose. This is the case of startups and companies working in fintech (new technologies applied to finance), many of whose purposes are aligned with the democratization of the economy. We find blockchain technology, and a multitude of cryptocurrency based on it, in that ecosystem, for example, as well as platforms such as Nexo, where you can obtain instant loans of up to two million dollars backed only by cryptocurrency. We can also find organizations like PayPal, whose purpose is precisely to democratize financial services, which are beginning to operate with cryptocurrency.

Another good example of a purpose-oriented ecosystem is the Alliance for Entrepreneurship and Innovation (AEI) created in Ecuador and Panama with over 150 private companies and public entities that share the same purpose: to promote entrepreneurship and innovation to improve the world. The ecosystem's various organizations share all kinds of communities and resources to empower entrepreneurs who want to create a positive impact.

Navigating new scenarios clearly requires new tools. With that in mind, in 2020, I published the book *Massive Transformative Purpose* together with Angel Maria Herrera. It describes a method and a tool, MTP Canvas, to help people and organizations discover and define their purpose as an initial step towards generating a positive impact.

It is precisely impact that has increasing prominence in the world of startups and corporations. In some ways, innovation methodologies have already offered us their value proposition, helping us correctly build new projects and develop organizations, minimizing risks and maximizing our chances of success.

Timeline of Noteworthy Innovation Methodologies

1940s: the concept of innovation is born

1950s: customer-centered creativity techniques (later Design Thinking)

1980s: agile product development frameworks (Scrum and others)

2004: product innovation (Blue Ocean Strategy)

2005: Customer Development (evaluation of customer and product hypotheses)

2010: business model innovation (Business Model Canvas)

2011: Lean Startup (*Build-Measure-Learn* and MVP)

2014: exponential organizations (ExO Model)

2020: purpose-oriented ecosystems (Purpose Launchpad)

8
The Impact Pyramid

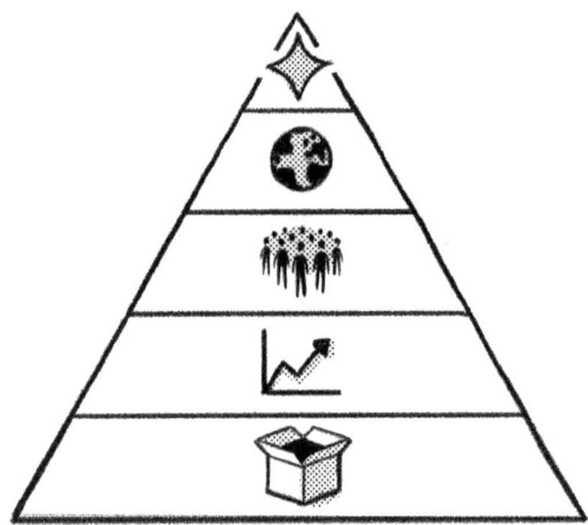

Over time, new methodologies and tools will emerge that will allow us to perfect the technique, but, beyond that, we must ask ourselves a question: To remain relevant in the world, is innovation enough?

A while ago, I had an interesting conversation with Daniel Truran, ambassador to Europe for the B Corp movement. He told me that "the role of companies is no longer just to sell products to their customers but to do good in the world." It should be noted that B Corp is the most prestigious global standard for recognizing for-profit and purposeful companies and certifies the company's social and environmental performance. Present in more than 78 countries already, it continues to take very firm steps to achieve its own purpose: to transform the global economy for the benefit of all people, communities, and the planet.

Society is increasingly aware that it's wrong to generate profits if those participating in the activity, whether employees or external communities, are not properly treated. And, of course, it's becoming increasingly evident that organizations must take care of the environment and the planet. It is therefore imperative to operate sustainably, which means performing an activity in the present without compromising future resources. In his book *The Triple Bottom Line*, John Elkington refers to the three parameters that every sustainable organization must meet: economic, social, and environmental, also known as the "3 Ps" of sustainability: profit, people, and the planet.

At the very least, every organization should try to be triply sustainable so that its activity does not compromise its own economic resources, social resources, or the planet's resources. Now, an organization can be sustainable and still leave no impression on the world, either good or bad. Just like the top layer of Maslow's pyramid indicates the need to transcend, to contribute our grain of sand to the evolution of the world around us, organizations can also go beyond sustainability and aspire to have a positive impact on the world. And, for that, they need to have a purpose.

These concepts are represented below in what I call the Impact Pyramid, which shows the hierarchy of objectives that an organization must set for itself in order to generate positive impact, both within the organization and in the world:

Figure 2.1. The Impact Pyramid

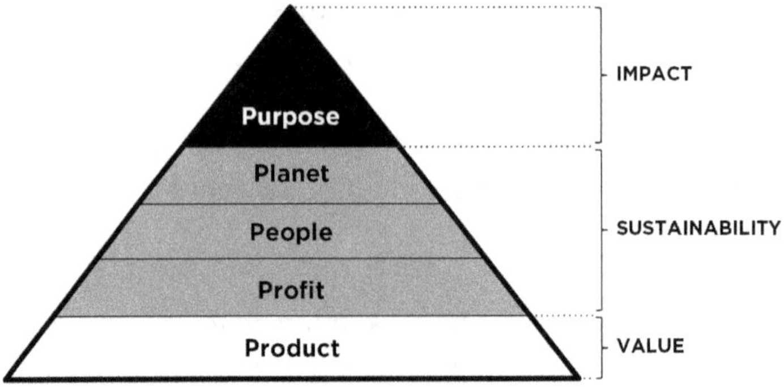

Source: Prepared by the author

This tells us that the basic need of any organization is to have a good product that adds value to its customers and that this is the starting point that allows it to be economically sustainable. But it must also be socially and environmentally sustainable. Only then can it aspire to generate a positive impact in line with its purpose. In other words, to generate real positive impact, both within the organization and in the world, it's necessary to own the "5 Ps" of the Impact Pyramid: product, profit, people, planet, and purpose.

As we saw in the previous chapter, innovation methodologies have helped us enormously in developing new products that add value to our customers to eventually generate income and economic benefits. But we cannot stop there, not only for altruistic reasons but because the scope of our organization and the total result of our actions will be much smaller if we only focus on profit. The result of that would be a much smaller pyramid:

**Figure 2.2. Incomplete Impact Pyramid,
Reduced to Economic Profit**

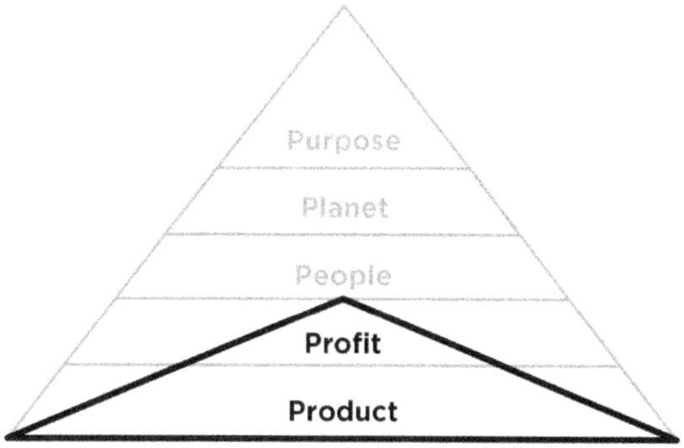

Source: Prepared by the author

You may end up with a profitable organization, but then you'll miss the opportunity to broaden your scope. If you elevate your pyramid to include purpose, you'll not only have a positive impact on the world, but your income will very possibly increase, since consumers are more and more mindful in their purchasing. You'll have the support of environmental and social movements that promote your project. Not only that, you'll enjoy a wealth of opportunities, as we saw in previous chapters.

Daniel Truran, who I've mentioned before, was very enthusiastic as he told me about Betterfly, a purpose-oriented and B-Corp-certified company, which has been valued at an astounding one billion dollars. Betterfly was founded in 2018 with the purpose of turning people's healthy habits into economic benefits. The organization offers companies of any size a benefits platform that rewards their workers' healthy habits with life insurance coverage that increases as they take actions to improve their wellbeing, such as playing sports, meditating, or choosing a healthy diet. Referring to his focus on purpose, Betterfly founder Eduardo della Maggiora notes, "When we made the decision to apply this structure, many people told me that it would hold us back from growing the company and increasing our capital, but the opposite has happened. I would venture to say that placing purpose at the center of everything we do is precisely why we've been able to grow the way we have."

Purpose is always the starting point, but, to create real results, it must be activated. This was the main reason that I began working on the Purpose Launchpad framework: to put purpose into action and turn it into true positive impact. Another reason, as we saw in the previous chapter, is that there are many innovation tools, and a framework that somehow integrated them all was needed. Purpose Launchpad is just that: a general framework that accompanies us at every level of the Impact Pyramid, not only when launching new projects or growing a business but also to develop sustainable projects that transcend and generate a positive impact on the world. Likewise, Purpose Launchpad helps established organizations leverage the new context in which purpose-oriented ecosystems are emerging to connect with them or evolve into an ecosystem model.

In the following chapters, I will explain in detail what Purpose Launchpad consists of. Later, in Parts 3 and 4, we will see how to apply Purpose Launchpad to your startup and to an established organization respectively. My goal is to help you avoid the mistakes I made when I didn't have adequate innovation models at the time and to inspire you to adopt the good practices that countless successful organizations have followed.

9
Discovering Purpose Launchpad

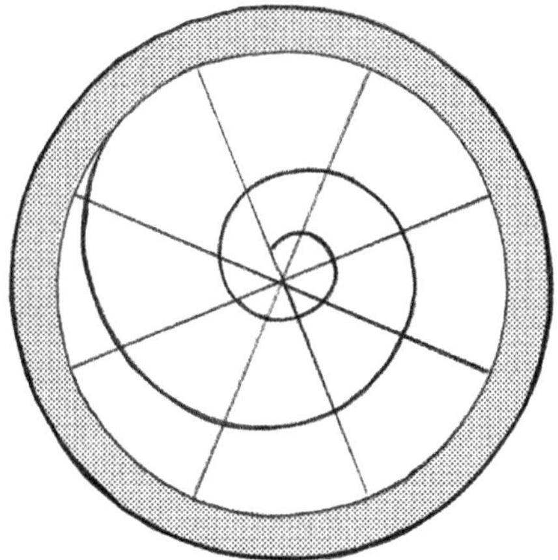

Let's start by defining the Purpose Launchpad. It is "an agile framework that relies on state-of-the-art innovation techniques to help people adopt the appropriate mindset to launch projects, such as new startups or new products or services, or to evolve established organizations so that they create a positive impact." Of course, as it's not a short or simple phrase, we're going to break it down.

To begin with, as you can see, we refer to a framework and not a methodology. This is not an arbitrary distinction. Methodologies are rigid and establish a series of processes and rules that must be strictly followed in order to obtain a specific result. Frameworks, on the other hand, are more flexible and offer principles and elements that guide us and let us obtain one result or another, depending on the path we choose. They don't force us to do things in a certain way; they instead give us principles to follow.

Secondly, this is an "agile framework." In fact, Purpose Launchpad is largely inspired by the agile product development frameworks that we reviewed in the last chapter (such as Scrum), although it doesn't only focus on the development of a product but on any project or initiative. Being an agile approach means that we won't base our progress on a static and predefined plan but that the framework always allows for changing the direction of our project's development in any of its stages to ensure maximum ability to adapt to the environment and the moment.

The definition also mentions "state-of-the-art innovation techniques," meaning that it incorporates and integrates different existing innovation tools and helps combine them most effectively. It makes the complex simple, as it simplifies the use of the various existing innovation techniques, helping you apply one or the other depending on the context, especially the timing, of your project. For example, the metrics we'll use in the very early phase of a startup, when it's still trying to find a fit in the market, will be different from what we'll use for a consolidated organization in its expansion phase.

I also say, "to help people adopt the appropriate mindset." In mentor certification programs, I insist on this point a lot, because a Purpose Launchpad mentor should focus less on achieving a project's success than on helping the people who are a part of it develop the appropriate mindset to achieve success on their own. We saw earlier in the book that mindset is the key. The Purpose Launchpad tools can also help us in this, since we experience new dynamics that let us understand and internalize new ways of thinking and acting, which will lead to better results. Evolving our mindset is essential in order to adapt to continuous changes in the environment.

Continuing with the definition, I said that this framework is appropriate "to launch projects, such as new startups or new products or services, or to evolve established organizations." The first part refers to innovative or disruptive initiatives, such as the creation of new products or services within an organization or a new startup, which should initially focus on exploring the environment to find the right path and eventually move to an expansion or optimization phase. Then I refer to consolidated businesses that must evolve by combining their daily operations with a continuous exploration of new opportunities to transform and adapt to the changing environment. This book follows this same distinction in fact, since, after this second part of the book, where we look at Purpose Launchpad features and basic elements, the third part refers to its application in new products and startups, and, in the fourth, we will see how to apply it to established organizations.

Finally, the description talks about "creating a positive impact." We've already talked about the importance of contributing to the world in a positive way, but it's worth remembering that humanity's main challenges are also the greatest business opportunities. Therefore, by creating a positive impact and generating value for the world, we will also have the opportunity to capture some of this value for ourselves.

Figure 2.3. Purpose Launchpad Logo

Source: Prepared by the author

In summary, and to simplify as much as possible, we can say that Purpose Launchpad is at the intersection of agile methodologies and impact and helps us not only do things correctly but also do the right things. Throughout the following chapters, we will see the different elements of the framework. In-depth knowledge of these will allow you to take your organization to the next level while contributing to creating a better world.

Key Points

- Purpose Launchpad is an agile framework, not a methodology.
- It integrates different existing innovation tools.
- Helps develop an effective mindset in an environment of permanent change.
- It is useful both to launch new projects and to evolve consolidated ones.

Resources

- *Purpose Launchpad* Guide: www.purposelaunchpad.com/

10
Values and Principles

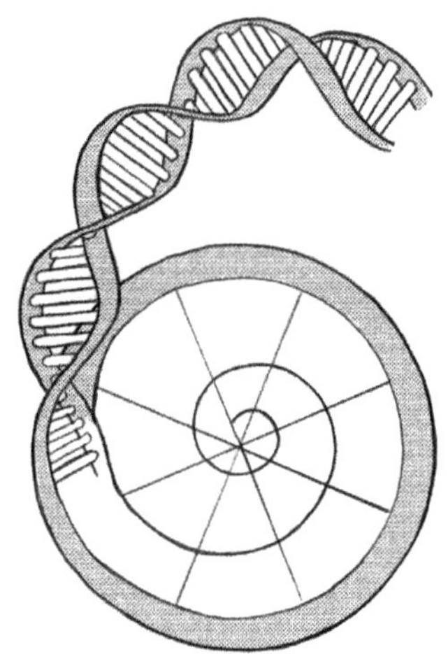

Some time ago, I saw the movie *Sully*, which recounts the incident that occurred on January 15, 2009, during a US Airways flight commanded by Captain Chesley "Sully" Sullenberger. (If you have not seen the movie and think you might, spoiler alert! I will reveal important details of the plot below.) Shortly after takeoff, his Airbus A320 hit a flock of Canadian geese, disabling both engines. Displaying cold-headed mental speed, Sully calculated that, under those circumstances, the plane could not reach Teterboro, the nearest airport, so he piloted the plane to an emergency water landing on the Hudson River. Thanks to this risky but necessary maneuver, all 155 passengers and crew were rescued without any casualties. The press presented him as a hero, but the National Transportation Safety Board accused him of not following protocol and attempting to land the plane at an airport and put him through legal hell before finally ruling that Sullenberger had made the right decision.

Captain Sullenberger had to make a very quick decision, as every second counted. He determined that it would be impossible to reach either of the two nearest airports as protocols demanded and chose the option he considered most appropriate at that time. He did not strictly follow the rules but acted on his values and principles.

In certain circumstances, standards such as those established by the US National Transportation Safety Board represent a challenge because they are so specific that they cannot contemplate all possible scenarios, especially in highly uncertain environments. This is the reason why most innovation frameworks are not guided by specific rules but by a series of values and principles that can be interpreted and adapted to each circumstance.

Purpose Launchpad has five values and ten principles inherited from the Purpose Manifesto (which you'll find at the end of the book) and adapted to the specific environment to which we apply Purpose Launchpad—that is, innovative and disruptive projects focused on developing new startups and products or transforming established organizations. Furthermore, these values and principles have been defined leveraging the experience of hundreds of successful innovators and entrepreneurs who collaborated in the creation of Purpose Launchpad.

Values

Values are those aspects to which we assign the most importance when implementing Purpose Launchpad. They are purpose, action, learning, abundance, and positive impact. I encourage you to keep them in mind in everything you do, not only to develop your initiatives in the right way, but also to develop the right initiatives.

1) Value 1: Purpose: Purpose Over Problems and Solutions

Sully's purpose was to save everyone aboard the plane. To do that, in a few seconds, he analyzed the problems and thought of different solutions, always keeping in mind the main reason for his actions.

Purpose is the North Star that illuminates our path and helps us always find the right direction. The solutions we implement to solve concrete problems may work or not, but the main thing is that they remain true to our purpose.

2) Value 2: Action: Actions Over Intentions

They say that "the road to hell is paved with good intentions," which means that good intentions are useless unless accompanied by positive actions. Impact equals purpose plus action. If we don't activate the purpose, we won't change or improve anything, either in our organization or in the world.

We only move forward if we act. Of course, when taking action, there will be many occasions when we're wrong, but that is not a negative; it's a learning opportunity.

3) Value 3: Learning: Customer Data Over Intuition

One of Steve Blank's most famous phrases, which I've mentioned before, is "No business plan survives first contact with a customer." And it's true. Our ideas and intuitions are very important, but they are merely hypotheses that we must evaluate through contact with our current or potential users and customers. We must talk to them constantly and gather data about our products and our business that will enable us to make evidence-based decisions.

The direct data and findings you get when you talk directly to customers is what we call "qualitative metrics." Quantitative metrics are still important, especially in certain phases of a project, but, in many cases, qualitative data is more important because it explains what really lies behind the numbers.

4) Value 4: Abundance: Purpose-Oriented Ecosystems Over Industry-Centric Competition

It's well known that Google's purpose is to organize the world's information, for which it offers not only a search engine for Internet web pages but a series of complementary products and services that have generated a community composed of billions of people aligned with that purpose. Many of them also use other tools. For example, Google Search users also search Wikipedia (whose purpose is to "benefit readers by acting as a widely accessible and free encyclopedia") and TED (whose purpose is to "spread ideas"); Google Docs users also use Microsoft products (Word, Excel, and others) to create or organize their documents; Google Calendar users sometimes combine it with apps like Windows Calendar or Apple Calendar, etc. Far from being a problem, this contributes to Google's purpose, which is being fulfilled thanks to an ecosystem that includes external elements and organizations oriented to linked purposes and that add value to its community. Community members belong to multiple ecosystems at the same time and make use of the value offered by each of them, collaborating without the need for a formal agreement. Purpose-oriented ecosystems, therefore, generate benefit for users and for all the component organizations. Everyone wins.

We shouldn't see competitors as a threat but as an opportunity to bring more value to our community. The key is to maintain a balance between competition and collaboration with other agents in the ecosystem.

5) Value 5: Positive Impact: Long-Term Positive Impact Over Short-Term Profit

According to Peter Diamandis, those who manage to positively impact millions of people will be the new millionaires. A clear example of this is Elon Musk, who, as I write this, is not only the richest person in the world but also someone who is generating a greater impact. With Tesla, which was the first company to massively market a new range of all-electric vehicles, he has managed to accelerate the transition to sustainable energy in the automotive industry. I dare say that, if it weren't for Tesla, most manufacturers would still be comfortably manufacturing and selling cars powered by gasoline or diesel. Musk's goal in creating Tesla wasn't short-term profits, for he was aware that it was going to take a long time for people to embrace electric vehicles. He thought about the long term. And, already now, when most vehicles on streets and highways are still not electric, Tesla stock has surpassed every other car brand.

In line with what we saw with the Impact Pyramid, this fifth and final value tells us that, if we focus on creating a long-term positive impact (rather than maximizing profits in the short term), we become an organization necessary to the world and, therefore, of greater value.

Principles

Principles are general guidelines that will help us implement these values and always act accordingly. As you can see in the summary table at the end of this chapter, each of the Purpose

Launchpad values is linked to two of the ten principles listed below. Simple and easy to understand, they are nevertheless not always easy to implement. At some point, you'll be tempted to skip them, but I suggest you don't because they only work if you really apply them. Over time, you'll see their power, internalize their essence, and prove their effectiveness. Are you ready for them?

1) Principle 1: Inspire People Through Your Purpose Rather Than Your Product

Simon Sinek, well-known speaker and author, is famous for his "Golden Circle" that explains how important it is to start every process of communication and inspiration with the why—that is, with the reason why we act. This way, we create trust and enhance the collaboration of the people who share our motivations.

If we start off by explaining what we do, the conversation will revolve around our product or service details—and even comparisons with other similar products, which can sometimes generate an unfavorable dynamic. And, if we begin by explaining how we do what we do, the conversation might get mired in technical details that might not interest everyone. However, if we begin by talking about why we do what we do, we'll be able to capture the attention, and surely the collaboration, of people who identify with and connect to our purpose.

In fact, according to Sinek, every organization knows how to explain what it does, and many of them can describe how they do it, but there are few organizations that really know how to convey the reason for what they do. So, I urge you to always begin your communication by explaining why you do what you do.

Figure 2.4. The Golden Circle

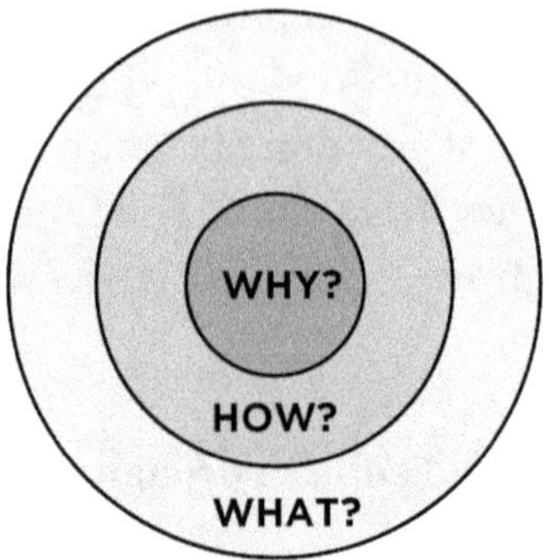

Source: Simon Sinek

2) Principle 2: Focus on the Purpose Before the Problem and on the Problem Before the Solution

When I began in the world of innovation and entrepreneurship, my mentors always told me, "At the beginning, don't focus so much on the solution you want to build but on the problem that you're trying to solve." And how right they were! Intuitively, we tend to focus on the solution (and fall in love with it) because it's more stimulating to build something new than to analyze something "old" that doesn't work. We all want a better world, a world without poverty, with clean energy, with democratic access to knowledge, etc. But we cannot forget that all these purposes are associated with many challenges—that is, problems that require a solution. Therefore, once our purpose (our "North Star") has been defined, the next thing is to identify the different problems that need to be solved to make that purpose a reality and, once those problems have been identified, to analyze the possible solutions for each one.

**Figure 2.5. A Purpose Includes Several Challenges
that Can Be Resolved in Various Ways**

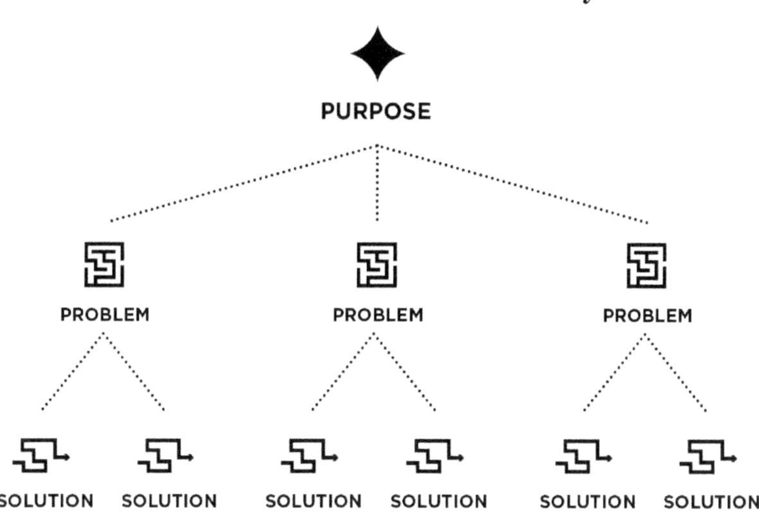

Source: Prepared by the author

3) Principle 3: Adapt Your Operating Style to the Context

It's not only about action but about always acting accordingly. This is just common sense, but, as they say, common sense is the least common of all the senses, so it's important to keep this in mind.

Over the years, I have met all kinds of people: innovators who are passionate about new challenges and are willing to be the first to try a new technology, conservatives who bring stability by making everything work properly and avoiding unnecessary risks, optimizers who love to improve something that already exists to take their performance and scope to the next level, etc. All these profiles are very necessary, but they also inherently imply a certain way of operating. It's essential that team members be aware of their personal style and continuously adapt it to the project's moment and specific needs.

As we'll see throughout the next chapter, Purpose Launchpad establishes three phases that represent an initiative's level of maturity (Exploration, Evaluation, and Impact) and that will indicate the way to evolve it.

Figure 2.6. Operating Styles

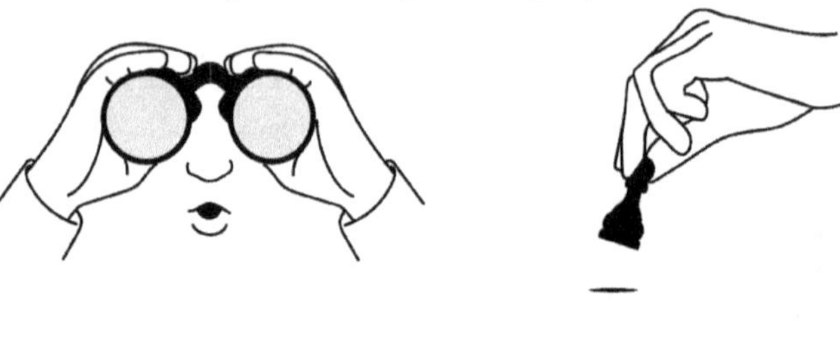

Source: Prepared by the author

4) Principle 4: Act with the Right Mindset Beyond Processes and Tools

A few years ago, in a meeting where we were trying to decide which management software tool might be best to organize our team, one of the attendees advised against using Trello. When I asked him why, he stated that it would lead us to a micromanagement style that could be counterproductive for the very initial and highly uncertain phase our project was in, which required autonomy and dynamism. I was surprised, because I had used Trello before in other projects and had not had that micromanagement experience. But I soon realized the reason for my opinion: I had used Trello while working with someone who was very detail-oriented and loved control. It was the mindset of the person implementing it that had led to micromanaging, not the tool.

In the end, we implemented Trello as a management tool but used a very different style and mindset. And it worked very well, because the mindset we use is more important than the tool itself. If you have the correct mindset, you'll use it correctly and implement the right processes, the ones your initiative needs at any moment.

Figure 2.7. Mindset Over Processes and Tools

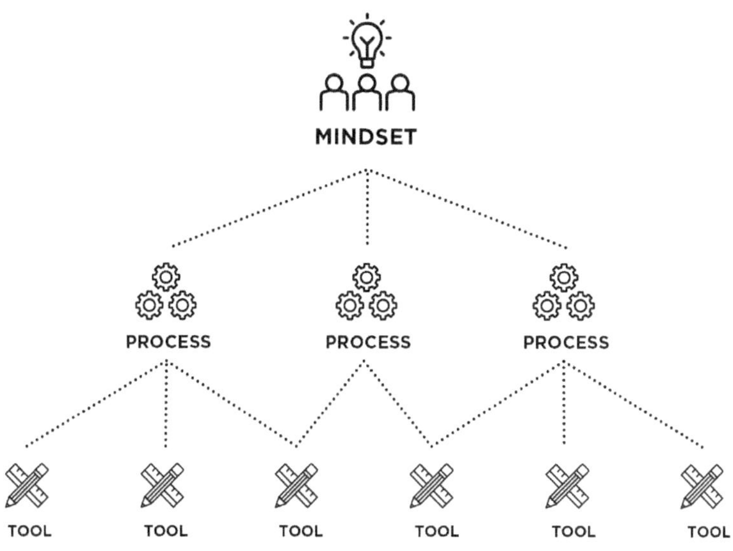

Source: Prepared by the author

5) Principle 5: Validate What You Learn Before Building

If we're going to build a new product, ideally, before creating it, we'd make sure that the market will accept it, don't you think? Well, though it seems obvious and makes perfect sense, that's usually not the way it's done.

One of the reasons is that sometimes we're so sure of the benefits of our proposal that we don't even consider the need to validate it, even more so if we have the financial resources to create it. Another reason is the fear of someone stealing our idea before it's launched, which doesn't make sense, since, by sharing an idea with potential customers, we get feedback that allows us to really improve it.

Whether we're thinking about creating a new product or expanding or improving an existing one, it's essential to validate in the market that it's really a good idea. This applies on many other levels as well, even when we're going to create a new internal process within the organization. The best way to do this is to conduct experiments that offer us real and demonstrable knowledge, a process we call "validated learning."

Keep in mind that there are degrees of validation. Customers' good intentions are not a complete validation. It's only complete when customers pay for our product and are satisfied after their experience with it. That's when our value proposition makes sense.

This not only applies to startups but also to corporations. An example: when Tesla launched their Model 3, they required customers to prepay, and, in doing so, they validated there was an actual demand before starting chain production.

Figure 2.8. Develop Your Customer Before Your Product

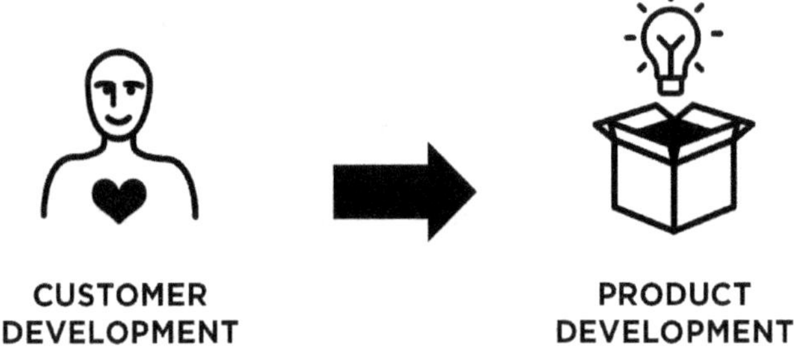

Source: Prepared by the author

6) Principle 6: Earn Meaningful Income Before Obtaining Investment

When a startup manages to "raise" financing, its founders usually celebrate this in style. However, while it's an important milestone that deserves recognition, getting a funding round does not in any way ensure a project's success. Moreover, it often dooms it to failure, especially when the business model has yet to be validated. Having more resources lets you hit the accelerator, but, if you're not clear about which direction to take, all you'll get is a full-speed crash against the wall of reality.

Money is always money, but it's worth much more when it comes from real customers, not investors, because they pay because they're convinced by our value proposition. In addition, their feedback is tremendously valuable to improve our products or services. It's not always simple, but, ideally, we get validation from real customers before going in search of investors. We'll see some ways to do so in the next chapters. We should only go to investors when we have market validation and need to take our business to the next level.

Figure 2.9. Earn Meaningful Income Before Obtaining Investment

Source: Prepared by the author

7) Principle 7: Unlock Abundance Through Purpose

The first thing that happens when an organization defines its purpose, which initially often seems much broader than its current business, is that a world of opportunities opens up that didn't exist before. Remember that a purpose contains many challenges and problems that must be resolved, which gives us the opportunity to launch a large number of solutions.

Throughout the book, we'll see that purpose not only unlocks an abundance of opportunities but also gives you access to talent and attracts communities.

Figure 2.10. Purpose is Linked to Different Opportunities

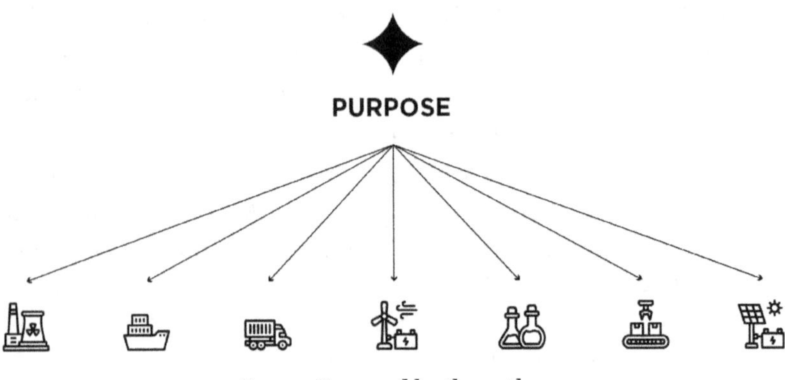

Source: Prepared by the author

8) Principle 8: Connect with and Generate Abundance Instead of Focusing on Managing Scarcity

When a business is oriented to a specific industry, it has no choice but to compete to get a piece of that market. Excessive competition can lead us to places where our survival is endangered, because it generates an environment dominated by scarcity.

On the other hand, when a business is purpose-oriented, a world of abundant possibilities opens up in the form of different types of purpose-linked challenges and needs, which the business will be able to satisfy with new products or services. Creating or connecting with purpose-oriented ecosystems helps us tap into abundance and escape the market-generated scarcity delimited by an industry.

Abundance, however, is about mindset. If we look at the world with eyes of abundance and can connect with sources of abundance and generate our own through strength of purpose and our strategy's scope, we'll be able to escape red oceans and access blue ones.

Figure 2.11. Abundance vs. Scarcity

Source: Prepared by the author

9) Principle 9: Maximizing Positive Impact Maximizes Benefits

As we saw with the Impact Pyramid, when we focus our organization on a purpose, we naturally connect with many opportunities and increase our income and profits. In addition, if we operate sustainably and responsibly, society and our customers will more strongly support everything we do, so we'll improve our positioning and maximize our results.

It's important to clarify that this principle also applies to non-profit organizations, which, while not focused on maximizing profits, also want to maximize revenue to maintain their activity and maximize their positive impact. In fact, impact and benefits are intimately related, since, without benefits, it's not possible to have an impact (due to lack of economic viability), and it's impossible to obtain benefits without positive impact (towards our customers at least). If we focus on the ultimate goal, positive impact, we'll be able to generate and maximize our benefits and contribute to fulfilling our purpose.

Figure 2.12. Maximizing Impact Maximizes Profits

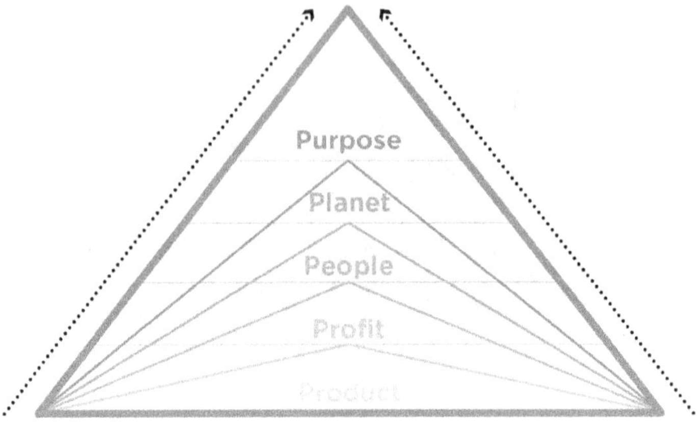

Source: Prepared by the author

10) Principle 10: Measure Progress Through Validated Positive Impact

Eric Ries, author of *The Lean Startup*, said that "validated learning is the unit of progress for a startup." Indeed, validated learning is very important for any type of initiative, but, to measure its progress, we need to know the validated positive impact. This will take into account and verify the following: the value delivered to our customers, the economic value generated for our organization, the degree of sustainability with which we carry out our activity, and the positive contribution we make to the world.

Only by measuring the validated positive impact will we know with certainty whether we're correctly developing our initiatives, as well as whether we're implementing the right initiatives.

**Figure 2.13. Measure Progress Through
the Positive Impact Generated**

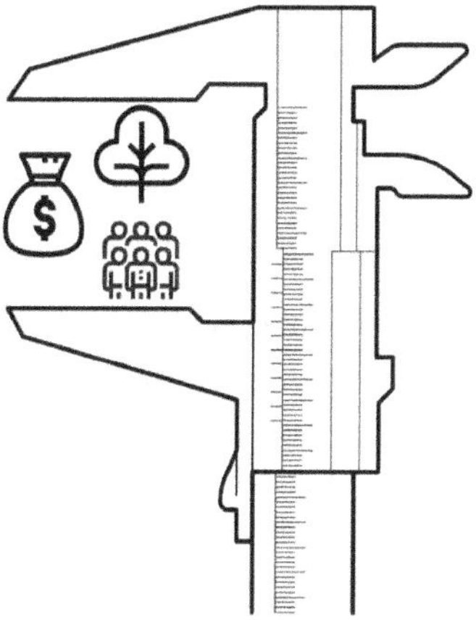

Source: Prepared by the author

Final Thoughts

These are the five values and ten principles of Purpose Launchpad. If we manage to keep them in mind and follow them (despite the temptation not to), we'll be able not only to create meaningful initiatives for the world but greatly increase our chances of success.

If you don't follow the values and principles, you may obtain short-term results, but you'll be compromising your chances for future success. In fact, to apply Purpose Launchpad, it's not even necessary to put everything that you'll continue to learn throughout the book into practice. Simply by internalizing and implementing the values and principles correctly, you'll achieve truly incredible results.

Even if you feel very motivated and convinced now, it's likely that you won't always take the values into account or won't always follow the principles. When that happens, it'll be important for you to be aware of it and learn from the experience. Mistakes will be useful for gaining more experience and a better understanding of why the values and principles have been formulated this way, as well as to continuously adapt your mindset to the environment.

I recommend that, from time to time, you review the values and principles, ask yourself if you're following them, and implement them as much as possible. With time and experience, with mistakes and successes, you'll internalize them to the point where you're not aware that you're applying them. The day this happens, you'll have incorporated the most important thing about Purpose Launchpad: the mindset.

Table 2.1. Purpose Launchpad Values and Principles

VALUES	PRINCIPLES
Purpose Purpose over problems and solutions	Inspire people through your purpose rather than your product
	Focus on the purpose before the problem, and on the problem before the solution
Action Actions over intentions	Adapt your operating style to the context
	Act with the right mindset beyond processes and tools
Learning Customer data over intuition	Validate what you learn before building
	Earn meaningful income before obtaining investment
Abundance Purpose-oriented ecosystems over industry-centric competition	Unlock abundance through purpose
	Connect with and generate abundance instead of focusing on managing scarcity
Positive Impact Long-term positive impact over short-term profit	Maximizing positive impact maximizes Profits
	Measure progress through validated positive impact

Source: Prepared by the author

Key Points

Purpose Launchpad has five values and ten principles derived from the *Purpose Manifesto* and defined from the experience of hundreds of successful innovators and entrepreneurs.

The **values** are:

- Purpose
- Action
- Learning
- Abundance
- Positive Impact

The **principles** are:

1. Inspire people through your purpose rather than your product
2. Focus on the purpose before the problem and on the problem before the solution
3. Adapt your operating style to the context
4. Act with the right mindset beyond processes and tools
5. Validate what you learn before building
6. Earn meaningful income before obtaining investment
7. Unlock abundance through purpose
8. Connect with and generate abundance instead of focusing on managing scarcity
9. Maximizing positive impact maximizes benefits
10. Measure progress through validated positive impact

11
Phases

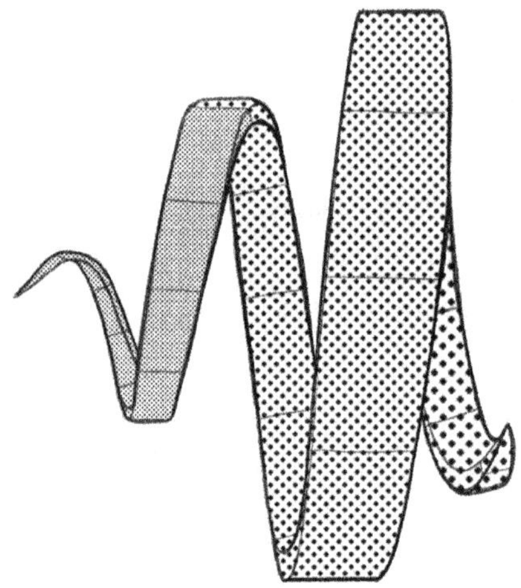

We all act in different ways depending on the circumstances. When we speak, for example, we express ourselves differently depending on who we're talking to: our best friend, our boss, a family member, etc. This is called "sociolinguistic register." When we drive our car, we change the way we drive depending on where we are: on city streets, on a highway, or on a country road. Our parenting style varies depending on our children's stage in life: childhood, adolescence, or young adulthood.

The same happens when we're developing a project or an initiative. Depending on the circumstances and your degree of maturity, we'll need to treat you differently. Purpose Launchpad establishes three possible phases for an initiative: Exploration, Evaluation, and Impact.

Figure 2.14. The Three Phases in Which an Initiative Can Be

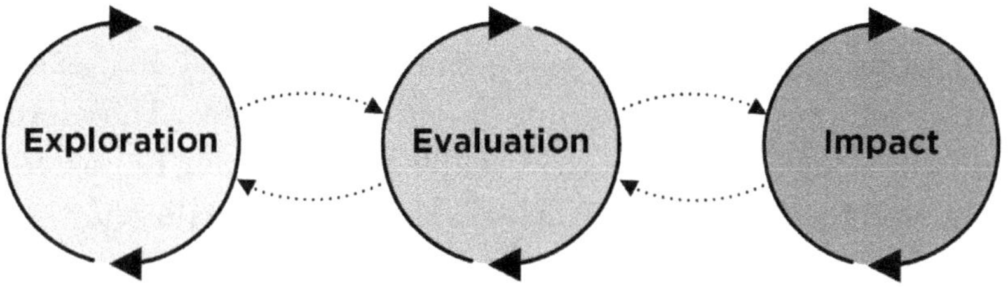

Source: Prepared by the author

For each one, it suggests a certain way of acting, even a different type of mindset. It's important to note that, as the arrows in the above figure indicate, the Purpose Launchpad phases are not a purely linear process; it's possible to move from one to another according to the initiative's status. For example, after moving from the Exploration to the Evaluation phase, it's possible to either move to the Impact phase or return to the Exploration one.

I'll explain the essence of each of these phases below, and, in the third part of the book, we'll see how to manage our new product or our startup in each of the phases in detail.

1) Exploration

In an initiative's early stages, it's important to apply Socrates' famous words: "I only know that I know nothing." You're innovating, doing something that no one has ever done before, at least not in the way and within the context you're doing it. Therefore, there's still much to discover until you find your way.

This is an exciting phase for projects, but, at the same time, it is also full of uncertainty, something that can be attractive for certain types of people and very uncomfortable for others. It's as if you were on a small heretofore unknown island of which no maps exist. You suspect that there's a deposit of magical minerals on the island that could be used to manufacture an anti-cancer drug, so, following your purpose (to eradicate cancer), you come to the island and start exploring.

During the Exploration phase, the goal is to maximize learning by minimizing the time and resources expended. Therefore, you don't start building a road to the site if you don't know for sure where it is. If you did, you would most likely waste your time and resources building roads that would turn out to be useless. The first thing you must do is look around and discover all the possibilities. For example, you'd climb to a high area of the island to observe the terrain in its entirety and determine possible routes. Then you would approach the beginning of each route to carefully assess which one seems more promising. Logically, we won't be able to know which is the right one until we walk along the route, but, for now, it's enough to find all the possibilities and make a preliminary analysis that helps you decide which of them to start with. Although some paths may seem more attractive, it's necessary to analyze them all before deciding.

In this Exploration phase, plans are useless, since each step we take reveals new information that could make the plan obsolete. Though I understand that plans offer a sense of security, they still don't make sense at this point, because what we need is to explore the whole island so that we're able to draw a map as soon as possible.

There are always different paths, and, for differing reasons, it's normal not to hit on the right one on the first try. One example is Instagram, which was called Burbn at first and included not only photos and videos but many other elements, such as games. The app didn't seem to work, so its creators decided to remove all but one of the features: photos. They rebuilt the app to focus solely on photography: it was clean and simple and clearly worth it. In other words, Instagram's founders explored the island, took one path, and, when they realized it was not the right one, they went back and focused on a more specific path that finally led them to success. In startups jargon, this is called "pivoting" and basically consists of changing your business model—in other words, changing the route towards reaching our goal. Most companies considered successful today pivoted at some point in their development: Twitter, Google, PayPal, etc. Many others who failed to find their way in time ended up failing altogether.

It's important that you assume from the onset that you'll probably need to pivot at some point and change routes. To minimize the risk that this represents, it's best that you explore the different possibilities in an initial phase, dedicating minimum time and resources to it. No one has infinite resources, so you must make the most of yours.

When talking about innovation, it's usual to use the term hypothesis, since any new idea is, by definition, a hypothesis. In the Exploration phase, we're not going to focus yet on evaluating whether the hypotheses are correct or not but on finding those hypotheses that we do not know. For example, imagine that you start a project focused on democratizing education and that, from the beginning, you clearly see that you should focus on creating an application to give any child in the world access to knowledge in specific subjects. It would be a mistake to start creating the app without first exploring any remaining options. There are many other segments of potential customers besides children: teenagers, university students, people actively working, and even retirees.

The first step, therefore, will be to detect all the possibilities, and the next one will be to examine each of them a bit to evaluate their potential. To do that, you can talk to people from each of these groups and evaluate how promising it would be to address one customer segment or another. This is what I mean when I say "take a peek" at the road without walking along it. We're not offering any product or service yet; we're trying to learn. As we'll see in the next chapters, there are specific techniques that will help you discover who your customers are and which ones you should discard.

This explorer attitude should also help you discover and define different types of products or services, to discover and evaluate potential team members, etc. In this initial phase, everything, absolutely everything, has yet to be discovered, and our inner explorer must help us change that. Of course, for that to happen, we must pass the controls over to our inner explorer and take them away from the perfectionist who also lives inside us, the one who will tirelessly want to create a plan and convince us of it. We must avoid the temptation to embrace the false security offered by plans and open ourselves to uncertainty. It's time to enjoy one of the things that makes us human: exploring beyond what is known!

2) Evaluation

Once all the possibilities have been discovered and preliminarily analyzed, it's time to embark on the adventure and try the most promising path. The moment of truth has arrived; we'll begin to put our ideas into practice and check whether they make sense or not.

Continuing with the island analogy, it's time to put on your backpack and start walking along the path that, after your initial exploration, you believe has more possibilities to take you to the site with the minerals. Every step you take from now on will be a new test, a new experiment, which will provide constant learning. You could find an insurmountable obstacle at any point along the way that forces you to go back and look for a different path (that is, return to the Exploration phase). This is something you must always keep in mind.

In the Evaluation phase, we must pay attention to details and make agile decisions. This means carrying as little baggage as possible so that we can walk lightly, make quick decisions, and even, if necessary, be able to switch paths. This phase's motto could be "minimum baggage, maximum learning."

At this point, we must be ready to begin real testing with a specific customer segment, to start offering our product to potential customers, and, even more interesting, to start generating value for them through real experiences. The key will be to do this without waiting to build a definitive and complete version of the product but with what is called a "minimum viable product" (MVP). This allows you to maximize learning with a minimum investment of resources and time.

It's about starting to deliver real value to your potential customers by minimizing product development (or even without creating the product). Otherwise, you'll carry more weight than you need to explore a path that you can't yet know will actually lead you to where you want to go. This involves conducting experiments on an ongoing basis that let you learn and, as agilely as possible, make the necessary changes.

Let's go back to the previous example, the project focused on democratizing education, and suppose that, during the Exploration, phase we've detected a very promising customer segment that we've decided to focus on: long-time unemployed adults, to whom we'll offer access to an application to update their skills to meet the demands of a new job market. As I mentioned before, we shouldn't create a very sophisticated app, because we're not yet certain that this customer segment will work or that the application will fit the market. What we must do is create an experience of some kind (maybe even without an app) that lets us start delivering value to that customer segment and see if what they receive has value for them or not. And we'll use their feedback to continue improving our service—that is, to iterate it until it fits perfectly in the market.

Like with the explorer's attitude, we'll also use the evaluator for this second phase, where everything is a hypothesis to be evaluated: the type of client, the type of product, the price model, the team's ability, work style, etc. If the evaluation confirms the hypothesis, move forward; if not, we'll make the necessary adjustments or change hypotheses.

This phase has very rewarding moments, especially when you see that the product or service that you've created so enthusiastically is liked and adds value. Feeling that you're on the right track is wonderful!

3) Impact

Once you've validated your hypothesis with real experiences (including satisfied customers) and know you're on the right track, it's time to move on to the next phase: Impact.

Let's go back for the last time to our imaginary island. You've explored all the possibilities, you've evaluated several of them, you've chosen a path, and you've validated it and have found the precious mineral deposit. Now you can fulfill your purpose and give everyone who needs it access to the magical minerals. It's time to think about how to best execute a plan, to focus on all kinds of details to optimize the mineral-extraction method. Now we must pave the road from the coast to the site so that trucks can circulate, get the minerals to the laboratories, and manufacture the drug that will eradicate cancer globally. In other words, the time has come to create a positive impact!

In this phase, there's much less uncertainty because we've validated our business model, our market, and even our value proposition through our products or services, and they all make sense. An even more rewarding time lies ahead: when we reap the first benefits after so much effort and broaden our reach.

The Impact phase doesn't always arrive as quickly as we'd like. Airbnb's founders began their first trials in 2007 and didn't begin scaling the business on a mass scale until 2010. They spent several years evaluating and iterating their services, which did not fully scale until they found the key to grow and go from an MVP to a scalable product based on an extraordinary user experience, leading them to become the largest lodging chain in the world. Through the constant application of experimentation techniques like Lean Startup, the founders of Airbnb realized that one of the keys for people to contract lodging on the Internet were the photographs on the webpage. They decided to work with experienced photographers and defined the appropriate guidelines for taking photos of the lodgings, which became the basis used by owners when posting their offered lodgings on the platform. Thanks to this new element, very focused on how to perfect what they were already doing, Airbnb experienced an exponential growth rate, going from one inflatable mattress in the founders' apartment to the world's largest lodging chain.

It's time to work on growth and increase the speed and scope of what we've previously validated. For this, we need an "impactor" attitude, centered on making the scope as massive as possible by focusing on execution and efficiency and making the necessary adjustments to make our initiative as scalable as possible. We have left the MVP behind and now have a product with a good customer experience that we want to perfect to take it to the next level.

Let's also return for the last time to our fictional project for democratizing education. Suppose that, after several experiments, we couldn't validate our hypothesis of targeting adults who have been unemployed for a long time but did identify a new segment: new college graduates seeking their first jobs while also getting practical training. We worked for a while with a group of users from this segment, and, thanks to the feedback obtained, we created and improved an app to access training programs until we had a product ready to offer the world. Now, in the Impact phase, we're considering how to scale our model and bring our application to as many people as possible. It's time to analyze our current processes to optimize them, find channels that help us mass promote the application, and perfect the product to the max to offer our customers the best possible experience—all this while constantly learning.

As impactors, we now view everything on a large scale and continually consider how to improve and multiply everything we do. And we look at everything through this prism: our product, which we try to perfect to the maximum; the team, which we may need to expand with execution-oriented profiles; the search for financing, which is easier now thanks to the fact that our model has already been validated; etc. In short, it's time to reap the fruits of all our previous work and show the world what we're capable of. It's time to make history and create a true positive impact!

Final Thoughts on Phases

The Purpose Launchpad phases represent different mindsets, different ways of viewing the world and acting when developing our initiatives. When we're in a specific phase, it's as if we were wearing lenses tinted with a certain color, which we will change when moving on to another phase to change our perspective.

As you've surely noticed, the passage across the three phases offers a divergent-convergent approach, as well as many innovation mechanisms in which we initially open and propose as many alternatives as possible, and, once evaluated, we concentrate on the most promising one to be able to develop it in greater detail.

Therefore, in the early stages, we'll view the world with a much more open outlook, and, as we move forward, we'll focus our attention on one path.

I want to insist on the idea that the three phases do not represent steps in a linear process but different operating states or mindsets. It's possible that, after carrying out an initial Exploration phase and moving to the Evaluation phase, the experience and learnings obtained will take us back to the Exploration phase, as Instagram once did, along with many other companies that pivoted their business models until they found the right path.

On the other hand, it's essential to understand that, when we're in a certain phase, to some extent we must always keep the previous phases in mind. For example, during the Impact phase, we cannot stop continuously exploring new possibilities, since the environment could change again or because we could find new paths that improve the previous ones. Airbnb continued to explore until it found the turning point (professional photographers) that allowed it to start scaling its sales.

The Purpose Launchpad logo reflects precisely this idea of always keeping the different phases present:

Figure 2.15. Purpose Launchpad logo icon

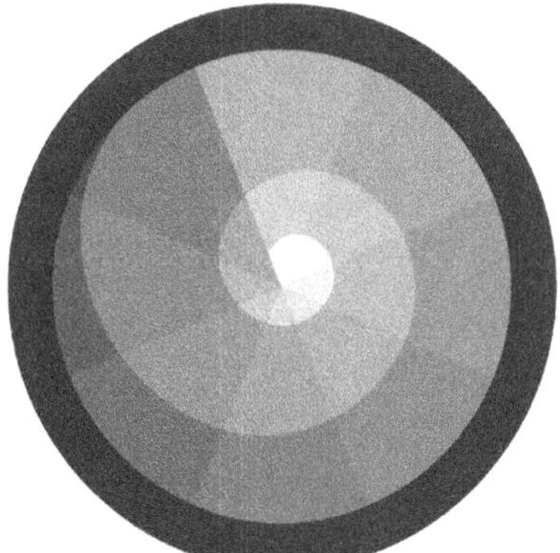

Source: Prepared by the author

If you look at the original Purpose Launchpad logo in full color, for example on the website (*www.purposelaunchpad.com*), you can see how orange represents the Exploration phase, blue represents the Evaluation phase, and violet represents the Impact phase. The version of the logo that you're looking at right now in the book, in black and white, only differentiates between the phases with grayscale, but it's enough for you to get an idea of what I'm talking about. In addition to the different colors, everything is represented by a spiral that aggregates each of the phases: we begin at the center with just orange, but, when we go to blue, we keep the Exploration base, and, when we're in the last of the layers, corresponding to Impact, we continue to keep the previous two, Exploration and Evaluation. It's not, therefore, a linear process but adds layers as our focus moves to the next stage. You carry the explorer, the evaluator, and the impactor inside of you at all times, but, in each phase, you give one of them prominence, the one who can best lead the project depending on its moment—in short, the one who can best help you achieve your purpose and create a positive impact on the world.

Key Points

Purpose Launchpad establishes three possible phases depending on the degree of maturity of a project or initiative and its circumstances:

1. **Exploration**: search for the different paths. This phase is characterized by the uncertainty and futility of the plans, something that some people experience as an exciting challenge and others as an uncomfortable phase. It's about assuming that all we know is that we don't know anything.
2. **Evaluation**: analysis of the different paths/hypotheses. This phase is characterized by the need to pay attention to details and make agile decisions, minimizing your baggage to maximize learning.
3. **Impact**: once the hypothesis is validated with real experiences with customers, we enter the optimization of processes and resources to maximize the impact. This phase is characterized by a decrease in uncertainty and the need to design and execute detailed action plans. It's time to maximize our positive impact!

12
Axes

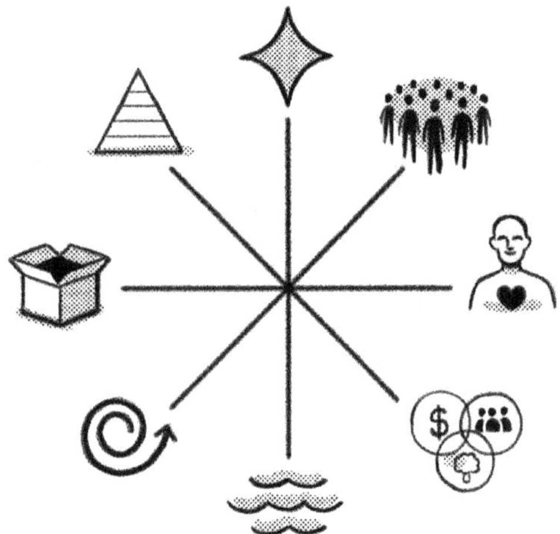

Everything is interconnected. We see it in ecosystems made up of different living beings that interact in the same environment. When one species disappears, the survival of the rest is threatened. That disappearance generates a chain effect that can ultimately lead to the demise of the entire ecosystem.

We also see it in living organisms, in our own body in fact. If our pancreas stops synthesizing enough insulin, our blood sugar levels rise, which can lead to kidney failure, blindness, etc.

The same thing happens in organizations, so Purpose Launchpad establishes eight totally interconnected axes: Purpose, People, Customers, Sustainability, Abundance, Processes, Product, and Metrics. When evaluating or evolving an initiative with Purpose Launchpad, it's impossible to work on only one of these axes without equally advancing the rest. Next, we'll see what each of these axes consists of and how they relate to one other. I'll also mention some of the tools that will help you when working on each of the axes. I won't go into too much detail, as we'll look at their application in more depth in the third part of the book. Remember that you can download the official guide on *www.purposelaunchpad.com*, where you'll find much more information and references to the different tools and methodologies associated with each of the eight axes that we will touch on below. Throughout the following chapters, you will also find links to download the different tools that will help you implement the axes (and much more) of Purpose Launchpad. These tools have been either developed or curated by the Purpose Alliance community, so you will see the links point to its official website. Are you ready to know what each of the eight axes hides and start implementing everything in your initiatives? Let's begin!

Axis 1: Purpose

As you'd expect, everything begins with Purpose, with your project's *raison d'être*. In this axis, you must describe the elements that define the initiative's identity: why the project exists, what it intends to become in the future, and how it will achieve this. Specifically, you should describe the following elements: purpose, starshot, vision, mission, and values. We talked about almost all of them already at the beginning of the book, so I'll simply give you a quick review using SpaceX, founded by Elon Musk, as an illustrative example:

- Purpose: This describes the world we would like to create and reminds us why the initiative exists. SpaceX's purpose is very clear: "to make humanity a multiplanetary species."
- Starshot: This is a quantifiable and time-bound goal that turns purpose into something measurable. It should focus on quantifying an external outcome on the change we intend to create in the world, not on an internal issue of our organization (otherwise it would be a Strategic Objective). In SpaceX's case, the starshot is "to take a million humans to Mars before 2050." When this happens, the human species will be a multiplanetary species. Starshot is formally located in the Metrics axis (Axis 8), but I chose to introduce it here since it's often used alongside purpose due to the direct connection between the two concepts. I'll also take this opportunity to mention that there's a concept called moonshot that you may already know about, since it's used in certain innovation and disruption environments to describe very ambitious goals and is like our starshot in some ways. However, in the Purpose Launchpad environment, we have called this concept starshot to link it even more to the Purpose, which usually resembles the star that guides each person or organization's path. In addition, it's important to keep in mind that this metric must be a quantifiable and time-limited objective, so the term we will use to call this concept will be starshot. We've already reached the moon, so it's time to aim for the stars!
- Vision: This is an initiative's long-term projection. If it becomes a reality, we will be contributing significantly to the purpose. Going back to SpaceX, its vision is "to become the next generation of space vehicles, reusable and capable of taking humans to Mars and other destinations in the Solar System."

- Mission: This defines how we will best be able to reach our vision. Its peculiarity is that it can change without affecting vision or purpose. At SpaceX, it consists of "designing, manufacturing, and launching advanced spacecraft and rockets."
- Values: This describes how we will operate to manage our initiative. Values are a key element of every organization's culture. SpaceX's values are innovation, risk, inclusion, and diversity.

There are multiple tools to define these elements—for example, the MTP Canvas. Another tool that allows you to visualize all the axis elements at once and manage them together is the Organization Identity Canvas.

The key to this axis is to define the purpose before the remaining elements. If you haven't done it that way from the beginning, I recommend that you stop for a moment and do so. Keep in mind that the Purpose will be fixed; it will be your North Star and will help you stay the course, while the rest of the elements may change over time as you learn, discover the environment, and evolve your initiative.

2) Axis 2: People

Any type of initiative you develop, whether it's a startup or a project within an organization, will always be made up of a group of people who will make it possible. The result will depend on the people who execute it, one way or another. These people can be part of the organization's internal team or the outside community.

- Internal Team: This is the group of individuals who collaborate within the same purpose, forming part of an organizational structure that favors their collaboration. In the SpaceX example, at the time of this writing, the team is made up of about 9,500 people in different locations in the US, led by Elon Musk, the organization's current CEO.

- Outside Community: This is formed by all those people and entities external to the organization that are aligned somehow with its purpose and, therefore, follow and support it in some way. The community is one of the most important assets of organizations, because, if we have a group of people and entities aligned with our purpose, we can garner great value from them. The community follows in the organization's footsteps, helps promote the organization's activity and purpose, and often carries out voluntary activities for the organization. In the case of SpaceX, its community is made up of the company's space exploration fans and people specializing in various technical aspects who sometimes support the organization by providing solutions and external talent. Companies like SpaceX with a strong purpose have no problem capturing the best talent, as many of the best qualified professionals share the company's purpose and are even fans.

There are multiple tools that help us organize and manage teams, such as functional organization charts or Team Canvas. Others, such as the Community Canvas, allow us to define who the community members of our initiative could be and help us ask ourselves the key questions that will allow us to attract people to our community and make it grow.

When you create a team, you must ensure that the people you incorporate are aligned with your initiative's purpose, as that will give them extraordinary motivation. As for community, the force of your purpose must act as a center of gravity, attracting the right people and entities—that is, those who are aligned with the purpose and willing to support it.

3) Axis 3: Customers

Every project has customers who must be served in some way. They are the people, users, or entities for whom we generate value of some kind (solving a problem or satisfying a need).

Let's go back to SpaceX. It currently has several types of customers: on the one hand, the federal government, including NASA itself, for whom they carry out specific projects such as transporting supplies to the International Space Station, and, on the other, individuals who want to go into space. SpaceX's first private mission, called Inspiration4, took four civilians into space. It was funded by one of them, Jared Isaacman, billionaire and founder of Ship4 Payments.

There are several tools to define your customers in detail, such as the Value Proposition Canvas, as well as methodologies that will help you discover which segments to focus on or not. In any case, the key to this axis is to always focus on understanding your customers' problems instead of obsessing over the solution, as I have mentioned earlier.

4) Axis 4: Sustainability

We define sustainability as being able to operate in the present without compromising future viability, ensuring a balance between economic growth, social welfare, and environmental care. Every project needs an economic viability model that makes it sustainable internally, whether it's a profit-oriented business or a non-profit organization. It must also be socially sustainable—that is, it must generate benefits for the people within the organization and surroundings. And, finally, it must carry out its activity without harming the environment.

Coming back to SpaceX, the company receives income for each space mission it performs for its customers, both government and private passengers, which makes it an economically viable entity. On the other hand, it offers its employees good working conditions and promotes education and support for society. For example, after Russia's invasion of Ukraine in early 2022, SpaceX donated many connection terminals to Ukraine for the Starlink satellite network to help keep the country connected to the Internet. Finally, in terms of environmental impact, we must not ignore that SpaceX rockets generate significant emissions, but, at the same time, the company is very focused on developing reusable space vehicles that avoid greater pollution on the planet and is contributing enormously to the aerospace industry's progress in environmental sustainability.

When developing your business model, you can use tools such as the Business Model Canvas, in addition to making financial projections that help you analyze the economic viability of your project. There are also other versions of this tool, such as the Sustainable Business Canvas, which help us consider the social and ecological costs and benefits of our model. Another reference is the ESG (environmental, social, and governance) model, widely accepted by entities dedicated to sustainability.

5) Axis 5: Abundance

In the first part of the book, we talked about how important it is to connect with abundance. Purpose Launchpad incorporates an axis focused on this essential idea.

This axis must include the possible sources of abundance that the initiative can leverage, as well as how to manage them. By connecting with abundance, we can position ourselves in much larger markets than those competitive spaces that focus on scarcity. In addition, connecting with abundance often allows us to offer greater value to our customers.

Several elements make SpaceX a project fully connected to abundance. SpaceX's own competitive environment—the universe itself—is abundant by default. The company also makes use of the latest technology, including advanced algorithms, to create reusable rockets, connecting the project to a greater abundance of resources.

When implementing this axis, it's enough that you ask yourself continuously how you could create abundance or connect with existing abundance and best manage it. You can count on tools such as the ExO Canvas for this, which will help you ask yourself the key questions. However, the most important thing is that you develop your mindset to continuously think in terms of abundance, as I explained in the chapter "Connect with Abundance."

6) Axis 6: Processes

How many apparently good ideas remain in the gutter because they are not well executed? Many. That's why it's important to always keep this in mind: an idea is worthless unless it's properly executed. As I've said, the *Agile Manifesto* was published in 2001 and has been followed by numerous frameworks and tools to facilitate the implementation of this type of approach in different types of organizations. That being said, it's essential to know when to apply agile approaches and when to implement more static and optimization-focused processes.

The team is responsible for executing the initiative in a way that leads to success. In the case of SpaceX, from the beginning, Elon Musk has promoted an agile culture within the organization, as well as in the rest of his companies, undoubtedly influenced by his beginnings as a software developer (where the first agile frameworks emerged). This has allowed it to move quickly, embracing failure as part of the process and as an opportunity to continuously learn to innovate and achieve unprecedented breakthroughs.

To define your processes, there are agile frameworks focused on the product, such as Scrum. You can also implement Purpose Launchpad for the entire initiative, as you're seeing throughout this book. There are other tools and techniques more oriented towards the definition and optimization of processes, including BPMN (Business Process Model and Notation).

The key to this axis is not to simply dwell on operations but to understand that the processes are the result of operating under a specific mindset. In fact, the very concept of "agility" attempts to synthesize a particular type of mindset.

7) Axis 7: Product

The way to add value to the different customer segments will be through a product or service. In other words, the product is what is created to respond to the challenges and needs of customers. In this sense, it will be essential that you properly plan the process of creating your products or services to avoid building something that no one wants to use.

It's very important to understand the difference between value proposition and product. An example: the value proposition could be to transport people from their city of origin to their destination city, while the products or services could be train travel, air travel, bus travel, etc. At SpaceX, the value proposition they offer to NASA, one of their main customers, is to improve the cost and reliability of space missions, and, to make it a reality, they have a very specific product: advanced and reusable space vehicles.

To define your value proposition, you can use tools such as the Value Proposition Canvas, which will help you connect your customer segments with a specific value proposition and, later, translate this value proposition into a specific product or service that you can define via user stories and other similar techniques.

The key to this axis is to work the product in a way that aligns with the specific needs of your customer segments (and, if possible, with the collaboration of real customers), always keeping in mind the relative value of the Purpose Launchpad purpose, which states, "Purpose over problems and solutions." In other words, always keep your purpose in mind—why you're doing what you do—and try to find challenges associated with this purpose.

8) Axis 8: Metrics

As Peter Drucker said, "What is not defined cannot be measured. What is not measured cannot be improved. What is not improved is always degraded." Whatever the nature and state of your initiative, you'll need to measure certain elements to constantly learn and improve.

The Metrics axis defines what we need to measure to know the status of our initiative and obtain relevant information that allows us to properly develop it. From the perspective of Purpose Launchpad, there are three types of metrics, arising in turn from three different types of accounting:

- Financial Accounting: recording, classifying, analyzing, and reporting in monetary terms the different economic operations of a company or project. There are different types of economic and financial metrics associated with this type of accounting.
- Innovation Accounting: evaluating the progress of a company or project in terms of the value contributed to the market in the process of generating new products or services. This type of accounting is very useful at a very early stage of the project, when economic and financial metrics offer us little or no information.

- Impact Accounting: assessing the value contributed to the world through the organization's activity. It's very useful when making decisions to maximize the impact beyond economic benefit or the value provided to our customers. In fact, starshot is considered an impact metric, thus closing the circle that begins with the Purpose axis and ends with the Metrics axis.

SpaceX's main impact metric is its starshot, "taking one million humans to Mars before 2050." At this time, this metric has a null value, since it has not yet sent any rocket to the red planet. What SpaceX does currently measure is the percentage of its rockets' successful launches and landings. They have gone from failing in practically all their attempts between 2013 and 2015 to a success rate of more than 95 percent as of 2017.

In short, don't forget to always measure your initiative's key data and analyze that information to obtain knowledge that allows you to improve.

Final Thoughts on Axes

As I said at the beginning of this chapter, it's essential that you understand that everything is interconnected and that, to advance an initiative, you must work all its axes equally.

That is precisely why Purpose Launchpad's main diagram, shown below, includes the eight axes in the same order that I have presented them to you and connects the pairs of axes that are related to each other the most. For example, the Customer axis is connected to the Product axis. There is also a great connection between Sustainability and Metrics, as measurements allow us to check whether we're being sustainable.

Figure 2.16. The Eight Axes of Purpose Launchpad

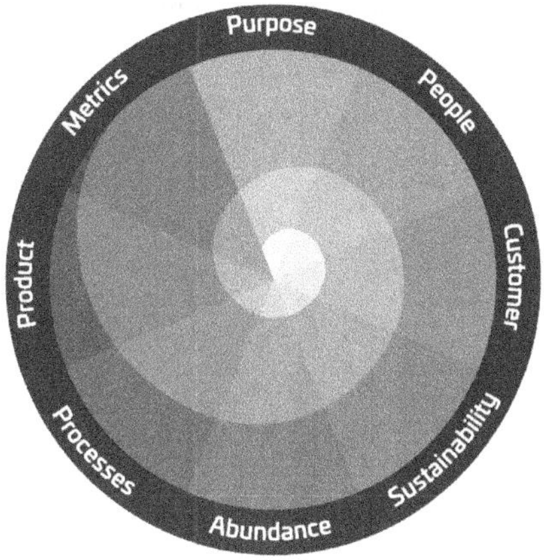

Source: Prepared by the author

In addition, the Purpose Launchpad diagram presents an iterative process by which we go through each of the axes to return to the beginning (Purpose) and start again. The fundamental idea behind the agile approach is to evolve all the axes in parallel, in an iterative way, which allows us to integrate the learning or progress of the different axes with the rest.

Purpose Launchpad Canvas, which we will see in greater detail in the next chapter directed at startups and new products, is a tool which allows us to easily work on the eight axes.

Purpose Launchpad also offers an evaluation tool (Purpose Launchpad Assessment) as a radar to know the status of the different axes in a specific initiative. This tool graphically informs us about each axis's stage of development. Here's a sample:

Figure 2.17. Graphic Representation of the Purpose Launchpad Assessment Tool

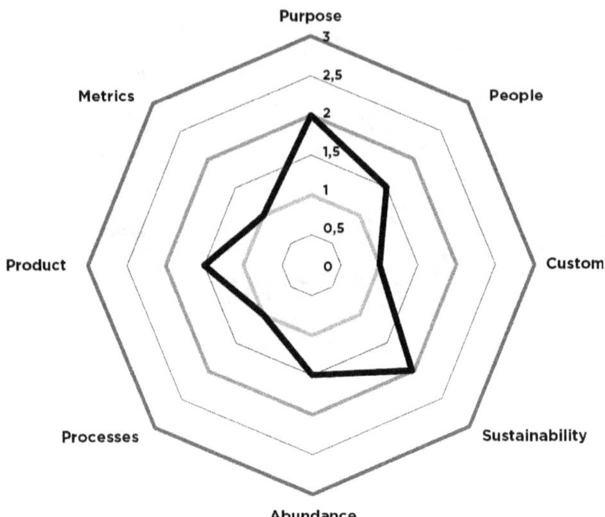

Source: Prepared by the author

If we want to develop our projects in the healthiest way possible, we will have to maintain a balance between the different axes. This means that we must first consolidate all the axes in the Exploration phase before moving conceptually to the Evaluation phase. If we have five axes in the Evaluation phase and three in the Exploration phase, we'll keep the project in the Exploration phase until we can develop the three axes that aren't at a sufficient level yet. And we'll do the same between the Evaluation and the Impact phases.

Finally, remember that you have more details in the official guide, downloadable on www.purposelaunchpad.com.

Key Points

Purpose Launchpad is structured around eight axes:

1. **Purpose**: the project's *raison d'être* and the North Star that guides you.
2. **People**: internal team and outside community, all related to the purpose.
3. **Customers**: people, users, or entities for whom we generate value of some kind.
4. **Sustainability**: necessary elements for our project to be sustainable at an economic, social, and environmental level.
5. **Abundance**: possible sources of abundance that can be leveraged by the initiative and how to manage them.
6. **Processes**: approach to always properly execute project operations.
7. **Product**: what we create to respond to the challenges and needs of customers and deliver our value.
8. **Metrics**: what we need to measure to always know the status of our project or initiative.

Resources

- Purpose Launchpad Canvas: *www.purposealliance.org/resources/purpose-launchpad-canvas*
- Purpose Launchpad Assessment: *www.purposealliance.org/resources/purpose-launchpad-assessment*

Part Three

Evolution of Startups and New Products

13
Being a Zebra Before Being a Unicorn

Creating something new is one of the most rewarding actions we can experience. If our creation also manages to generate a positive impact on the world, we will feel that what we do—and our lives—have meaning.

I remember a conversation I had years ago with my friend Clarence Tan, who is an investor and founder of the EPIC (Exponential Positive Impact Capital) impact investor platform. I was explaining my Cognocare project, a system based on artificial intelligence to personalize and improve cancer treatments, when he suddenly blurted out, "You're creating a zebra!" Seeing my surprised face, Clarence explained to me that "zebras" are startups that not only seek profitability; they also try to generate a positive impact. Zebras are black and white, the colors used to represent those two objectives: profit and impact—in my case, to generate business and save lives by improving cancer treatments.

The startup movement explosion in recent years and the large economic benefits some of them offered generated a new gold rush that attracted entrepreneurs and investors from all over the world. In some cases, they generated unbelievable returns on investment. Andy Bechtolsheim, one of Google's first investors, was an example of that. His initial contribution of $100,000 ended up becoming $2 billion!

Never in the history of business has anything like this been seen before. Investor Aileen Lee coined the term "unicorn" in 2013 to refer to this class of startups capable of exceeding a valuation of $1 billion in a very short time. Some of these unicorns deflated, but the ones that managed to bring value to the world and create a massive positive impact continued to grow.

An increasing number of startups are looking to generate both profit and a positive impact on the world. Creating one is a great motivation for entrepreneurs. Larry Page, one of the founders of Google, put it this way: "If you're changing the world, you're working on important things, and that will motivate you to get up every morning." Google not only generates profits but creates a massive impact (as stated by its own purpose) by organizing the world's information and making it accessible to anyone. Like so many other startups that have ended up as unicorns, Google started out as a zebra with a focus on generating both economic benefits and a positive impact. In fact, thanks to the positive impact it creates in the world, it has been able to expand globally in a short time, and, thanks to its profits, it has been able to amplify its positive impact. The biggest challenges in the world are best business opportunities, and it is precisely the zebras that can best take advantage of them.

Several communities and platforms, such as Zebras Unite or Purpose Alliance, have recently emerged in which entrepreneurs and investors collaborate to create zebra-type startups. These are startups that seek to generate a positive impact to be relevant in the world and to give meaning to their organization. And they don't necessarily scale globally; they can be limited to a local range of action. In short, they choose to be zebras rather than unicorns.

In the next few chapters, I'll explain how to leverage the Purpose Launchpad mindset and framework to minimize risks and maximize your zebra organization's impact. But, above all, remember that being a zebra is mandatory—being a unicorn is optional.

14
Purpose Launchpad
for Startups and New Products

You already know what Purpose Launchpad is, but now you'll have the chance to put it into practice, so you'll not only evolve your projects and create a positive impact, but your mindset will evolve too. Remember that Purpose Launchpad is not only a framework;, it's also a way of thinking. In fact, in the next chapters, I'll focus on this mindset, since you can find the methodological and technical aspects in the official guide.

Let's start at the beginning: what is a startup? Steve Blank, father of the Lean Startup movement, defines it as "a temporary organization designed to search for a repeatable and scalable business model." This very brief definition is full of meaning. The term *temporary* refers to the fact that, if the organization fails to find its business in time, it will cease to exist; if, on the contrary, it finds the right business model, it will cease to be a startup and become an established organization. In any case, startup is only an initial and temporary state. Steve also states that a startup is not implementing a pre-determined plan; it's looking for a business model that will make it viable (we'll come back to this later.) Finally, it mentions the need to create a project that is *repeatable* and *scalable*, although Purpose Launchpad can also be applied to local projects.

Eric Ries, Steve's top representative in the Lean movement, says that "a startup is a human institution designed to deliver a new product or service under conditions of extreme uncertainty." Ries doesn't talk about business but about delivering new products and services, to which we can also apply the Lean Startup method in their implementation. On the other hand, the element of "extreme uncertainty" could be considered true for any type of project, especially if it's attempting to be innovative.

While the two definitions are effectively complete, I find a core Purpose Launchpad element is missing: impact. We're not only trying to create an innovative business but also to have a positive impact on the world. That's why mindset is so essential to Purpose Launchpad, because we understand that any type of project we launch should always strive for a positive impact. If we incorporate this idea into the versions offered by Steve Blank and Eric Ries, it could look something like this: "A startup is a temporary organization in search of a business model to create a positive impact under conditions of extreme uncertainty."

When I talk about startups on Purpose Launchpad, I agree with Steve Blank's idea that they're organizations that hasn't yet found their way to fit into the market and that, once they do, they will cease to be considered a startup and become an established organization. The nuance that I try to incorporate is that the objective of those organizations is not only to find a business model to generate profits but to create the right conditions that enable them to have a positive impact.

Startups share many characteristics with innovative products or services from established companies. Both must face a lot of challenges, which makes their success rate very low. Some of the reasons why they fail are a lack of focus, the people who lead the initiative, or the difficulty in generating income and obtaining satisfied customers. Sometimes it's not difficult to find a first group of customers, but, later, it's not possible to scale to a level that lets you reach your objectives. There are other important challenges to face, such as managing liquidity so as not to continuously depend on external investment. This is the dream of many entrepreneurs and innovators, but, unfortunately, in most cases, it doesn't come true.

Ideas are worth little; the key is in the implementation. How should we focus our processes so that our ideas materialize properly? Building a product is not usually complicated: the key is to build a product that the market readily accepts. By applying Purpose Launchpad in a startup or a new product, we'll get the team's mindset to evolve and focus on managing the most common challenges that usually arise in this type of project. To do that, in each phase (Exploration, Evaluation, and Impact), we must manage the eight axes proposed by the framework (Purpose, People, Customers, Sustainability, Abundance, Processes, and Metrics.)

At the end of the axes chapter, I mentioned the Purpose Launchpad Canvas tool, which consists of a simple canvas that will help you easily define each of the eight axes, as you can see in the following image. Keep it handy throughout the following chapters, as you might find it useful.

Figure 3.1. Purpose Launchpad Canvas

Purpose	People	Customers	Sustainability
Abundance	Processes	Product	Metrics

Source: Prepared by the author

Another tool that I also mentioned is the Purpose Launchpad Assessment, which evaluates each axis's status in each of the three phases. This tool generates a radar-like graph showing the evolution status of the different axes at a glance. If you are currently working on your startup's or new product's development, the first thing I would recommend before moving on to the following chapters is that you visit the official Purpose Launchpad website and generate your project's radar. That will let you know your starting point, and you'll be able to see how the axes are evolving at the same time as your project.

However, remember that the most important thing is not applying one tool or another or following a series of steps. The key is your mindset. You'll have the opportunity below to keep evolving your mindset to bring your startup or innovative product to success while creating a positive impact on the world. Let's get started!

Key Points

- A startup is a temporary organization in search of a business model to create a positive impact under conditions of extreme uncertainty.
- Startups and innovative products have many challenges in common that can be solved with Purpose Launchpad.
- By applying Purpose Launchpad in a startup or for a new product, we'll get the team's mindset to evolve to maximize the chances of success and the impact generated.

15
Define the Purpose of your Startup

Twitter, like so many other startups, started off traveling a very different path than the one that finally led it to success—that is, becoming the top Internet platform for sharing short text messages. One of the keys of that success was maintaining their purpose while experimenting with different paths, strategies, and even teams.

In this chapter, we're going to talk about the importance of the Purpose axis in startups and new products, specifically how to properly manage it so that, without losing its essence, you can propose different strategies until you discover the right path. I'll tell you Twitter's story in greater detail, since it is a good example that will help us understand the challenges we'll encounter and how best to face them.

It all began in 2004 in the apartment of an American programmer named Noah Glass. Glass created a project called Odeo that allowed you to send a recorded message over your phone and store it in the cloud so anyone else could hear it later. Odeo went on to become a podcasting platform with fourteen employees, but then Apple launched its own competing podcast platform with iTunes. The startup needed to somehow reinvent itself. It was time to pivot.

They didn't at first know how, but they were clear about their purpose: to allow people to connect and share their thoughts with a large audience. The podcast format clearly wasn't the only one they could use. Jack Dorsey, who would later become the company's CEO, was the one who thought that SMS could be used to generate conversations between groups of people (which is why messages were initially limited to 140 characters). Twitter was born, though they went through various names, such as Twttr, before settling on that one. The first tweet in history was written by Jack Dorsey on March 21, 2006:

In 2007, Twitter officially became an independent company and Jack Dorsey its CEO. Users and traffic began to increase rapidly. In August of that same year, almost by chance, user Chris Messina invented the hashtag concept, which would later be implemented on the platform and on many other social networks.

The platform continued to grow and increase in popularity. Jack Dorsey was ousted, and Evan Williams was named CEO. Soon afterwards, Williams was also fired, and the board of directors put Jack Dorsey back at the helm.

I'm explaining all this so you can see that, throughout their history, Twitter experienced numerous changes in name, direction, and even team members, but one thing that never changed and that allowed them to keep their focus on point was their purpose: to enable people to connect and share their thoughts with a larger audience. Thanks to their perseverance in their purpose, they remain a pacesetter for social networks, and, although Facebook and Instagram have more users, they can't compete with Twitter when it comes to comments going viral. It has been and continues to be revolutionary in human communication.

Twitter's story underlines the importance of having a purpose to guide you. In projects with a high level of uncertainty, like startups and innovative products, sometimes purpose may be the only thing to hold on to. It can be a firm "axis" to cling to when pivoting (I urge you to review the Axes chapter if you feel it's necessary). In Twitter's case, the essence of their purpose never changed, although its wording did. The initial purpose was to "allow people to connect and share their thoughts with a large audience," and currently it's "serving the public conversation," which is essentially the same thing.

We all have a North Star that helps us remember who we are and which direction to take. Purpose is a project's north star. If it changes, so does the project's direction; you can change your vision, mission, and values because they represent the way to achieve your purpose. In fact, when Twitter was still Odeo, its vision was to become the go-to platform for podcasts. Later, after pivoting the business model, the vision evolved into becoming the top platform for text messages. And it has subsequently continued to evolve; the vision expressed on their website as I'm writing this is "to become the world's most diverse and inclusive company." Their mission—that is, the path to their vision—has also changed a lot over time. So have their values, which are currently trust, speed, freedom, fun, and union of benefit and purpose, and, of course, their leadership and management style, currently in the hands of Parag Agrawal, their former CTO, who took over from the legendary Jack Dorsey. But the essence of its purpose remains the same, as does the ecosystem created around it.

Twitter is not an isolated case but rather the general tone of all the startups and products that have managed to find their way to success. To this end, they have maintained their purpose throughout the three phases described in Purpose Launchpad: Exploration, Evaluation, and Impact. Let's take a look at how to do that.

Purpose During the Exploration Phase

It all starts for a reason, even if we don't initially know what it is. Sometimes, the purpose is given by the organization you belong to, which has decided to launch a new product or service.

At other times, especially if you are an entrepreneur, you or the original group of the startup's founders define the purpose. After all, a startup is nothing more than a vehicle to realize its founders' purpose.

Defining a good purpose is not always simple or easy. It can take weeks, months, or even years to translate it into a concise and inspiring sentence. Therefore, in the exploration phase, you shouldn't obsess over defining the perfect purpose but instead try to connect with the essence of what you want to do and express it in some way to begin communicating it. Remember that, in the exploration phase, we generally don't try to optimize anything; we're discovering different alternatives. Regarding the purpose, it will be enough for you to start thinking about it, to try to somehow express it in writing (knowing that it will change), and that you try to do it as soon as possible since, as I insist, your purpose should be the starting point and the North Star for your next steps.

You may be at an advanced stage of your project but have never stopped to define your purpose. It happens—don't worry. In that case, stop for a moment and think about the real reason why you are doing what you do—that is, what change you would like to see in the world as a result of your project. And it's not enough to say that you want to make gobs of money, because, although that's a valid goal, the purpose is not about your goals but about what you want to create in the world.

If you're willing to spend a little more time defining your purpose, a good way to do that is by using the MTP Canvas tool. If you are the only founder, I encourage you to access the open (and free) program I mentioned in the first chapter, under "Discover Your Purpose," and give serious thought to establishing your personal and your startup's purpose. If there are several founders, you can each do it individually and then share all the purposes and try to find a common one.

Figure 3.2. MTP Canvas

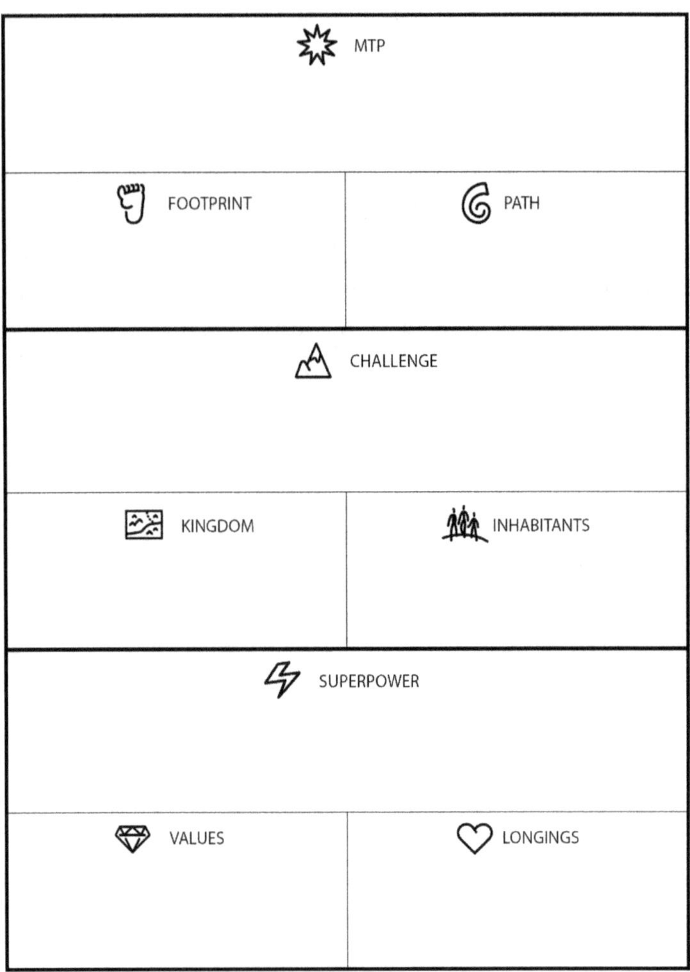

Source: Francisco Palao and Angel Maria Herrera

Once your purpose is clear, it will serve as a guide to seek different opportunities. Remember that, in the exploration phase, we're still trying to detect the different paths that could lead us to our destination. With the purpose, our reason for being, we'll try to determine the rest of the strategic elements that will establish our initiative's identity. The first of these will be the vision, which will define what we would like to become in the future. Next is the mission, which will describe how we can achieve our vision. In fact, you might already have these elements before you even begin to define the purpose. That's fine—the important thing is that you're open to changing them once you define your purpose and as you move forward in developing the project, since, at the beginning, everything is hypotheses. I also recommend that, in this phase, you define an initial set of values for your initiative, but remember that they, too, are hypotheses and will most likely change at some point.

Purpose During the Evaluation Phase

To enter the evaluation phase, your purpose must have been defined, along with the rest of this axis's elements: vision, mission, and values. Once in this phase, you should do several things related to the purpose. On one hand, share it and get feedback on it. On the other, check whether the vision and mission you have defined make sense. To do that, you must continue advancing with the rest of your initiative's axes. If you manage to validate all the hypotheses defined in them, it will mean that the vision and the mission indicate a good path. If, on the other hand, you invalidate any important element (which is very normal), you'll have to review the vision and mission.

During the early phases of your project, there may be discoveries and changes in the environment that could change an element as important as vision. Remember when Twitter's founders invalidated their platform's initial vision, based on podcasts, and had to propose a new one focused on becoming the preferred platform for text messages? This meant not only changing their vision and mission but also many other elements, including the company name.

It's also possible that you maintain your project's vision but change its mission—that is, the way to make your vision come true. This also happened to Twitter: years after generating great traction, with millions of Internet users, they changed the way their business worked to start monetizing the value they were generating. At that time, the mission incorporated monetization through ads on the platform, something they had not done previously and which finally allowed them to become an economically sustainable entity. By validating the rest of the axes (in this case Sustainability in reference to their economic viability), they were able to validate the strategy to make their purpose a reality, which included the vision and mission.

In short, during the evaluation phase, you should not change the essence of your purpose, but you do have to be very open to making quick changes in your vision, mission, and values to find the best way to make your purpose a reality.

Purpose During the Impact Phase

At this point, you not only have a clear purpose and a way of expressing it; you have also validated your vision and your mission with the support of the rest of the axes. Now the challenge is to take your initiative to the next level in terms of quality (improving everything you have been doing so far) and possibly also in terms of scale (replicating your activity globally). To do that, you'll have to put yourself into execution and optimization mode.

It's time to communicate your purpose in the best possible way, to make it reach as many people as possible, and to make the world (or the environment in which you want to position yourself) know about the existence of your startup or your product, as well as the reason why it exists. By communicating your purpose, you'll attract communities, clients, and talent to your team, including impact investors aligned with the essence of your project.

As for the vision and mission, at this stage, they shouldn't change, at least in their essence, though the way of expressing them can be improved. If you change your vision or your mission for any reason, it would mean that you're pivoting your model and, therefore, that you should review the previous phases. If we're in this last phase, it's because we've already found the right path, and we will now focus on scaling our business, our reach, and our positive impact on the world.

Values, on the other hand, can change at any time, especially when there are changes in the management team, as each leader imprints a different leadership style that usually spreads throughout the organization.

Final Thoughts on the Purpose Axis

Remember: Purpose is where it all begins and ends. By following the iterative process indicated by the eight axes of Purpose Launchpad, purpose will guide you in your decisions and make it easier for you to find the path that will eventually make your purpose a reality. In fact, as we'll see later, the last axis (Metrics) will help you define one of the fundamental elements: the starshot. Starshot is the way to tangibly ground purpose into a measurable and time-delimited objective. This closes the circle and makes it an iterative and continuous process in which everything is connected.

There is a simple tool, called *Organization Identity Canvas*, that you can use while working on the purpose axis, which not only includes purpose, vision, mission, and values but also the starshot to constantly remind you of the metric you must pursue to make your purpose a reality. I recommend that you download the *Organization Identity Canvas* and use it to continuously update these important and strategic elements, as well as to communicate them to your team and collaborators. It's as important to find and know the right direction to which we're heading as to communicate it to the people who will make it a reality, as we'll see in the next chapter.

Figure 3.3. Organization Identity Canvas

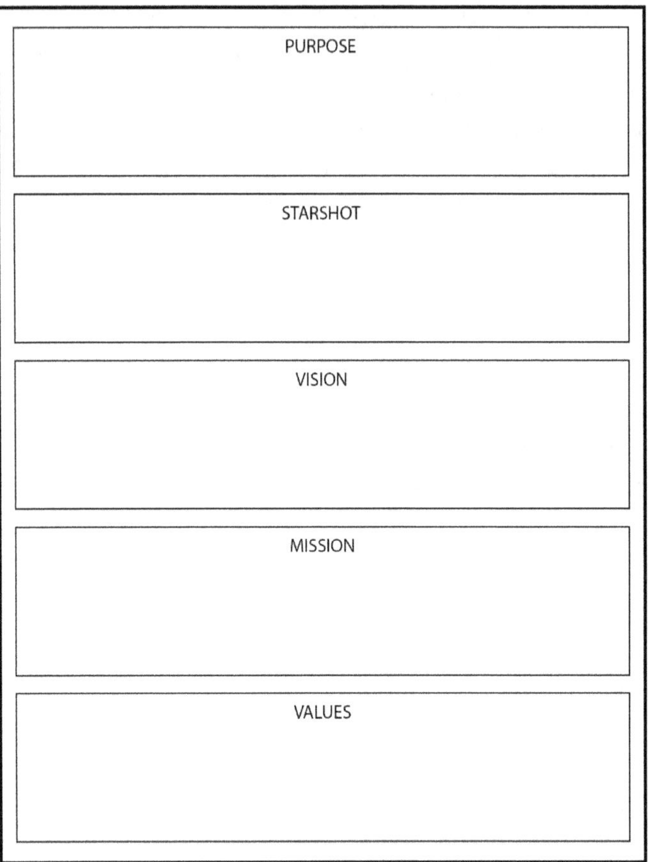

Source: Prepared by the author

Finally, I would like to remind you of something important, especially if you're working on developing your startup. Once you're in the impact phase, there will come a time when you'll stop formally being a startup (especially once you have an economically viable business) and become an established organ-ization. At that point, as we'll see in the fourth part of the book, purpose will not only help you move in the right direction but also generate new initiatives to create an ecosystem oriented to your purpose. The strength of purpose goes far beyond what you see in this chapter, and I hope that you can gradually continue to discover it.

Table 3.1. Summary of the Purpose Axis in Startups and New Products

	PURPOSE AXIS		
	EXPLORATION Discover the initiative's purpose and define an initial version of your strategy	**EVALUATION** Experiment with the strategic approach you determined and review as necessary	**IMPACT** Boost your strategy to reach your Purpose
WHY	Begin to think about the essence of your Purpose	Share and review how you will express your Purpose, maintaining its essence	Promote the Purpose
WHAT	Frame an initial version of the initiative's Vision for the future	Review the initiative's Vision according to what you've learned	Boost the Vision to make it happen
HOW	Review the initiative's Mission according to what you've learned	Review the initiative's Mission according to what you've learned	Optimize the Mission to improve how you perform your activity

Source: Prepared by the author

> **Activity**
>
> Take your own project (startup or new product) or, if you don't have one, think of a case that you're familiar with and do the following activities:
>
> 1. Define the purpose if you don't have one. You can use the MTP Canvas or the Open Purpose Launchpad program to discover your personal purpose.
> 2. Describe the rest of the elements of the Purpose axis. You can use the *Organization Identity Canvas* to do this (you don't need to include the starshot yet).
>
> Remember that you'll have to manage the previous elements in different ways depending on which phase you're in. Reflect on how you should act according to the phase your project is in.

Resources

- MTP Canvas: *www.purposealliance.org/resources/mtp-canvas*
- *Organization Identity Canvas*: *www.purposealliance.org/resources/organization-identity-canvas*

16
Connect with the Right People

Wikipedia is the largest encyclopedia in the world, with more than 45 million entries in over 300 languages. It was created in 2001 and hasn't stopped growing since. Most amazing is that it's a project created by over 250,000 volunteers worldwide. The key to its success has undoubtedly been attracting (and then managing) a community of people contributing to a common purpose.

In this chapter, we are going to talk about the People axis, about how your startup or your product can attract communities and how you can form a team aligned with your purpose to achieve extraordinary results. To do this, let's take a closer look at Wikipedia's story.

In March 2000, Jimbo Wales created Nupedia, a free encyclopedia project with articles of comparable quality to professional encyclopedias. This was possible thanks to an ambitious peer-review process involving selected experts consisting mainly of doctoral students and academics. The project was progressing slowly, however, so, in early 2001, Larry Sanger, editor-in-chief of Nupedia, proposed starting a parallel process to create articles in a more agile and fast way. The idea was to use a wiki, a system to allow a virtual community to create, modify, and share content. And Wikipedia was born.

Nupedia was soon overshadowed by the new, small side project and ceased to function, and Jimbo Wales and Larry Sanger continued to work together as co-founders. Wikipedia is currently among the ten most-visited sites on the Internet. It's not only the largest encyclopedia in the world but also the most up to date. If a relevant event occurs, someone from Wikipedia's community of volunteers and contributors captures the event before anyone jumps in to verify it.

Wikipedia has a truly inspiring purpose: to be an accessible and free encyclopedia for everyone. Both Nupedia and Wikipedia had the same purpose, but the results they obtained were completely different. What made the difference? The answer is very clear: community. While Nupedia was focused on the creation of articles by selected think tanks, Wikipedia made content generation open to the community, using a wiki-like system. In the words of Jimmy Wales, its founder, "Wikipedia has more and more power, but it is in the hands of the people." The first articles were created by the founders, but, once they communicated their purpose to the world, they managed to attract a growing community of people who, inspired by the purpose, began to contribute entirely voluntarily, creating new articles and improving existing ones.

In addition to the more than 250,000 volunteers who contribute content to Wikipedia around the world, the organization has an internal team responsible for managing the system and keeping it running. It started out as two people, Larry Sanger and Jimmy Wales, who were soon joined by Harry Geitner, who had been the managing editor for Nupedia. The team has grown to 250 people at the time I'm writing this.

People During the Exploration Phase

Your goal in this phase should be to connect with the right people to discover information relevant to your startup or your product, as well as to start laying the foundations of what could be your community (in case you plan to have one). Of course, it is not yet time to create a community, since there may be many changes in the project direction that could confuse its members. Now you should just connect with people (talking to them or reading books or articles) and with communities linked to your purpose to continue understanding the environment. Jimmy Wales, for example, was inspired by economist and philosopher Friedrich Hayek's essay "The Use of Knowledge in Society," which he read as a student and which was fundamental to his way of managing Wikipedia. Hayek argues that better decisions are made when information is decentralized and each person knows only a small fraction of collective knowledge. Wales reconsidered Hayek's essay in the 1990s as he began to connect with open-source communities, which advocated for wide-spread distribution of free software. He was particularly moved by the essay "The Cathedral and the Bazaar," written by one of the founders of the open-source movement, Eric S. Raymond. Wales claimed that this essay "opened my eyes to the possibilities of mass collaboration."

So, for now, get informed. I recommend that you make a list of communities or organizations that are somehow related to your purpose or that have a related purpose. Then approach them and start interacting with the people who form them. This will keep you in touch with the most important trends related to your purpose, detect the main challenges you will encounter along the way, and even discover possible customer segments that you could focus on (we'll talk about the Customer axis in the next chapter). By connecting with communities tied to your purpose, you may well find people who want to join your team, including a co-founder for your startup.

If you plan to create your own community, once you have explored the environment, you can begin to imagine it but without building anything yet. Remember that, in this phase, all your ideas (as well as those related to the Community) are simple hypotheses that you will have to test before continuing. There are important tools that can be useful in this regard; one is Community Canvas, which includes blocks with seventeen key issues such as: What is the mechanism of entry of new members to a community, and what are the rules that govern it? This canvas has three sections, one to define the community's identity, where you will find important elements like purpose, which you've already defined by now and must coincide with the purpose of the startup or product you are developing. Another section is aimed at defining the experience of the members of your community, where you will find elements such as the entry selection mechanisms or the operating rules. The third section is oriented to defining the structure of the community, where you will find blocks in which you can raise issues such as how you'll manage the data or what platform (if applicable) you'll use to host your community members.

Figure 3.4. Community Canvas

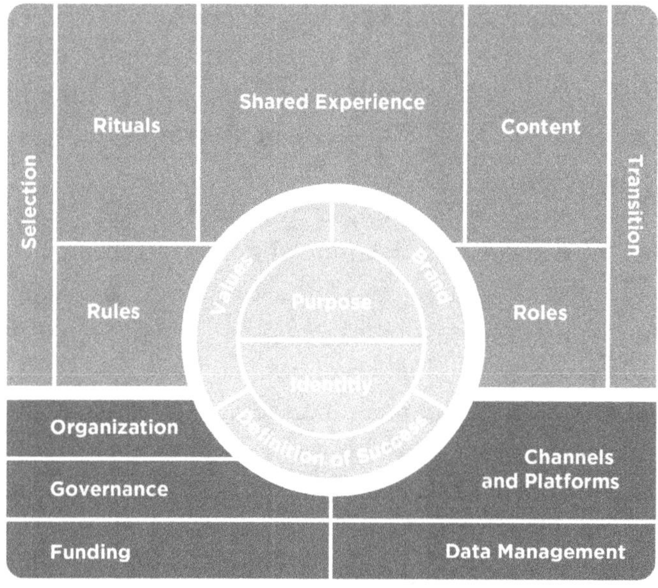

Source: Fabian Pfortmüller, Nico Luchsinger, and Sascha Mombartz

One of the most common failures at this point is to believe that, if we launch our own online platform, the community will magically emerge. Platforms are merely the tool; people are the key. The individuals who could potentially join our community are out there, and creating that community stems from attracting them with the right motives and offering them a space to interact. In fact, there are many communities that do not have a platform, and that's OK. Therefore, don't obsess over creating a platform until you have properly validated your hypotheses.

In *The Art of Community*, Charles Vogl introduces us to seven fundamental principles or aspects that can serve as a guide to establish the foundations of your community:

1. Boundary: this is about establishing a clear line between the people who belong to a community and those who do

not. To do this, you must define entry requirements, registration mechanisms, etc.

2. Initiation: the activities that mark a new member's entry into the community—for example, communication welcoming the new member or their introduction to the community.

3. Rituals: the actions we perform periodically in the community that have a meaning aligned with the purpose.

4. Temple: the place where the people of the community gather. It can be a platform, a physical place or network of places, or a combination of both.

5. Stories: the experiences that are shared between members of the community and how to share them. These stories are crucial when it comes to generating empathy and connection between the members, as well as communicating their values and the reasons why the community itself exists.

6. Symbols: elements, icons, or badges that represent important community concepts. They may mention the status of community members or distinctions given to certain people for concrete actions they have performed.

7. Inner Rings: groups within the community made up of people with something in common, such as a type of experience, a status, etc.

The People axis also includes your team. It's just as important to connect with outsiders linked to your purpose as it is to find the right people to be part of your team. Here the search is internal, because we must look within to know whether we have the right team or not, for which you must keep two very important issues in mind. First is whether the people on your team are aligned with the project's purpose, strategy, and style. The ideal is to have people who are looking for something more than a job and an income (something totally valid, in any case), people who are aligned with the purpose and who embrace it as their own. If the people on your team are inspired by the project's purpose, they'll always have the extra passion that will make a difference. It's also important that they are aligned with the vision, mission, and values. There is no point in sharing a purpose if you're not aligned regarding how to achieve it. The second aspect to consider is whether the people on your team have an exploration mindset. There are individuals who feel more comfortable when working according to a set plan, execution-oriented people who like to have everything tightly controlled and optimized, but that's not what we need in the Exploration phase. Here we need adventurers, people who feel comfortable without a defined plan and who like to improvise—in short, people who do not need a way forward but are able to create the path out of nothing.

Projects require people with an optimizer profile as well as people with an explorer profile, but, in the initial phases of a startup or when creating a new product, only the latter type will be able to break through the unknown. Does this mean that we don't need people with optimizer profiles during Exploration? No, provided they understand that, at the present time, exploration must prevail over optimization. If they can understand and support that, even if they sometimes feel uncomfortable due to the lack of planning, we can keep them in the organization—provided, of course, that we have enough explorers.

I wasn't there, so I can't talk about the Wikipedia team during their Exploration phase, but I can talk about my own experience. Over time, both with IActive and in many other projects in which I have participated, I have come to recognize a pattern that I have seen repeated and that I now recognize and can manage correctly. Most people have been trained to "do things right." which means passing the exam or not making mistakes. This generates a way of thinking and acting focused on avoiding failure. We try not to make mistakes and create plans that tell us what to do and why. However, any plan in the initial phase of an innovative project is nothing more than a bunch of hypotheses that are almost never confirmed.

In my experience, entrepreneurs with an explorer spirit often have to devote part of their time and energy to calming people with an optimizing profile or to continuously justifying changes in plans, which generates internal tension. In the Exploration phase, "doing things right" does not mean not making mistakes; it means being able to make mistakes and learn from experience as quickly and agilely as possible.

If you have an optimizer profile, don't worry: the time will come when your qualities will be crucial for the project to reach the top. However, you must control your need for a plan now and leave the way open to people searching for which paths to follow. If, on the other hand, you're an explorer, now it's your turn. Try to find and evaluate the different paths as soon as possible and try to explain to the optimizers why things need to proceed now without seeking perfection and instead embracing failure to learn from it. Now, don't expect them to follow you, because normally they won't (and possibly it will be better that way). The important thing is that everyone knows who they are and takes the lead (or empathizes with those who should have it) when it's time for them.

There are also tools that can help you evaluate the profiles of your team members and even your own. One of them is the BOSI Quadrant, created by Joe Abraham and described in detail in his book *Entrepreneurial DNA*. Abraham explains that there are many different types of entrepreneurs and that we all have one type or another inside. The important thing is to know which kind of entrepreneur we are so that we can dedicate ourselves to the right type of project and combine our profile with the right team. The quadrant represents four types of entrepreneurial

DNA, which constitute the acronym BOSI: *Builder, Opportunist, Specialist,* and *Innovator.* Everyone's personality will be more associated with one of these types of primary entrepreneurship and with a secondary one. The combination of these variables offers sixteen combinations, which means sixteen different types of entrepreneurs. In my case, I am a builder and innovator, as I have always focused on creating new projects in an innovative way. You can check which one you are by responding to a short survey on the official website of the BOSI test; you'll find the link with the resources recommended at the end of this chapter.

Another tool that can be useful in the initial phases of your startup or your product is Team Canvas. With your purpose at the center, the canvas suggests you fill in a series of areas, including one dedicated to the team and each person's functions.

Figure 3.5. Team Canvas

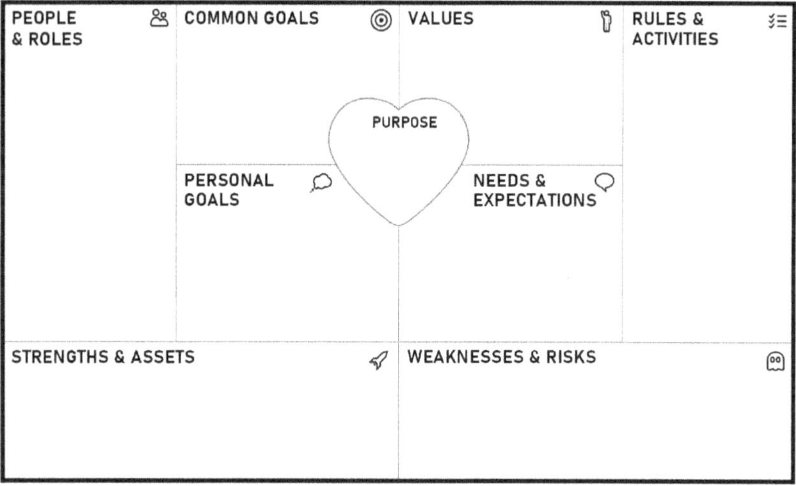

Source: Alex Ivanov and Mitya Voloshchuk

It's a very useful tool to fill in together as a team and ask yourselves questions about how each person fits into the project, whether changes need to be made, and how to best align them to achieve your goals.

Since we're in the Exploration phase, anything we define about the team is just a hypothesis, as with the other axes. Even the team members themselves are a hypothesis, since we'll have to evaluate whether we're really the right team or not. It's important to keep an open mind, to analyze whether the team is the right one, and to increase your self-awareness. You're sure to discover and learn things you didn't initially expect, and those findings will be important for the future and the success of your initiative.

People During the Evaluation Phase

At this point, you already know and have contacted communities related to your purpose. You've surely interacted with people and organizations with whom you could collaborate in one way or another. In fact, some of these groups may have been classified as customer segments and you're already working on them from the Customer axis (which we'll talk about next). You've also managed to put an initial team in place (it may be just you, which is also fine) aligned on the key elements: Purpose, Vision, Mission, and Values.

Now, in the Evaluation phase, the important thing is to put into practice everything that was proposed and learned in the Exploration phase. If you plan to create a community, start conducting experiments to make sure, before you grow it, that it really is the kind of community you need. This will also allow you to continue learning and even find your first customers and collaborators.

The Purpose Alliance is one case I've experienced on the front lines. This is a global community with a clear purpose: to empower extraordinary people and organizations to create a better world. It all started, almost by chance, at the beginning of the COVID-19 pandemic in 2020. On March 12th of that year, I launched a worldwide challenge in an online format so that anyone could join and offer solutions to the pandemic. Over three hundred people joined in just one week, and more than twenty solutions were generated. After that, many members of the community, which began to grow spontaneously, asked me for support in organizing similar challenges. A few months later, fifteen other events were launched in different countries and with different problems.

In May 2020, after a short but intense Exploration phase, I decided to give what was happening a shape and created Purpose Alliance with the vision of becoming a purpose-oriented community focused on creating a better world and with the mission of awakening people to become aware of their abilities, unlock their real potential, and offer them the appropriate tools and the mindset to create a positive impact.

The community developed easily and naturally for two reasons. On one hand, we had a very strong purpose that attracted thousands of people and organizations from all over the world who wanted to create a positive impact. In fact, thanks to Purpose Alliance, I have met many people who are now a fundamental part of my life, and I feel very fortunate. On the other hand, we were joined by people from communities where I had previously played a key role, such as OpenExO and Singularity University, where consultants from around the world are focused on helping transform corporations using the ExO Sprint methodology, which I created in 2015. Many of these people are still active in the Purpose Alliance community, fully aligned with our purpose and essence. Some, on the other hand, did not fit. In fact, there came a time when we had to make the community's identity very clear so that the people who truly fit the purpose, with their vision, their mission, and their values, felt at home, and those who did not left the community. Through this movement, we created a harmonious environment and built a solid foundation with people who are fully aligned with the essence of Purpose Alliance.

Sometimes, we are at risk of getting carried away by what we call "vanity metrics" (we'll talk about them in detail in the Metrics axis). This means that we focus exclusively on growing the community without being sure that its people understand the purpose and are aligned with it. And that's a mistake. It is the chronicle of a death foretold.

You'll only know if you're right and that the path is correct when you start to travel it. Therefore, in the Evaluation phase, you must start putting the different concepts that you've previously defined around your community into action. To do this, you can be guided by the three-stage process that Kevin Huynh and Kai Elmer Sotto propose in their book *Get Together*. Using fire as a metaphor, they explain how to build a community of people in three steps that align perfectly with the three phases of Purpose Launchpad:

1. Spark the Flame (Exploration phase): In this first stage, identify the people who should really be part of your community; having open conversations, starting joint activities, and learning from all these interactions will be key for the first "sparks" to "ignite" the community.

2. Stoke the Fire (Evaluation phase): Once the flame is lit, the goal will be to attract new members to the community while staying alert, learning, and detecting possible deviations from our original vision. In addition, it will be time to define and confirm the community's identity.

3. Pass the Torch (Impact phase): It's time to grow and expand, to attract more leaders who make the community able to scale to achieve your goals, whether it's massive growth or more localized.

As you interact with your community and draw conclusions, you will make the necessary modifications to the approach until you find not only the community's identity but the mechanisms that will allow you to scale it too.

As for the team, it will be essential to maintain alignment and coordination throughout the project's evolution. During the Evaluation phase, the day to day will test it and show us if it's necessary to reconfigure it. The first customers will arrive, the first real challenges, the strong pressures, and even the "failures," which will require a complete review of the project. The important thing in this phase is to implement a culture of continuous experimentation and maximum agility. The entire team must be open to admitting that initial ideas may not be accepted by the market. It is about eliminating the egos and not seeing these invalidations as personal failures but as part of the process. Invalidating a hypothesis is really a gift, as we learn that there is a path we should not follow, saving us a lot of trouble in the future.

It's about being able to collect feedback and react quickly to make any necessary changes in our product or service (including in our general approach to the project) and adapting it quickly according to what we've learned. It's not about doing things perfectly but about creating something quickly to be able to learn, both from successes and failures. Being agile is not implementing a process but having the mindset to be agile. We'll see more of this in the next chapter, which is dedicated to the Customer axis, and, above all, in the chapters dedicated to the Process axis and the Product axis. For now, just remember Mark Zuckerberg's famous phrase: "Move fast and break things."

The Evaluation phase ends when, among other things, we have customers who are satisfied with our product, and, for this to happen, we had to pay attention to the details and greatly improved our initial offer. This means that you will gradually have to incorporate into the team people with a more detail-oriented profile or who are able to remove their explorer and evaluator hat to put on their optimizer hat.

People During the Impact Phase

If your goal was to create your own community, at this point you will have already created it and will have a growing number of satisfied members. Regarding the team, you will have overcome the difficulties of the first phases. Now you all have aligned visions and collaborate properly to evolve the project, which is already beginning to fit into the market.

In the Impact phase, the challenge is to multiply and replicate the initial achievements. To do this, we will learn to scale the community (if we've created one, of course), and we will take the team's performance to the next level.

Regarding the community, the time has come to "pass the torch" to as many people as possible. You must propose growth strategies, such as promoting a network of ambassadors or evangelists. Make sure that those ambassadors are clearly aligned with the project's purpose.

The time has also come to create (or improve, if you've already created it) your own technology platform for the community—if doing so adds real value to members. The platform alone will not grow the community but will be a "place" where members will come so long as it adds something and they feel it makes sense.

As for the team, if we were to continue giving the explorers prominence, we would run the risk of continuing to open new fronts instead of taking advantage of the findings obtained so far. That is why, in the Impact phase, we must give way to optimizers--that is, people focused on executing a plan and making the path we've found easier to travel more efficiently and effectively. Just as people focused on optimizing and executing had to give way to explorers at the beginning of the project, now the explorers must give way to optimizers. The time has come to take advantage of the findings and make the most of them without losing focus. It's important, of course, to never stop learning, since the environment is always uncertain and ever-changing.

There are numerous tools to optimize the team and organization, like classic organization charts, among others. It's advisable to create one in the Impact phase and to establish missions, functions, and another series of attributes linked to each area of the organization. This will make it easier to organize functional departments and coordinate collaboration between different teams. Try not to create a structure that is rigid or too hierarchical—that is, always maintain some flexibility to adapt to unexpected changes in the environment. As Darwin said, "the species that survive are not the strongest ones, but those that best adapt to change." So, activate your growth and optimization mode without losing agility, and take your impact to the next level!

Final Thoughts on the People Axis

The power of people is the key that allows us to make our purpose a reality. Throughout this chapter, we have seen how to contact the right communities to learn and find opportunities and how to create our own community if it makes sense to us and allows us to take the project to the next level. Sometimes it will not be necessary to create a community, as it will already be part of the environment in which you move. In that case, you should leverage it for feedback and support.

We've also seen that having the right team and evolving it throughout the different phases of the project is another key. This might be the area with the greatest difficulties when analyzing and making decisions—on the one hand because you are part of the team and, on the other, because, when it comes to people, it's seldom clear-cut; it's grayscale and full of subjectivity and diverse perspectives. It will be of great help to be aware at all times of which phase you're in and to act accordingly, trying to find an appropriate balance between search-oriented and execution-oriented approaches.

Finally, I would like to share a thought, possibly one of the most important ones in the whole book. As you may have noticed throughout this chapter, by working on the People axis, you will not only evolve your project but also how the team understands the project's situation and contributes to it. That's why the key to a successful project is the team's (and your own!) constantly evolving mindset.

Table 3.2. Summary of the People Axis

PEOPLE AXIS			
	Exploration Learn by connecting and interacting with people linked to your purpose	**Evaluation** Find your community's and your team's identity with real experience	**Impact** Scale by boosting your connection with the community and increasing your team
External Community	Connect with communities linked to your purpose in order to learn	Maintain the connection with communities to find your first customers	Broaden the connection with communities to reach the mass market
Your Own Community	Define your initial approach to your community (if you plan to have one)	Test the approach with your community to learn and find your identity	Grow your community and build your own platform (if you need to)
Team	Begin to build a team of explorers aligned with your purpose	Test the team and create an agile culture that accepts learning-based failures	Evolve and expand your team based on execution and optimization

Source: Prepared by the author

Activity

Take your project (startup or new product), or, if you don't have one, think of a case that you're familiar with, and do the following activities:

1. Determine what stage your initiative is in. Remember that, although a specific axis (such as People) is at a more advanced stage, the initiative will be in the same phase as the least-evolved axis. Use the Purpose Launchpad Assessment to do this; I referred to this in the axes chapter in the second part of the book (www.purposelaunchpad.com/assessment).

2. Make a list of communities to connect with that are linked to your purpose to learn and find new opportunities.

3. If you plan to create your own community (or if you already have one), define how it should work. Remember that you can use tools like Community Canvas. Establish a series of experiments or next steps for the community based on the phase your initiative is in.

4. Describe your current team, either with Team Canvas if you're in the Exploration/ Evaluation phase or with a functional org chart if you're in the Impact phase. Next, set up a series of experiments or next steps for your team based on the phase your initiative is in.

Resources

- BOSI Test: *www.purposealliance.org/resources/purpose-launchpad-bosi-test*
- Community Canvas: *www.purposealliance.org/resources/community-canvas*
- Team Canvas: *www.purposealliance.org/resources/team-canvas/*

17
Discover and
Develop Your Customer

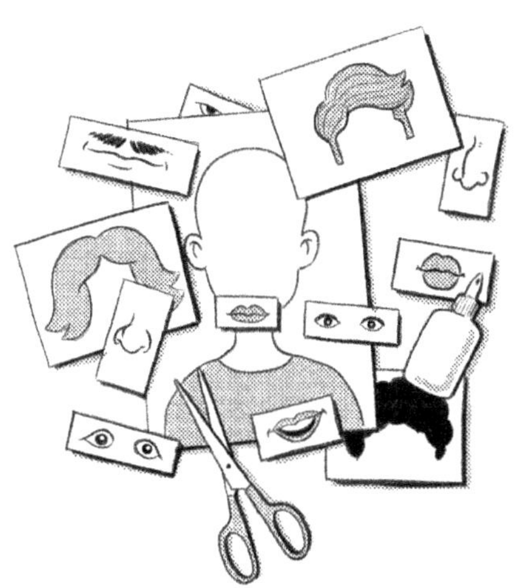

Towards the end of 2013, a travel company called SBTUR bought our startup, Nativoo, which offered customized tourism plans based on user preferences. Nativoo used artificial intelligence technology that I had previously developed at the University of Granada, together with my partners, as part of my PhD thesis. We had begun to develop this technology and its applications in 2003, but almost ten years went by before the project found its niche in the market and it was able to bring real value to users. In fact, though we had finally done it, we had to sell the company to cover the debts we had incurred in the meantime.

In hindsight and with the experience accumulated over the years, I understand now that we could have traveled that road in much less time and with a much lower investment. We could have found our customers and our fit in the market quicker and more efficiently, which would have meant complete success for Nativoo, for us ... and for the world of tourism.

In previous chapters, we've discussed how to adequately define a startup's purpose and how to connect with communities related to it. In this chapter, we'll focus on the Purpose Launchpad axis related to customers. The challenge will be finding the right customer segments for our startup. To that end, I will present some innovation methodologies and tools that will help you when you're working on the Customer axis. But, first, I'll tell you a bit more about Nativoo's history.

Several factors led us to create Nativoo. First, we had developed an award-winning AI technology to perform automatic planning and scheduling. Second, we lived in Granada, one of the greatest tourist cities in Spain, and we had some contacts on the city council. We added it up and thought we could provide the city with an intelligent system to customize tourist visits, thus attracting more visitors and boosting the local economy. With this idea in mind, and without any hesitation whatsoever, we set out to create a new app that could be integrated with the city's web page as a smart assistant for customizing tourist plans based on each visitor's preferences and budget. After a few months in development, we trotted off to show the Granada city council a first version of the product.

This was our first mistake: developing a product without having first talked to any customer; we were motivated only by our own idea. Despite this, the first meeting with the city officials in charge of tourism went relatively well, and they bought the idea. A few months later, our system appeared in the national press, and the city of Granada boasted of offering its tourists the most recent developments in AI. But that, which had been a success beforehand, made us run headfirst into our second big mistake: we invested hundreds of thousands of euros in developing a much more complete version of the product, and we hired a sales team to sell the new version to the remaining city councils in Spain. After several years of developing the product and carrying out commercial activities, we had only one more client, which meant a significant loss of both time and money.

I couldn't understand it at first. Everything seemed to have been well planned: we had a state-of-the-art product and a great first client. I set out to learn why we had failed—despite all we had going for us. Fortunately, in 2011, I had the chance to attend a program at the University of California at Berkeley on innovation methodologies for startups. The program was run by Steve Blank, the creator of the Customer Development model, whom I've mentioned previously in this book. This experience completely changed my way of thinking. The first thing I learned was that we cannot begin by developing a product; as Steve Blank warns, this path leads to disaster. The correct path begins with developing the customer.

Another important lesson I learned as a student of Steve Blank was that all our wonderful ideas are just hypotheses, so the only way to find the truth is by talking directly to our customers. That's the reason why Steve always advises entrepreneurs to "get out of the building!" Following his lead, I went out and began speaking with Nativoo customers and users. Among other things, I learned that one of the main reasons why the city of Granada had contracted Nativoo was to position itself as an innovative tourist destination. I also learned that the other cities didn't have as much interest in our AI system because they wouldn't be the first city to have it anymore, and it would therefore no longer be newsworthy.

I also learned that tourists prefer to download their own apps rather than visit a city's website to manage their visit. We offered huge value with Nativoo, but we needed to find a different channel and format. So, after discovering that our customers weren't cities but rather tourists, we completely reworked the app, combining Customer Development with agile product development. Thanks to all these lessons I learned after 'getting out of the building,' we were able to successfully position the new version of Nativoo in the market. A while later, we received an offer from the Brazilian company SBTUR to buy the app and decided to accept it since it would allow us to pay off the debts incurred during the entire failed development process. All we had left was one very valuable thing: the lessons learned, which enabled us to continue working in the right way on other startups and projects by developing the customer before developing the product.

Steve Blank's Customer Development model is one of the first tools created specifically for startups. Today, it continues to be totally relevant to any entrepreneur, letting them discover and validate their customers as well as other elements of their business models. This is essential, because, as we said in previous chapters, inside a startup, it's all connected.

In 2005, Steve Blank published *The Four Steps to the Epiphany*, where he described his model based on four steps:

1. Customer Discovery
2. Customer Validation
3. Customer Creation
4. Company Building

Figure 3.6. Steve Blank's Four-Step Model

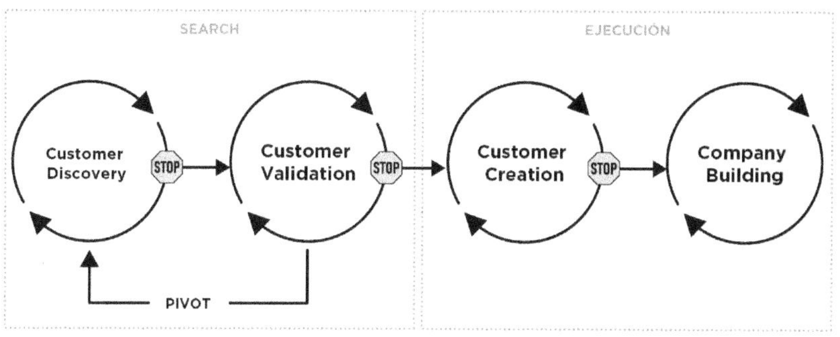

Source: Steve Blank, *The Four Steps to the Epiphany*

In 2012, he published *The Start-up Owner's Manual,* co-authored with Bob Dorf, which included an update of the model focused on the first two steps. These two books have been my basic references since I discovered them, and I strongly urge you to check them out to complement the high-level overview on Customer Development we will see in this chapter.

As you would expect, Purpose Launchpad makes use of Customer Development across its three phases (Exploration, Evaluation, and Impact) to evolve the Customer axis in order to eventually help you make a positive and massive impact on the world. In the following pages, we'll see how.

The Customer Axis in the Exploration Phase

It's important to be honest with yourself when the time comes to question whether you've performed an adequate evaluation of your hypotheses regarding your customers or not. If you haven't, it's important that you stop and do so, even if you are already selling to real customers.

During the Exploration phase, you should analyze the different types of customers you can target and, without actually developing a real product, perform certain experiments to find the most promising customer segment. You are in the step that Steve Blank calls "Customer Discovery."

Figure 3.7. The "Customer Discovery" Step

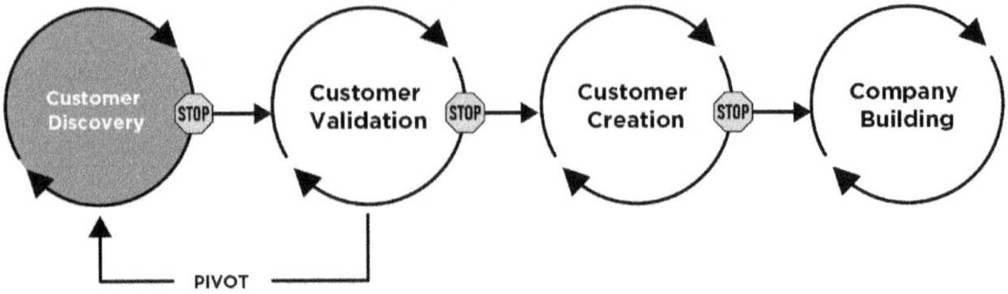

Source: Steve Blank, *The Four Steps to the Epiphany*

To go through the "Customer Discovery" step, you should follow the following phases:

1. State your hypotheses: Keeping in mind that most of them might change in subsequent steps, for now, it's enough to merely state the customer hypotheses: the list of possible customer segments, the segmentation variables to classify them, the problems they may have, and the value proposition you'd like to offer them.

2. Test the problem: It's time to "get out of the building" in order to know whether people care or not about our ideas. It's essential that you speak with actual customers and start to learn directly from them. To do that, you should interview potential customers. Careful! I don't mean massive surveys (you don't even know what questions to ask yet); I mean interviews focusing on knowing your potential customer better and evaluating their problems. The goal is not to sell them something but to evaluate whether the problems you think they have are real or not.

3. Test the solution: Based on what you learned in the previous phase, modify the starting hypotheses, as some of

the problems have probably been invalidated and you've discovered some new ones. This might also make you modify the solution you had initially envisioned. With your revised proposal in hand, it's time again to "get out of the building!" This time, you should present to customers the solution you have in mind for them and learn from their feedback in order to continue modifying the initial hypotheses. The goal is to continue learning, not to sell. Imagine that you close a sale with a customer for a product that you haven't built (nor validated) yet and that, after the sale, the rest of your customers invalidate your solution. You'd have a problem, since you've committed to creating a product for a single customer.

4. Pivot or proceed: After all the testing you've done, you must analyze the data and reach your conclusions. If you haven't found the fit between your value proposition and the market's needs, you'll have to go back to the first step, pivoting and establishing new paths in the search process. If, on the other hand, you've found a fit between the proffered value proposition and a real problem detected in the market, it will be time to move forward. You can consider the Exploration phase in the Customer axis completed and move on to Evaluation.

The process suggested by the Customer Development model is tremendously useful, and there are facilitating tools that let you continuously define and evolve the status of the hypotheses. I recommend that you use the Value Proposition Canvas created by Alex Osterwalder, which helps you define your customer segments and the value proposition for each of them. Just as I'm not attempting to provide you with an in-depth explanation of the Customer Development model but merely going high level through it, the only thing I'll say about the Value Proposition

Canvas is that it consists of a canvas with three blocks to define the customer segment (jobs to be done, pains, and gains) and three more blocks to define the value proposition (pain relievers, gain creators, and a list with products and services). Like other canvases used for innovation, this one allows you to define and communicate your hypotheses about your customer segments and the value proposition for them in a very easy way. If you want to learn more about it, I suggest you read the book *Value Proposition Design* by Alex Osterwalder.

I recommend that, during the Customer Development process, you create a Value Proposition Canvas for each of the potential customer segments you identify or discover as you move forward and that you continuously evolve it during the process based on what you learn, as summarized by the following diagram:

Figure 3.8. Sample of Customer Hypothesis Evolution on Several Value Proposition Canvases Across the Customer Development Process

	CUSTOMER DISCOVERY			
	Define your Hypotheses	Test the Problem	Test the Solution	Pivot or Continue
Customer Segment #1				
Customer Segment #2				
Customer Segment #3			CONTINUE	

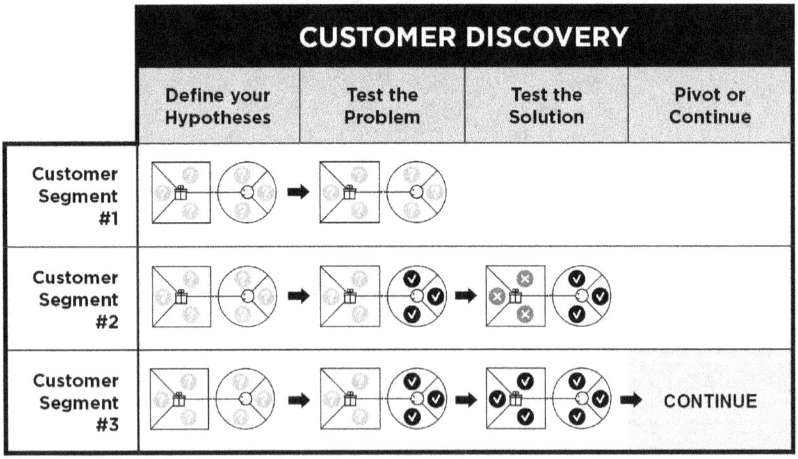

Source: Prepared by the author

As seen in the example in the diagram, which has been simplified to show the main idea, segment #1 was invalidated after testing the problem; segment #2 validated the problem but not the value proposition after testing the solution; and only segment #3 validated both the problem and the solution after going through all the Customer Discovery phases. Therefore, in this example, you would only move forward with customer segment #3, which was probably modified based on learnings obtained from the interviews performed during the different phases.

The more customer segments you analyze in this phase, the better. Remember that it's quicker and cheaper to talk to customers than to develop a product that the market ultimately doesn't want. If you do your homework, you will find the right path, discovering the right customer segments and value proposition to offer them. This is enormously valuable!

The Customer Axis in the Evaluation Phase

Once you've performed certain tests to learn and discover the most promising customer segment for your startup, the moment of truth has arrived. Now is when you validate whether you were right or not. Many times, the potential customers can confirm your initial ideas in an interview, but definitive validation will happen when you have customers spending their time and money on your product.

Figure 3.9. "Customer Validation" Step

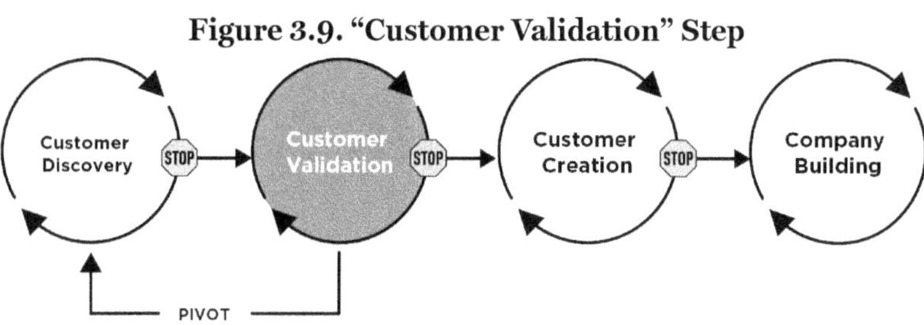

Source: Steve Blank, *The Four Steps to the Epiphany*

During this Evaluation phase, you should find the first customers who will pay for your product. Also, you will use what you've learned from your first customers' experiences in order to keep improving your product. In this Purpose Launchpad Evaluation phase, we can benefit very much from step two of the Customer Development model, called "Customer Validation." Here's what you do:

1. Get ready to sell: The time has come to present your value proposition to customers, and, to do that, you may need to create certain assets. It's not about developing a product to deliver real value (it's too soon!) but about defining your product's positioning and creating what you need in order to communicate your value proposition—for example, some sales materials or a landing page to communicate your product to end users. It's about getting ready to present your product to real customers and learning how to sell.

2. Get out of the building and sell: The best validation is for your customers to pay for your products and/or to dedicate time to using them. And this is exactly what you should obtain in this phase. However, I don't recommend you do it with any customer. You are still in a very early phase, so you should avoid attracting pragmatic customers. You should concentrate on a very specific type of customer called Early Adopters, who share your vision and are willing to accompany you on the road of constant improvement of the product (even if it's not perfect at first, since it won't be!). Selecting the right customers at the very beginning will be key.

3. Product developing and company positioning: After the tests focused on trying to sell, you'll have learned a lot, which will help you define your company's and the

product's positioning in the market. You will be able to start feeding the Product axis and combine Customer Development with agile product development in order to start working on your minimum viable product, as we will see in the corresponding chapter for the Product axis.

4. Pivot or proceed: If you have found product-market fit, it's time to move on to the next phase and begin scaling your impact; otherwise, you will need to either keep iterating your product or pivot and go back in the Customer Development process.

In this Evaluation phase, like we will see in the Impact phase below, the key is combining Customer Development with an agile product development approach, because all the feedback you receive from real customers after they use your product will be very important when you're evolving your product. That's the reason why the Customer and the Product axes are connected in the Purpose Launchpad model, and that's why it will be essential to coordinate their progress.

**Figure 3.10. Combination of Customer Development
with Agile Product Development**

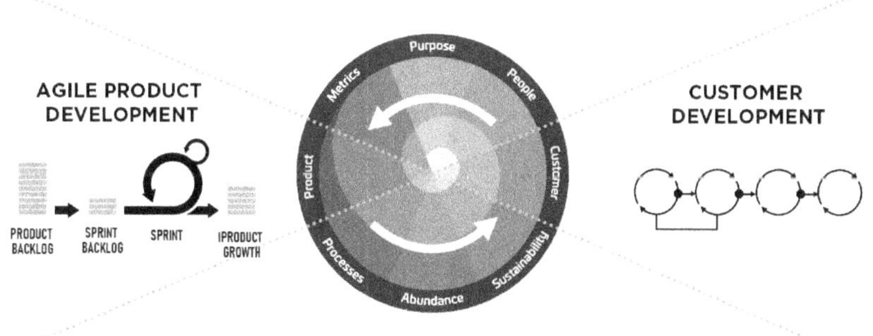

Source: Prepared by the author

At the end of the Evaluation phase, you should not only have paying customers and/or users dedicating real time to using your products, but they should also be satisfied customers. That's when you'll be able to say that you have validated your customers and your product. Congratulations! Now, it's time to scale your business and your impact on the world!

The Customer Axis in the Impact Phase

At this point, you've found and validated the appropriate customer segments, who are pleased with the real value provided by your product. It's time to replicate and scale what you've achieved so far so we will be able to start making a massive impact on the world. However, most startups tend to face a very common challenge at this point: after selling the product to a few early adopters, they struggle with increasing sales in the mass market, where customers have a much more conservative mindset.

Figure 3.11. The Execution Moment

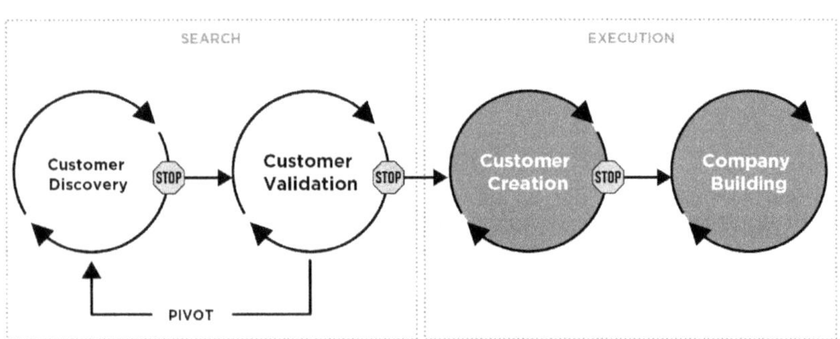

Source: Steve Blank, *The Four Steps to the Epiphany*

Here, you can again refer to the Customer Development model—specifically the last two steps, which are aimed at execution: Customer Creation and Company Building. By following this process, among others, you will obtain support to launch your product in the best way, to create demand in the mass market, and to develop the company to properly manage growth.

In a complementary way, the model that Geoffrey Moore presents in his book *Crossing the Chasm* will also come in handy. The title refers to the crucial moment for startups that we've mentioned before: beginning selling in the mass market after having sold to early adopters.

Figure 3.12. Phases for Crossing the Chasm

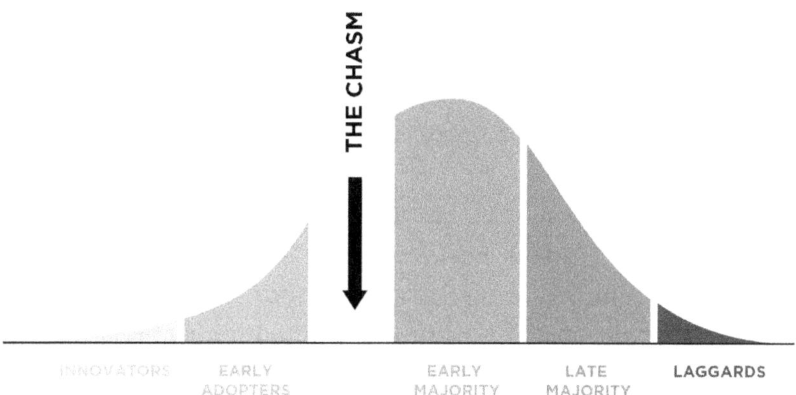

Source: Geoffrey Moore, *Crossing the Chasm*

To do that, Moore suggests defining a concrete market niche and creating and executing a strategy to conquer it, for which you need to answer the following questions:

- *Who is your niche customer segment?* In other words, which specific niche (within the early majority) are you going for? Imagine that you're offering a new book-reading product for people who use digital devices (digital readers). A more defined target customer group could be digital readers who are also entrepreneurs and who seek to broaden their knowledge with new innovation methods (probably someone like you). This way, you can focus all your efforts on a much more concrete niche, which will make the job easier when it's time to cross the chasm. In a way, what you're trying to do is identify a "rock" on the other side of the chasm where you'll try to land when you leap from the early market to the mass market.

- *Where is your niche customer?* To answer this question, you'll have to think about the communities or locations (both physical and online) where you can find your niche customer. This will allow you to properly promote your product. In the aforementioned case, you could find digital readers who are also entrepreneurs in specific groups on certain social networks, in some training programs especially aimed at them, and among followers of certain influencers.

- *How will you reach your niche customer?* Keeping in mind your niche customer's profile and where you can find them, you'll have to create communication strategies and even specific promotions. Communications should include satisfied customer testimonials, because mass market customers will want to see success stories before making a decision. In this example, you would prepare an online promotion directed at digital readers who are entrepreneurs using testimonials from early adopters and launch it together with training centers where they study with specific offers for them.

- *What will you offer your niche customer?* As the mass market customer is much more pragmatic and demanding, it's time to move from a minimal viable product to one in which the user experience plays a key role. It's time to review the entire functionality and the user experience and add new customer-support functions as well to ensure the value received is as high as possible.

The Impact phase in the Purpose Launchpad framework is never completely finished, as, after conquering the mass market early majority, you'll have to jump again to the next group of customers, the late majority, and later jump again to the last group, which Geoffrey Moore calls the "laggards." To do that, you can (and should) complement the tools I've mentioned with other traditional techniques for acquiring customers, such as the four Ps of marketing mix (price, product, promotion, and placement). The basic idea is that you continue learning how to conquer new market groups by using the learning and reputation you already have. The only way to do create a massive market impact is reaching the highest possible number of customers!

Summary and Final Thoughts on the Customer Axis

As we have seen, there are different innovation methodologies and tools that allow you to develop the Purpose Launchpad Customer axis. In fact, aside from those mentioned in this chapter, there are many others. The most important thing will be knowing how to use them and when to apply them according to the startup's Evolution phase.

Lastly, it is essential to remember that, though you might be in an advanced phase, such as the Impact phase, you should keep exploring continuously, so you should never stop talking with your customers. Like one of the Purpose Launchpad principles states, "Exploration outcomes over execution." This means that, even if you're executing a plan based on the validation you obtained beforehand, you must always stay alert and maintain some parallel exploration activity, because you could find new insights that completely change your plans.

In short, if you develop your customer before your product, you will not only find the right path, but you'll also spend fewer resources and less time trying to fit into the market, which will allow you to create a positive impact on your customers and on the world!

Table 3.3. Summary of the Client Axis

	CUSTOMER AXIS		
	Exploration Discover on which customer segments your should focus	**Evaluation** Verify that the selected segments are correct	**Impact** Scale the number of customers in the mass market
Hypotheses	Define a list with different customer segments	Propose mechanisms for selling to early adopters	Identify a niche in the mass market where you can grow
Experiments	Talk to customers to learn about their problems and possible solutions	Combine product development with customer development	Learn so you can constantly adapt your product and sales approach
Results	Choose the most promising customer segment (without selling anything yet)	Continue until you have satisfied customers who pay for your product	Scale your sales in the market niche and find others to continue to grow

Source: Prepared by the author

Activity

With your own project (startup or new product) in mind, do the following activities (if you don't have a project, think of one that you're familiar with).

1. Determine what phase you are in. Remember that, although a specific axis (such as People) might be at a more advanced stage, the initiative will be in the same phase as the least-evolved axis. Remember that you can use the Purpose Launchpad Assessment to do this (www.purposelaunchpad.com/assessment).
2. Define what actions you should implement to manage the Customer axis properly based on its actual state, using some of the techniques described above (Customer Development, Value Proposition Canvas, Crossing the Chasm, etc.).

Resources

- Value Proposition Canvas: *www.purposealliance.org/resources/value-proposition-canvas*

18
Achieve Triple Sustainability

Google's story began in 1995. Larry Page was considering studying at Stanford University, and Sergey Brin, who was already studying there, was in charge of showing him the campus. Soon after, Larry and Sergey began developing a search engine that used links to determine the importance of each page on the web. This first search engine was called Backrub, but, soon after, it was renamed Google, just like the company they co-founded in 1998. At first, they didn't even know how they were going to generate income; in fact, they were against putting advertising on search engines. Obviously, they ended up changing their minds, and Google is currently one of the most profitable companies in the world, with a turnover in 2020 of more than $180 billion, of which over $140 billion corresponded to advertisements.

In addition to being an economically sound and profitable company, Google has also managed to be a sustainable organization in every way. As far as environmental sustainability is concerned, it has been carbon neutral since 2007 and aims to reach zero emissions by 2030. In terms of social sustainability, the organization fosters positive values and encourages its employees to promote their own projects, allowing them 20 percent of their working day for that. In addition, it has launched programs to democratize access to educational resources and knowledge, with initiatives such as the free distribution of over 10 million applications to Malaysian students.

It could be said, therefore, that Google has achieved triple sustainability, a concept coined by John Elkington, as I said earlier:

- Economic: carrying out our activity profitably or, at least, without generating financial losses. This favors job creation, tax collection, and wealth generation.
- Environmental: reducing or eliminating your carbon footprint, reducing the use of natural resources, or regenerating them.
- Social: treating well all employees, families, customers, suppliers, communities, and any other person who is part of, or is affected by, the organization.

When it comes to raising your initiative's sustainability at these three levels, there are models that can help you define the most relevant aspects to analyze and manage, including the aforementioned ESG (environmental, social, and governance) model. We'll talk more about this topic in the last chapter of this section called "Measure Your Progress and Impact on the World."

**Figure 3.11. Triple Sustainability
(Economic, Social, and Environmental)**

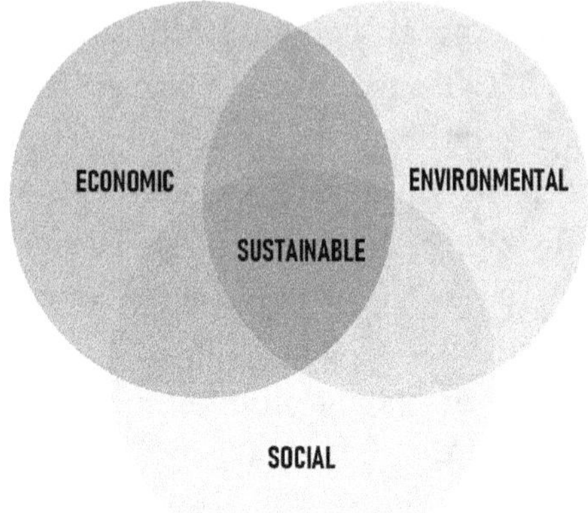

Source: John Elkington

It isn't necessary to achieve triple sustainability from day one. In fact, Google started out like most startups: without a clear (let alone validated) business model. Larry Page and Sergey Brin had a clear purpose and had found an opportunity in a new market, Internet search, so they focused on creating a better search engine than the existing ones. After their first technical results, they found in Andy Bechtolsheim, co-founder of Sun Microsystems, a business angel who gave them a check for $100,000, providing the boost they needed. In 1999, after continuing to move forward in the project and achieving important milestones, they received a $25 million investment from different venture capital companies, Sequoia among them. In 2000, they began selling ad space through keyword-based ads. After accumulating some $20 million in continuous losses during their first years of operation, in 2001, they managed to get in the black with a net profit of $7 million. Finally, in 2004, Google went public, getting $1.6 billion for investors.

In the following graph, you can see the different phases of financing that a startup usually goes through:

Figure 3.12. Financing Phases of Scalable Innovative Projects

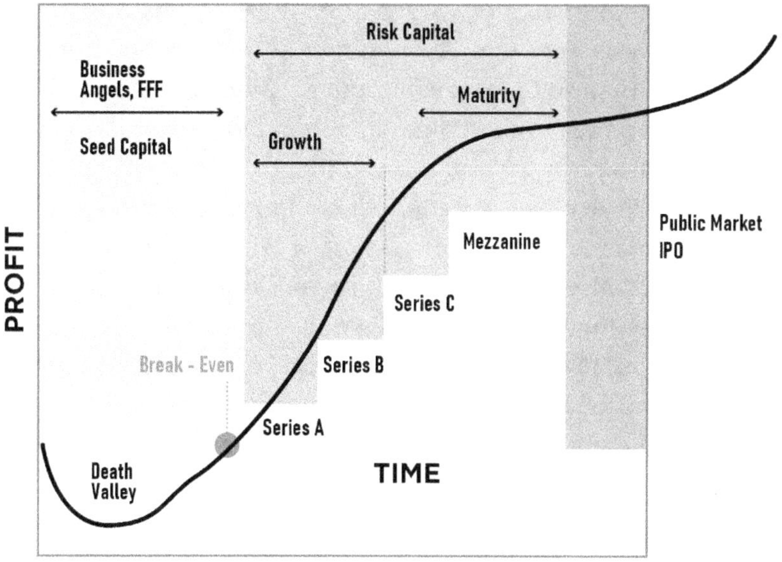

Source: Mario W. Cardullo, *Technological Entrepreneurism*

At the beginning are the "3 Fs"—namely, family, friends, and fools—who are followed in the early stages by business angels, a more professional figure. Investment amounts at this stage are usually low, usually between $50,000 and $500,000. This level of investment is mostly based on personal trust and usually takes place before the startup has even reached the break-even point—that is, before it's financially sustainable.

At the next level, we find venture capital firms, a much more serious type of investment supported by the real results that the startup has obtained. This investment can be several million dollars and often occurs when the company has already reached the break-even point and is financially sustainable.

The third and final stage is when the startup goes public through an initial public offering.

As in any model, reality and theory never fully coincide, so consider the above diagram a mere reference, not a process to follow to the letter. In fact, we can already see certain differences in Google's case. For example, they got a venture capital group to invest more than $20 million without a validated business model, something that would be practically impossible today (those were the Gold Rush days on the Internet).

In the next few pages, we'll see how Purpose Launchpad can help you navigate the different stages of your project to achieve economic sustainability. But, first, so you have more references, I'd like to also mention the "camel model" approach, which focuses on ensuring the survival of the project (our camel) even if we don't have resources (water) during the complex process towards sustainability (the desert, until we arrive at the oasis). Camel projects don't focus on obtaining funding from the beginning but on speeding up the company's income generation, even if it implies having to deviate slightly from the path. The idea is to generate short-term revenue and focus on long-term goals. A good example of this is Amazon, which was already earning more than $20,000 per week within a month of its launch, thanks to their initial focus on selling books on the Internet, without losing sight of their vision of selling practically anything online. This initial revenue not only helped them validate their business model from a very early stage but provided them with a base of operations. The camel is less dependent on external resources and finds a way to continue advancing, even if the environment changes, making its way through adversity until it achieves its objectives.

In terms of social sustainability, Google evolved a lot during its first years to achieve a model that let them offer their employees and the community the benefits they currently enjoy. Nor was it environmentally sustainable from the start. It wasn't until 2007 that it managed to be a carbon-neutral organization, and its goal is to reach zero emissions by 2030. Like at the economic level, the key is to propose a model of social and environmental sustainability from the start and promote a plan to achieve it as quickly as possible.

Remember that, before creating a positive impact on the world, we must above all avoid creating a negative one, and, to do that, we must be sustainable. In this chapter, we'll look at the way to achieve triple sustainability throughout the three phases of Purpose Launchpad.

Sustainability in the Exploration Phase

The Exploration phase is about discovering and analyzing options to make your project viable at an economic, social, and environmental level. The steps to follow are:

1) Define and simulate your business model

For your project to be economically sustainable, you need a business model that generates profits and allows you to reinvest in your project and continuously improve it. If your project is non-profit, you still need income to meet your expenses, even if you later reinvest the profits in the project.

According to Alex Osterwalder, author of *Business Model Generation*, a business model is how we create, deliver, and capture value. According to this definition, in the Exploration phase, we'll define these three elements:

- Creation: how we're going to generate value for our customers, something that we already deal with in the Customer axis.

- Delivery: how we're going to deliver value to our customers—that is, the channels we'll use.
- Capture: how we'll retain part of the value generated, capturing economic resources that let us achieve economic sustainability.

As I explained earlier in the chapter "A Brief History of Innovation Methodologies," Alex Osterwalder created a very useful tool to help define our business model: Business Model Canvas. This canvas has nine blocks and will help you establish the key issues of your business to define how your project will create, deliver, and capture value. This is a widely known tool, so I won't describe the different blocks in detail here. I'll only show you the canvas with its nine blocks to give you an idea if you're not familiar with it (you can easily find more information on the Internet):

Figure 3.13. Basic Canvas – Business Model Canvas

Key Partners	Key Activities	Value Propositions	Customer Relationships	Customer Segments
	Key Resources		Channels	
Cost Structure			Revenue Streams	

Source: Alex Osterwalder, *Business Model Generation*

When considering your business model, it's essential that you ask yourself whether you want to create a scalable business (with a global scope) or a linear one (with a local scope). Technologies allow us to propose and implement scalable business models and multiply our positive impact considerably. In general, they're businesses that connect with abundance (the next axis we'll look at). There are many successful abundance-related business models, and I'd like to list a few brief examples to inspire you:

- **Platform**: These are business models where there are at least two customer segments, one acting as the "producer" and one as the "consumer." Our mission is to act as intermediaries and build a platform that enables the value transition between the two parties. In this model, the source of income usually comes from periodic fees paid by consumers, from campaigns or promotions paid by producers, and/or from a transaction commission. One example could be Airbnb.
- **Communities**: This business model is based on facilitating and enhancing interactions between people and entities belonging to one community, so the more members it has, the more value is generated for them. The source of income here comes from advertising or from the cross-selling of products. Facebook is one example, where community members generate and consume content with one another, and the main source of revenue is advertisers' ad campaigns.
- **Automated services**: This makes intensive use of digital systems and algorithms to automate some type of action that adds value to the client or the user. In this business model, revenue can come from pay-per-service or through advertising (especially when we have a large volume of users). An example of this model is Google, which is based

on the use of algorithms to connect with the abundance of information and allow an abundance of searches on the Internet. It generates and delivers value to users while, on the other hand, it has companies that pay to promote themselves in the search results.

- **Software as a service**: Also called SaaS, this is a business model where users are offered access to software through the Internet without having to pay for a license and install the application on their own computers, as it's accessed through a web browser. In addition to the software itself, the added value is that no installation is required, updates are automatic, and access to the application is ubiquitous. In this business model, income is usually generated by periodic installments. On many occasions, a revenue system called *freemium* is implemented, which means that there is a free version of the basic software and a premium version that must be paid for. An example of this model is Dropbox, which offers cloud file storage services, both free and paid plans.
- **Anything as a service**: Also called XaaS, it consists of offering anything, even physical objects, as if it were a software service that we manage through the Internet. The value offered to the user is access to the goods they require without having to acquire them. Like the SaaS model, here the revenue is typically based on the payment of periodic fees or pay-per-use. An example is Zipcar, a company that allows you to use a car for a few hours by booking it on an Internet app.

Here's the Business Model Canvas of Airbnb as an example, which, as I said before, is a platform business model:

Figure 3.14. Business Model Canvas for Airbnb

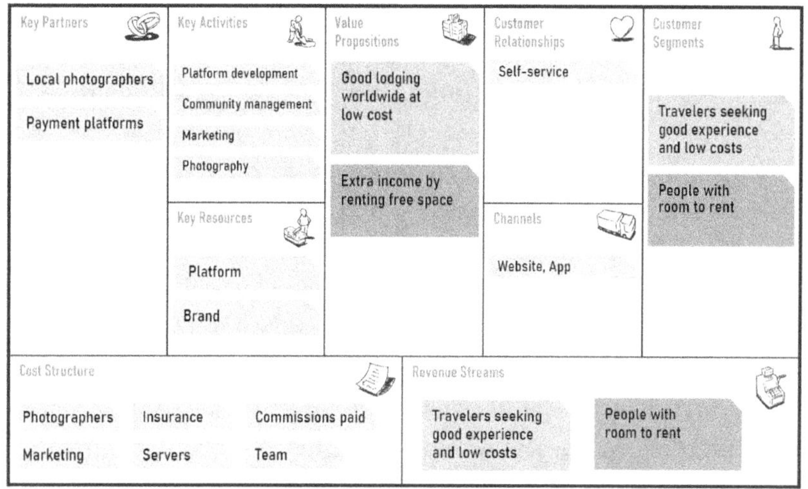

Source: Thiago Paiva, *Startupbizmodel*

Using the Business Model Canvas to design a business model can make it look very nice, but we could even design it on a paper napkin. The important thing is that it allows us to quickly explore different alternatives. Just like we did with the Customer axis, we'll have to experiment to see which business model is the most promising and continue developing it in the following phases. To do that, I recommend that you pay close attention to the progress and learning coming from the rest of the axes—for example, the results you get from experimenting in the Customer axis—since they may change your approach towards your business model. Initial conversations with potential customers can lead you to invalidate some of your customer segments or even discover a new one, which will have repercussions on the business model you've proposed. That's why you must be very agile and use tools and techniques that allow you to quickly change your business model description. In this phase of Exploration, it's not recommended to write up your business plan, which is an extensive, time-consuming document and expensive to alter. Let's revisit Steve Blank's famous statement: "No business plan survives first contact with customers." In the initial stages, the only sure thing is that everything will change in the future.

I also don't recommend that you try to raise money at such an early stage of your initiative. Maybe you could get funds from individuals close to you due to their personal trust, but it's not good to involve them in your project when you still have so much to learn and so many hypotheses to invalidate in the future. The good news is that, if you do things well, at this stage, you practically won't need to spend any money, since it's all about proposing different avenues and experimenting to try to glimpse the most appropriate path. If you wait a little longer to get your financing, it'll be easier, because you'll transmit more confidence to your investors and avoid problems in the future.

You can still make financial projections to simulate scenarios. We already know that these projections are hardly ever fulfilled, but they will help you determine the viability of your proposed model. So it's not about defining an achievable financial plan (since it'll never happen) but an experiment that lets us view the path we're proposing before we start to travel it. That way, we will be able to see whether, if validated, that path could be economically sustainable.

2) Define your corporate social responsibility (CSR) model

In traditional management models, when talking about generating a profit, the only people who are taken into consideration are the shareholders. However, there are many other people you should consider. You have to think about how to give back and treat your employees, how to interact with communities, how to relate to people along the supply chain, and even how to benefit your own customers.

To propose a socially sustainable model, I suggest that you review existing models, such as ESG, which can help you identify and define the criteria and metrics that you should analyze and manage when considering the needs of all the people linked to your organization and your actions. Remember that these types of models are not yet perfect and that you may have to complement them with similar ones (we'll talk about them in the last chapter of this part of the book, which focuses on the Metrics axis).

Your CSR model could, for example, include policies and actions to ensure gender equality in your teams, create a healthy and safe work environment, ensure fair trade with suppliers, and prevent child recruitment. Many of these criteria may seem too obvious, but it is important to ensure that they are met throughout the supply chain.

Just as it's not yet time to create a detailed business plan, we're also not going to create an overly elaborate corporate social responsibility model or plan. We should start thinking about these issues and raise them at a high level from the early stages of your project.

3) Define your corporate environmental responsibility model

In the same way that responsible and educated people take care of the environment when they go out to the countryside for a walk or collect their waste when they have a picnic outdoors, your startup or product will have to find a way to carry out its activity without damaging the natural environment. In fact, society is increasingly aware of climate change and the negative impact that many organizations have on the planet, so it will also be essential that you achieve environmental sustainability to have a good image and maintain your customers. Environmental sustainability is the most profitable path for a company in the long term.

I recommend that you simulate your organization's sustainability chain (a concept that we will also introduce in the chapter on Metrics) and the different actions you're considering for your activity to be environmentally sustainable. This will also include your suppliers, since it will be useless for you to carry out a sustainable activity if your suppliers aren't on the same page. For your initiative to be environmentally sustainable, you will have to consider how you produce and market your product, including policies that minimize waste and emissions and that maximize the recycling and use of renewable energies.

When considering your models of corporate social and environmental responsibility, you can take another look at models such as ESG and references such as the 17 Sustainable Development Goals (SDGs) published by the United Nations in 2015 so that they inspire you to implement your business in an environmentally sustainable way.

Figure 3.15. The 17 Sustainable Development Goals

Source: United Nations

It's useless to generate a positive impact relative to our purpose if we're creating a negative impact with our activities. We should always seek a balance between the benefits we bring to the world and the cost that our activity extols on the environment and society.

From the beginning, it's important that you take into consideration your project's sustainability, not only economically but also environmentally and socially. A tool that can help you is the Sustainable Business Model Canvas, which adds two blocks to the Business Model Canvas that we've seen before: one to write down the benefits that our initiative brings to the environment and society and another to write down the cost we generate in these same areas.

Figure 3.16. Sustainable Business Model Canvas

Key Partners	Key Activities	Value Propositions	Customer Relationships	Customer Segments
	Key Resources		Channels	
Cost Structure			Revenue Streams	
Eco-Social Costs			Eco-Social Benefits	

Source: Loïc Bar

In short, in the Exploration phase, you should focus on thinking, ideating, and designing how your startup or project will achieve triple sustainability. Define your starting hypotheses in regard to achieving economic, environmental, and social sustainability. You're not going to get anything going yet, nor is it time to invest resources. You're only in the world of ideas right now.

Sustainability in the Evaluation Phase

In this phase, the goal of sustainability is to move from theory to practice—that is, to experiment to try to put our plans into action. On paper, it all works, but it's different in the real world. Now you must validate (or invalidate) your starting hypotheses.

1) Test your business model with real revenue

One of the first investors to enter Google's venture capital phase was John Doerr, who invested $11.8 million to get 12 percent of the company and a seat on the board of directors. In one of his conversations with the founders, Doerr asked about the size the company might have in the future. Larry Page replied, "$10 billion someday." Doerr replied in amazement: "You mean the market cap value, don't you?" Larry clarified that he was referring to revenue and that the market valuation would be about $100 billion. Over time, these forecasts have been far exceeded. Current revenues exceed $100 billion, and the market value is more than $1.8 trillion.

With most projects, reality is seldom so splendid. 90 percent of startups do not meet their financial projections for various reasons—sometimes due to entrepreneurs' lack of experience, something you can avoid if you follow the advice in this book, sometimes because of their founders' inflexibility and lack of agility, their unwillingness to change the plan when it begins to fail. Remember that the founders of Google had to pivot their business model towards a type of income which they had previously even rejected publicly. In any case, you must be prepared for not fulfilling your projections, because there will be times when that will surely happen, and you'll have to manage the situation and make the right decisions, implementing specific actions that allow you to adapt your path to reality.

My message here is that, to avoid problems, you must dream while keeping your feet on the ground. Therefore, in this phase, you must evaluate your previously defined hypotheses regarding your business model by carrying out experiments on the external market and less so regarding how to operate (this will come in the Impact phase). If you take the Business Model Canvas as a reference, experiments should focus on the blocks on the right half of the canvas (customer segments, customer relationship, channels, value proposition, and revenue streams). Of course, always keep an open mind to changing any aspect of your model. Remember that a startup is a temporary entity in search of a business model. Google didn't find its own until its second year, when it decided to launch a keyword-based ad-selling system.

It may still be too early to try to raise funding—first, because we could generate expectations in our investors about an initial plan that could change when we don't validate it and, secondly, because it's easy to get carried away by having resources and focus on building on our hypotheses before determining whether the path is the right one.

Following the principles of Purpose Launchpad ("earning meaningful income before investment"), it is preferable to earn income from visionaries to validate the business model before obtaining external financing (even before investing our own resources if we have them). This will allow you to confirm that you really have a valid value proposition and business model for your potential customers while also getting feedback to continue improving it (or even to pivot it if necessary).

As we saw in the chapter on the Customer axis, you must present your early adopters with a value proposition before building a final product. The income you obtain will allow you to develop your product in an iterative and agile way and minimize the investment (we'll learn how in the Product axis).

This model does not work for projects where heavy investment in research and product development is required. If this is your case, I recommend that you be creative when it comes to capturing early adopters. For example, you can pre-order the product with a crowdfunding campaign before raising private funding. And, once you have initial sales, you can seek complementary financial help to develop the product.

Another way to earn meaningful income rather than resorting to financing, especially when the development of our product involves a significant investment, is to offer consulting services to the same clients who would eventually buy your product. This way, we generate revenue in the short term and gain valuable learning about our customers and their real needs that we can use in the iterative process of building the product. This approach is in line with the "camel" strategy that I spoke about earlier in this chapter.

Whatever you do, the important thing is to sell before developing your product. While you try to sell to early adopters or visionaries, you will learn about your value proposition (how to create value), about the channels you are going to use (how to deliver value), and about the pricing model (how to retain value). Keep experimenting and iterating.

In this phase, you already begin to have real expenses, and, at some point, you also have income. Therefore, we no longer talk about hypotheses but about real data. This allows you to conduct experiments, learn, and make decisions. For example, you can experiment with the price of your products, with the length of the free period you give your users before they start paying (if that's the case), etc. Then you can see how your financial model really behaves and continue adjusting it until you find a business model that leads to economic sustainability.

At this point, you could also invalidate your business model and find that you must pivot, which would mean you'd need to go back to the Exploration phase to consider other possible paths. Or you could validate your business model but find that it is not yet economically sustainable due to lack of volume. In this case, you'll have to continue adjusting the different parameters of the model to optimize it and achieve a greater volume in the Impact phase.

2) Start putting your models of corporate social responsibility and corporate environmental responsibility into practice

In addition to starting to measure the economic results of your project, you should also start measuring the results related to environmental and social sustainability. Take as a starting point the hypotheses you defined in the Exploration phase and gather the necessary data. For example, if you are using the United Nations SDGs, I recommend that you delve into their definition. Each SDG is broken down into a series of quantifiable and measurable targets, allowing you to start monitoring your activity and evaluate with real data both the benefits and the costs you're generating at an environmental and social level. It's possible that you're not yet fully socially and environmentally sustainable at this stage. That's normal, but you must aim along those lines and make the necessary adjustments and improvements to fully achieve it in the next phase. Remember that it's only possible to create a true positive impact if we do it sustainably.

Sustainability in the Impact Phase

At this point, you have already managed to demonstrate that the business model leads the project to economic sustainability. Although you may not have yet reached the break-even point, you are moving in that direction. You have also shown that the project can be environmentally and socially sustainable. Although it is not yet totally so, you are moving towards it. So now, in the Impact phase, the goal is for your project to really reach that desired triple sustainability. To do this, you will continue to boost your business model by trying to optimize your operations and scale your activity sustainably.

1) Improve your business model's scalability

When Google closed its $25 million funding round in 1999, venture capital fund Sequoia suggested hiring a CEO with an executive profile. Soon after, in 2001, Larry Page and Sergey Brin hired Eric Schmidt for that position. This was one of Google's first moves towards scaling its business. In fact, after Eric's arrival in 2001, Google's main source of revenue (ads) began to grow exponentially, going from $70 million in 2001 to more than $36 billion in 2011.

Figure 3.17. Advertising Revenue for Google from 2001 to 2020 (in billions of dollars)

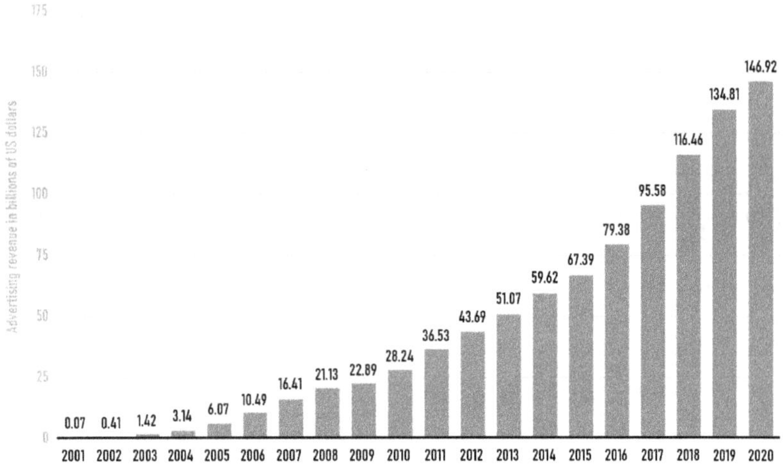

Source: Google, Alphabet

If you have a scalable business model, the key to making it grow will be to focus on enhancing access to abundance (of customers, resources, etc.) and optimizing operations. If you take the Business Model Canvas as a reference, you should focus on reviewing the blocks on the left of the canvas (partners, key activities, key resources, and costs). In fact, the team is one of the key resources, which is why Google made such an important change in the company's leadership and execution at the time. For you, it's also time to complement your team if necessary and to review the rest of the organization's gears (including funding) to scale it and achieve your goals.

The last time I raised funding for a project, it was quite simple. After preparing some documentation to communicate the investment opportunity and make it known to potential stakeholders, the investors appeared almost by magic. But it wasn't magic: we had a validated business model and an economically sustainable organization. We didn't need the capital to keep the organization alive but to grow (expand the team, dedicate resources to promotion, etc.). The organization was Purpose Alliance, and we managed to reach this point without investment, following the very steps I'm explaining in this chapter and throughout the book.

If you can wait to get financing until you have validated your business model (even if you have not yet reached the break-even point), you can attract investors much more easily. If the amount is less than $500,000, you will probably have to consider the "3 F" model or find business angels. If the amount is higher, I recommend that you seek venture capital. Of course, at a certain point, you may want and need to consider making an initial public offer (IPO) to have your company's shares listed on one or more stock exchanges. In any case, it moves forward step by step and iteratively. You can start a first round with business angels that validate the model from the investor's point of view and help you reach certain important milestones and, after that, consider a larger round with venture capital.

In the Impact phase, you must prepare a full-fledged financial plan with budgets that help you control spending, sales objectives that help you get the necessary income, etc. You've already accumulated experience and an important validation of your model, so you must start making forecasts from your previous results and meet them. In fact, your financial plan can help you communicate your business's real performance to investors and offer realistic expectations.

Remember that, even if you raise funding and have more resources, you should not stop exploring and learning while trying to scale the organization. Don't neglect good practices, such as continuous hypothesis evaluation. I have seen many startups that, having obtained more funding, have tried to go too fast and have crashed. Don't speed up if you're not ready to take the curve or you'll miss it. Keep moving forward, learning, and, once you validate with real data that you're ready to accelerate, do it. It will be time to reach your break-even point or multiply your economic benefits. Go for it!

2) Achieve and maintain social and environmental sustainability

Just like you've been able to create a financial plan to help guide your steps to economic sustainability using actual experience, you must do the same to achieve environmental and social sustainability. I advise that you create a document (or use a tool that can help you do so) in which you set down your sustainability goals and define a series of actions that will help you achieve them. In the chapter on metrics, we'll see in greater detail how you can achieve that, and I'll also provide some models and standards that will help you monitor your level of social and environmental sustainability.

Remember that it's not about touching on social and environmental sustainability and forgetting about it but about doing it continuously, just as we manage economic viability.

Final Thoughts on the Sustainability Axis

As I said at the beginning of this chapter, by applying the Purpose Launchpad approach towards achieving your project's sustainability, you can minimize the risks of creating a startup or a new product. However, it's important that you also keep in mind that this chapter is totally related to the one on metrics at the end of this third part of the book, since you'll need to be able to measure your results and your progress in order to continuously improve your economic results and your social and environmental footprint. I recommend, therefore, that you do not apply everything you have seen here separately without considering what you will find in the Metrics chapter.

I would also like to give you one last piece of advice regarding economic sustainability, because, in the world of startups, it is very common for entrepreneurs to focus on raising capital too early. In fact, as we have already mentioned, the key in the Exploration phase is to hold off on investing capital, either your own or external. In the Evaluation phase, you must get income from real customers (before creating your product!), which will validate the model and provide a good source of financing. Only if you are working on a project with a strong research and development component should you consider obtaining financing from investors in the Evaluation phase before developing your product—and, in that case, always after having obtained some income from customers to validate your value proposition. In projects without a high R&D component, we will only seek investment in the Impact phase once we have validated that our model is scalable. Please don't be tempted to raise money from investors too soon. Try, rather, to follow the camel approach we reviewed at the beginning of the chapter.

Figure 3.18. Recommended Funding Sources in the Purpose Launchpad Phases

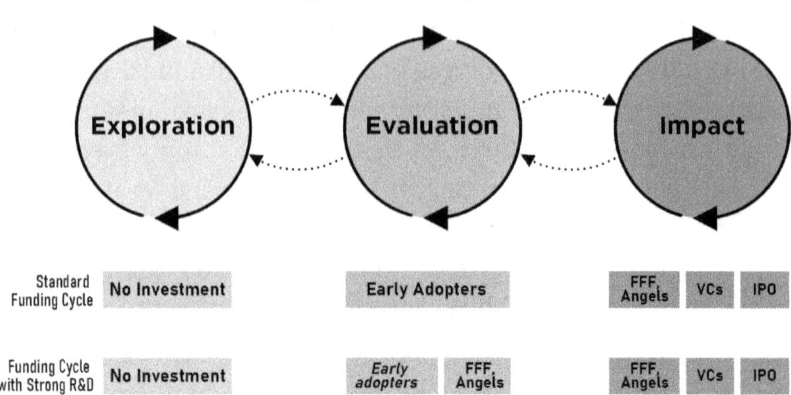

Source: Prepared by the author

However, remember that sustainability is not only about economic viability; we always propose it as triple sustainability, which includes social and environmental aspects. Janez Potocnik, European Commissioner for Science and Research between 2004 and 2009 and for the Environment between 2010 and 2014, expressed this dynamic uniquely: "If you think economy is more important than environment, try holding your breath while counting your money."

The type of innovative impact-oriented projects we are developing, therefore, also require social and environmental sustainability—that is, a triple sustainability that helps you generate a double positive impact: on your project and in the world.

Table 3.4. Summary of the Sustainability Axis

	SUSTAINABILITY AXIS		
	Exploration Propose how you can be economically, socially, and environmentally sustainable	**Evaluation** Verify whether your sustainability model works and iterate if necessary	**Impact** Enjoy your triple sustainability ad use it as a basis for creating real impact
Profit	Define and simulate your business model (without seeking funding)	Test your real income model	Scale and optimize your business model
People	Define your Corporate Social Responsibility model	Start putting your Corporate Social Responsibility model into practice	Reach and maintain social sustainability
Planet	Define your corporate environmental responsibility model	Start putting your corporate environmental responsibility model into practice	Reach and maintain environmental sustainability

Source: Prepared by the author

Activity

Using your own project (startup or new product), do these activities (if you do not have a project, think of one that is familiar to you).

1. Determine what phase you're in. Remember that, although a specific axis (such as people) might be at a more advanced stage, your initiative will be in whichever phase the least-evolved axis is in. Remember that you can use the Purpose Launchpad Assessment (www.purposelaunchpad.com/assessment) to determine this.

2. Depending on the phase your project is in, do the following:

   a. Exploration phase:
   - Define your business model, identifying how you will create value, how you will deliver it to your customers, and how you will retain it (revenue model).
   - Create a simulation of your income/expenses for the first year of project operation.
   - Define a model of corporate social responsibility.
   - Define a model of corporate environmental responsibility.

   b. Evaluation phase:
   - Evaluate the most important hypotheses of your business model based on experience and propose a possible pivot or improvement based on the results obtained so far.
   - Try to think about how you could earn income from early adopters if you haven't already.

- Consolidate the financial evolution of the project so far (income and expenses) and, depending on possible changes you plan to make and as a continuation of the previous results, project the coming months.
- Get insights from real experience and improve your corporate social responsibility model.
- Get insights from real experience and improve your corporate environmental responsibility model.

c. Impact phase:
  - Think about how you could scale and optimize your business model.
  - Define the best strategy to obtain financing for growth if you really need it.
  - Make a financial plan or review the one you have to evaluate possible adjustments or set goals to break even.
  - Get insights from real experience and improve your corporate social responsibility model.
  - Get insights from real experience and improve your corporate environmental responsibility model.

Resources

- Business Model Canvas: *www.purposealliance.org/resources/business-model-canvas*
- Sustainable Business Canvas: *www.purposealliance.org/resources/sustainable-business-canvas/*

19
Leverage Abundance

Imagine for a moment that you are sitting by the seashore, observing the immensity of the ocean and trying to imagine everything that must exist under that endless mantle of water: beautiful seascapes, living beings of all colors and shapes, many secrets waiting to be uncovered. As Carl Sagan said, "Somewhere. something incredible is waiting to be discovered," and not just in outer space but here, in our own planet's vast oceans.

Sitting on the beach and observing the immensity of the sea connects us with our essence as human beings and with the magnitude of the universe in which we live. Our gaze lost on the horizon, we know that the sea continues to extend far beyond what we can see, acquiring a dimension that we are barely able to grasp with our imagination. The sea is a clear representation of the abundance of the world in which we live.

There is abundance, in fact, almost anywhere we look. Those who see it and can connect with it achieve success unimaginable to others. Such was the case for the founders of GitHub, a social network where software developers worldwide host and share their projects. It was founded in 2008 and acquired by Microsoft in 2018 for ... $7.5 billion! How was it possible?

There is evidently an abundance (increasing daily) of free software developers—that is, of source code that can be consulted, modified, and used freely by other programmers for any purpose and redistributed with changes or improvements. Thanks to this movement, important systems have emerged, such as Linux, Mozilla Firefox, and numerous applications. In fact, many of them make it possible for your mobile phone and computer to work. What did GitHub do? Well, it offered them the perfect platform where they could find useful source code for their projects and share their code with others who wanted to use it. The key was to take the needs and desires of users and developers into account and help them interact with other colleagues, sharing, commenting, and learning continuously from feedback. In addition, when the platform had an internal need, it opened its own code up to developers to collaborate as staff on demand.

Today, GitHub has more than 73 million users who continuously create and share source code on the platform, making it the world's largest software repository, where we can find applications for almost anything we could imagine. The platform also has a badge system to recognize the most active users, those who write the best code, etc. That way, it manages to maintain a community that is not only involved but committed to the project.

It's not enough to connect with abundance; you must also know how to manage it properly. GitHub did this by creating an extraordinary user experience with its simple interfaces, which allow any developer to use the platform easily and intuitively. It also enables the GitHub team itself to make use of the platform, creating dashboards that offer statistics and key metrics about the system's millions of users and repositories. In fact, GitHub encourages its teams to drive new ideas, iterate them, and learn from failures and successes on an ongoing basis. In addition, the teams have total autonomy, as decision-making is completely decentralized.

Besides managing the abundance of developers and code, GitHub also manages the abundance of comments and questions from its users by allowing them to talk to one another. This greatly speeds up communication, since it would be impossible for GitHub to address each of the programmers when they have any questions or need assistance.

There are increasingly many other organizations that have found ways to connect and manage abundance in an amazing way, which has led them to achieve exponential growth. Salim Ismail, Yuri Van Geest, and Michael Malone explained this phenomenon well in their book *Exponential Organizations* published in 2014. As I mentioned before, a year later, I began collaborating with Salim Ismail. One of the projects I promoted from the beginning was the development of a tool called ExO Canvas, which collects the eleven attributes that exponential organizations implement to connect with abundance and manage it:

1. MTP (Massive Transformative Purpose): the purpose of the initiative, which is positioned as transformative (since

it will have a world-changing effect) and massive (since the idea is that the initiative has a massive positive impact).

2. Staff on Demand: people who are not employees but who perform tasks to carry out the main activity of the organization dynamically when they are needed.

3. Community: people and organizations linked to the organization in some way who can live together under a set of rules or share common interests.

4. Algorithms: systems and applications that automate the organization's activities.

5. Leveraged Assets: Resources that, without formally belonging to the organization, are used flexibly as they are needed.

6. Engagement: mechanism we use to retain and keep the community active.

7. Interfaces: applications and graphical interfaces that allow us to offer a good user experience to our customers and community members.

8. Dashboards: control panel that allows us to define and trace the most relevant metrics for our initiative.

9. Experimentation: experimentation techniques and culture used to evaluate our hypotheses.

10. Autonomy: how we will offer decision-making and operational freedom to our teams and even to our customers and community members.

11. Social Technologics: mcchanisms and softwarc that allow our customers, community members, and even our team to communicate in an agile way.

Figure 3.19. ExO Canvas

MASSIVE TRANSFORMATIVE PURPOSE	
STAFF ON DEMAND	INTERFACES
COMMUNITY & CROWD	DASHBOARDS
ALGORITHMS	EXPERIMENTATION
LEVERAGED ASSETS	AUTONOMY
ENGAGEMENT	SOCIAL TECHNOLOGIES

Source: Francisco Palao and others

The left-side blocks (also called SCALE) are usually useful for connecting and generating abundance, while the right-side blocks (usually called IDEAS) are more focused on abundance management. It is advisable that you use a combination of these elements that allows you to balance access to abundance and its management.

Next, as an example, you can see GitHub's ExO Canvas, whose success factors we saw at the beginning of the chapter:

Figure 3.20. ExO Canvas for GitHub

MASSIVE TRANSFORMATIVE PURPOSE	
Social Programming	

STAFF ON DEMAND Community members who contribute to the development of the GitHub platform	**INTERFACES** Internet platform
COMMUNITY & CROWD Free software developers	**DASHBOARDS** Real-time user statistics
ALGORITHMS Version control	**EXPERIMENTATION** Constant agility-based experimentation
LEVERAGED ASSETS Software code from millions of programmers	**AUTONOMY** Teams are automatically formed and organized
ENGAGEMENT Badge system	**SOCIAL TECHNOLOGIES** GitHub social layer

Source: Prepared by the author

Leveraging the abundance of programmers allowed GitHub to generate an abundance of source code and deliver enormous value to its users, as well as to define a fully scalable business model. Therefore, the key is to consider how you can connect with abundance (the type that relates to your project) to create new sources of abundance. It is quite possible that, when you find the sources of abundance relevant to your project, you'll rethink the value proposition or even the business model of your startup or product.

Beyond the tool you use, the important thing, as always, is the mindset with which you develop your initiative. Let's look at the most appropriate mindset in relation to abundance in each of the three phases of Purpose Launchpad.

Abundance in the Exploration Phase

The goal in this phase is to discover the different sources of abundance and raise your first hypotheses. You can start by imagining what extraordinary value you would like to be able to offer your customers through abundance. When you have something truly amazing in mind, think about how you could make it happen. It doesn't matter that it's a crazy idea, because it could come true by connecting it with some source of abundance. Remember the case of Wikipedia. Creating the world's largest free encyclopedia accessible to anyone might initially seem like an impossible idea, but they managed to connect with the abundance of knowledge and the people willing to share it. That way, they generated an unprecedented abundance of content.

Another way to connect with abundance in this phase is to imagine a replicable and scalable business model in a way never seen before and then think about how to make it possible. Again, it is very possible that different sources of abundance come to mind that could allow you to make it happen.

The ExO Canvas can also be very useful. The very process of reflection on the different attributes will naturally lead you to propose different sources of abundance and how to manage them. And contact with potential customers and the community can also give you clues to paths to abundance that you haven't thought of before. Remember that you are exploring. Therefore, you must find all the possibilities before taking a path. Spotting the right source of abundance can change the course of your project and take you into a new world full of possibilities.

Abundance in the Evaluation Phase

The objective in this phase will be to verify that we can really access the abundance that we have identified and even generate the abundance that we have imagined—in other words, to validate hypotheses regarding the sources and generation of abundance.

When the founders of GitHub started with their project, they were already aware that the source of abundance existed, because they themselves were software developers and knew the magnitude of the free software programmers' community and the abundance of source code. However, they had to validate that they were able to connect with that abundance. To do this, after interacting with potential users, they decided to create a first beta version of the platform, where they received about 10,000 software projects. Their experience confirmed that they were on the right track when it came to connecting with a source of real abundance and showed that they could generate an abundance of software projects of great value to the world.

I recommend that you do the same—that is, that you evaluate through conversations and experiments of different types that the source of abundance that you have identified is real and that you are able to connect with it. Try to do this without investing a lot of time or resources, because you are still in the evaluation phase and you must minimize the investment and maximize learning. If you are using the ExO Canvas, you should focus on evaluating and iterating hypotheses focused on connecting with abundance or generating it—that is, the ones in the blocks related to staff on demand, community, algorithms, leveraged assets, and engagement.

Abundance in the Impact Phase

It's time to learn to swim in the sea of abundance you just threw yourself into. It's time to show that you are able to manage abundance properly to finally create a powerful value proposition or scalable growth in your business model.

You may have to make changes to your project to get it. GitHub only managed to scale exponentially when it optimized its platform interface to deliver an extraordinary user experience. It achieved this thanks to its agile culture, the continuous experimentation of a fully autonomous team, and the large social component of the platform, which allowed users to support one another without centralized control.

In this phase of impact, you must optimize to scale and bring abundance to many customers, users, and/or members of your community. If you are using the ExO Canvas, at this stage, you should be open to improving the necessary elements related to the right-side attributes of the canvas: interfaces, dashboard, experimentation, autonomy, and social technologies, which are suitable to best managing abundance.

Final Thoughts on the Abundance Axis

Connecting with abundance and managing it is key today in order to find a market niche and survive. Those who fail to do so end up disappearing. However, not all projects should be approached with a global or exponential approach, since it is perfectly admissible and feasible to propose initiatives whose scope of action is limited to a more local environment. In other words, generating abundance is mandatory, while scaling is optional.

We could create a world with democratic access to resources of all kinds in which abundance removes barriers to competition and expands the possibilities for collaboration. It's up to you. You can continue to look at the world through scarcity lenses and compete for resources or look at it through abundance lenses and enhance collaboration with other people and organizations to take your projects to the next level. Abundance, after all, is not just something you connect with externally; it is mostly a mindset that takes you into a world of endless opportunities.

Table 3.5. Summary of the Abundance Axis

ABUNDANCE AXIS			
	Exploration Discover outside sources of abundance and how to generate it for others	**Evaluation** Learn to connect with the sources of abundance, to generate it and manage it	**Impact** Increase your connection to the outside sources of abundance and your generation
Connect	Find sources of abundance to make your purpose happen	Find sources of abundance and learn from experience	Increase the sources of abundance
Generate	Define how you'll generate abundance for your customers and environment	Begin to generate real abundance and learn from experience	Boost the generation of abundance
Manage	Visualize how you will manage abundance after connecting with / generating it	Learn from experience and re-define how to manage abundance	Test and evolve how to manage abundance to scale your impact

Source: Prepared by the author

Activity

Considering your own project (startup or new product), do the following activities (if you don't have a project, think of one that you're familiar with):

- Define the sources of abundance you could use and how to manage them. To do this, you can use the ExO Canvas.
- Define experiments that allow you to evaluate your hypotheses, whether they are related to how to connect with abundance (if the project is in the Evaluation phase) or how to manage it (if the project is in the Impact phase).
- Determine how the Abundance axis could affect the rest of the axes—for example, improving your value proposition or even the business model itself.

Resources

- ExO Canvas: *www.purposealliance.org/resources/exo-canvas/*

20
Implement the Right Processes

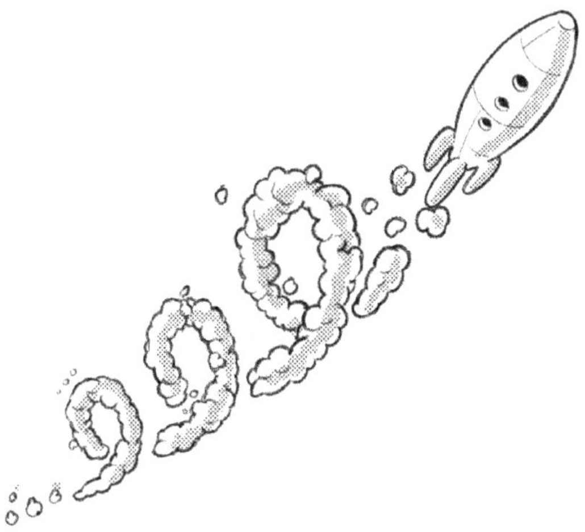

Until the early 2000s, software development methodologies forced engineers to generate a large amount of documentation that was a waste of time and money, since the final version was almost always very different from the initial one. They realized that doing a detailed analysis and a development plan did not work because, among other things, it was impossible to know in advance how users were going to interact before launching the software. In addition, the environment was increasingly dynamic and uncertain, so it was impossible to foresee months in advance what the market would need. All this caused a lot of frustration for the engineers.

To try to solve this problem, on February 12, 2001, a group of sixteen people met in Snowbird, Utah, to try to find a different way of working. The result was the *Agile Manifesto*, the seed of a global movement that has given rise to well-known frameworks such as Scrum, which facilitate the implementation of agile principles. The *Agile Manifesto* sent a very important message to the world, as it defined a series of principles that completely changed software development. The agile approach is based on quickly creating a small first version of the software and iterating it from users' feedback. It does not start from an established plan but allows developers to change the direction of the project based on the input received.

Today, most software companies and computer engineers work under agile techniques. And they're not the only ones, as there are more and more business profiles certified in this type of techniques. It is a movement that has not been limited to the world of software but is already present in most industries in one way or another, helping navigate an environment of high uncertainty and rapid changes.

Figure 3.21. Agile Approach

Source: Prepared by the author

Agile approaches are not always the best way to achieve our goals. When there is no uncertainty, we are clear about what we want to do, and we're sure that our actions will lead us to the right destination, the best way forward is to define a plan and execute it as optimally as possible. For this reason, traditional techniques and methods with a linear approach still make sense in many contexts. These types of approaches follow predefined plans or processes that are executed from beginning to end and, therefore, in many cases, are called waterfall approaches.

Figure 3.22. Waterfall Approach

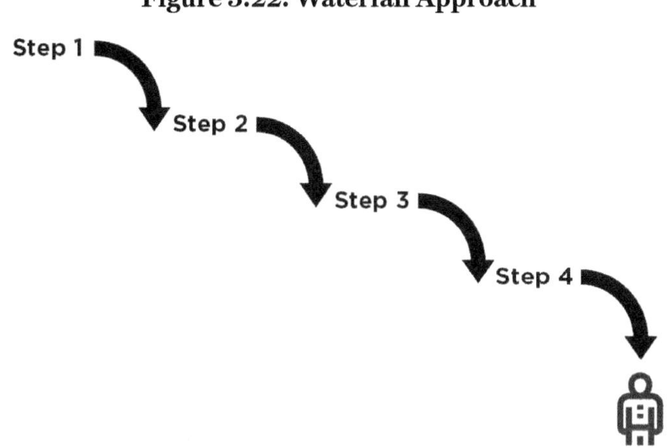

Source: Prepared by the author

Waterfall approaches are useful both for running an organization's day-to-day life and for manufacturing a product in a familiar environment and with a high degree of certainty. An example is Airbus's A380 aircraft, considered the largest passenger aircraft in the world. Its manufacturing process, assuming all parts are available, takes around 80 days and involves a team of 800 people. It is a very complex production, with a very well-defined plan from the beginning, since the manufacturing design is clear and the environment quite controlled.

A very different case is IMVU, co-founded in 2004 by Eric Ries, whose vision was to create an environment for people around the world to connect with one another. At first, they didn't even know very well what to offer users, so they applied agile techniques. They started by developing a basic chat, and, after conducting multiple experiments that allowed them to receive significant feedback from users, they evolved into a virtual 3D chat environment in which users could dress up with an avatar, create a homepage, and connect with new people. A few years later, IMVU had more than six million active users and the largest catalog of virtual objects in the world.

Not only do we find uncertainty when we want to develop a new product, sometimes it's also present when organizing our day-to-day work. Imagine, for example, the IT department of an organization that must continuously respond to all kinds of requests from users (installation of new equipment and systems, breakdowns, questions about doubts, etc.). In this case, it is not only useless to have a predefined action plan but even pre-established priorities, because you could change the team's tasks at any time. It is necessary to use agile approaches or even techniques that allow greater flexibility.

Next, let's see how Purpose Launchpad can help you recognize the type of approach and tools you should implement regarding construction or execution processes in low- or high-uncertainty environments. You'll see that the way to approach processes is different when you are focused on developing a product or a startup than when the focus is on day-to-day operations.

Processes in the Exploration Phase

In this phase, as in the other axes, the objective will be to search for the most promising path but without finding it. In fact, you could say that, at the beginning of a project, the best process is the absence of processes, because you still don't know anything, not even what you don't know. It's not yet time to develop a product or design how the organization will work.

During the first months of creating my second startup, IActive, I attended a training program for entrepreneurs in which they taught traditional business management techniques. One of the tasks I was assigned was to draw a map of my organization's processes. I never hesitated: I downloaded a process design software and got to work. In fact, I must admit that I really enjoyed the exercise, since I was finally beginning to visualize how my startup could work, something that had been totally unknown until then. I defined a process to invoice our customers, another one to develop and test the software, another to manage and coordinate the team, etc. The problem is that we had no software, no equipment, no customers; we were at a very early phase in which all we had was ideas. As I've said before, we love and are, above all, reassured by creating plans or designing solutions to feel that we have everything under control. But, when the time comes to face the truth, they rarely work. As you can imagine, that's what happened then: none of the processes I had defined were good for anything.

After that, I never again designed processes at such an early stage. Now I always wait for the project to be more advanced, and, with real experience, I draw the processes that have emerged almost naturally and try to improve them.

Not having processes doesn't mean doing nothing. In fact, as you already know, in the Exploration phase, you must discover the possible paths to your destination by considering all the axes (going through all the axes can be a process in itself). You must dedicate some time to each of the axes until you take them all to a level that allows you to move on to the next phase. My recommendation is that you do it following the order suggested in the chapter on the axes: purpose, people, customers, sustainability, abundance, processes, product, and metrics. For each axis, you must define hypotheses and carry out experiments that allow you to validate or discard them. Once you go over all the axes a first time, you may need to give them a second pass, a third, etc. The idea is to work your project in an iterative and agile way to implement the changes you require depending on what you learn. You can do it informally or by implementing a mechanism that gives you greater rigor, such as Purpose Launchpad Sprint, synthetically represented in the following diagram:

Figure 3.23. Purpose Launchpad Sprint

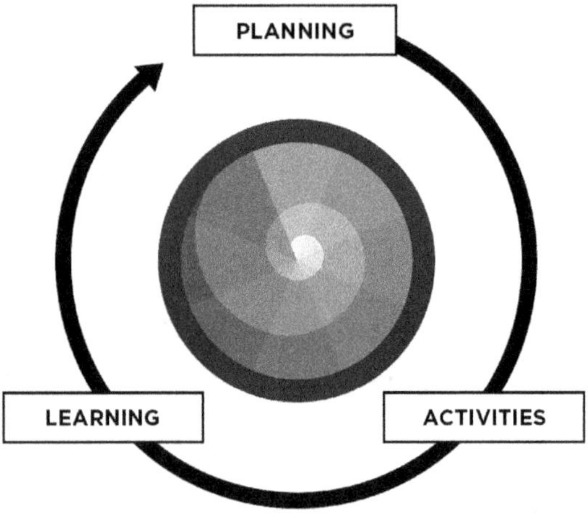

Source: Prepared by the author

Each loop will let you learn anew with real results and advances. Personally, I don't like to spend a lot of time on the Exploration phase, just enough to observe and analyze the different possibilities. I try to jump into the Evaluation phase as soon as possible, and, if necessary, I go back to explore alternatives again if the chosen option has not worked.

Processes in the Evaluation Phase

The goal here is to start experimenting to learn how to best carry out your activity. In environments of high uncertainty or where the solution to be developed is not clear from the beginning, I recommend that you use agile approaches such as Scrum, which will allow you to have a list of prioritized features (backlog) you will develop over periods of between one and two weeks (sprint). After each cycle, you will change and prioritize the feature list in a specific session (planning) based on learning and user feedback.

Figure 3.24. Agile Development Process Based on Scrum

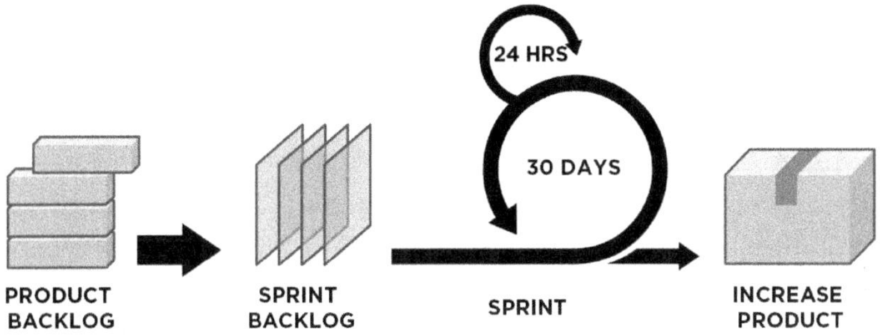

Source: Lakeworks

Let me emphasize one important aspect: it is not just about developing your product but your entire initiative comprehensively. That is precisely why Purpose Launchpad is also an agile framework that guides you to evolve all the aspects (axes) that you must develop to correctly build your startup or your product, continuously iterating your initiative based on validated learnings until it fits into the market, gradually creating a real and positive impact.

One of the most complicated moments for any startup or product is when the first customers arrive. It's very exciting to start providing real value, but, at the same time, everything is complicated because now you not only have to develop your initiative but also serve your customers and users on a day-to-day basis. This will burden you with many more demands, which your customers will always consider urgent. When this happens, remember one thing: in this phase, above all else, the goal is still to learn. When you serve a customer or user, in addition to doing your best and trying to provide their satisfaction, the key will be to learn. Even if you don't manage to make them happy, the important thing is to learn for the future. As we saw in the Customers axis, in the Evaluation phase, the objective is not for all early adopters to be content (you must assume that you will lose some of them) but to learn from their experience to create something that satisfies all future users and customers.

In this Evaluation phase, we will still operate under conditions of great uncertainty, so I don't recommend that you define any processes yet. Manage your activity in the best way but without planning, not even plans based on short cycles of one or two weeks, like the Scrum sprint. In this environment, you will also need agile approaches, but perhaps you will do better with other types of frameworks, such as Kanban, which simplifies the approach by eliminating the concept of cycles (sprint) and allows you to change priorities at any time. You can also use Kanban for agile product development.

As you can see in the image below, Kanban proposes a series of columns that represent the status of tasks (pending, in progress, finished, etc.).

Figure 3.25. Kanban

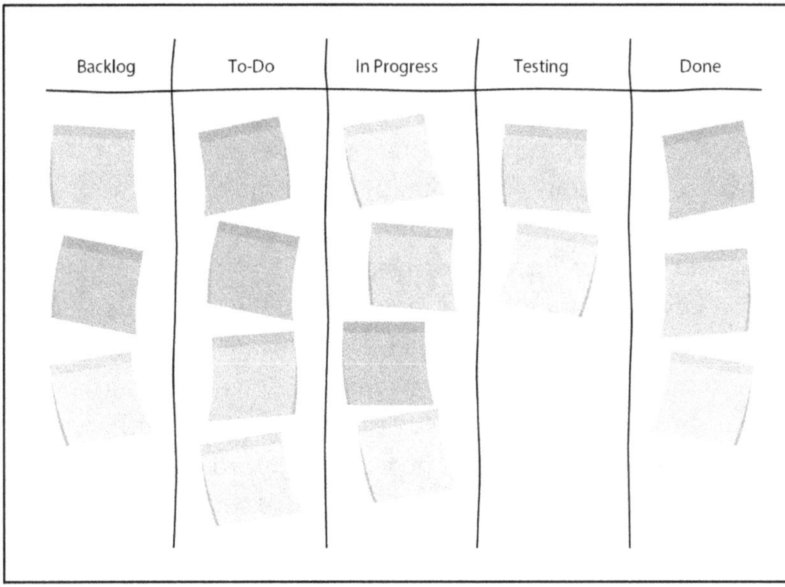

Backlog	To-Do	In Progress	Testing	Done

Source: Prepared by the author

The tasks at the top of the column have a higher priority than those at the bottom. When a person on the team is available, they go to the "to-do" column and choose the one at the top, moving it to the "in progress" column and start working on it, until they finish it and pass it to the "done" column. At this stage, we could dispense with this last column, in fact, because it's all about learning rather than executing. You could name the "done" column "evaluating" and then add two more columns: "invalidated" and "validated." The most important thing, in any case, is not to have the maximum number of actions completed but to maximize learning.

Processes in the Impact Phase

The goal in this phase is to improve the way you do things to optimize your results. After the previous learnings and getting the initiative into the environment, there will be less uncertainty, so you can start implementing processes and follow plans in some cases—without ever stopping your learning of course. If I advised you earlier to learn while you were running, now it's time to execute without forgetting to learn.

The work of exploration, innovation, and continuous adaptation to the environment never ends. In IMVU's case, for example, although they have millions of users, they continue to use agile techniques to keep evolving their product. The difference is that, while in the Evaluation phase agile approaches allowed us to find and develop the right type of product for the market, during the Impact phase, they will allow us to improve our current product or service. Now the question is not to decide whether to develop one product or another but how the product we already have should evolve.

It could also happen that we must manufacture a product that has already been previously tested, both technically and at the market level, so the uncertainty will be very low at all levels. In such a case, defining a predetermined plan for the product's mass production will possibly be the best option. That is the scenario in which Airbus manufactures new units of any of its aircraft. Although it is a very complex manufacturing process, it is possible to define a plan from start to finish and adapt it to any possible changes in the environment that we detect as we go.

For activities in which the result we must obtain is very clear from the beginning and in which the environment will not undergo major changes, we are able to know quite accurately the time and resources we will need to successfully carry out our mission. Therefore, to plan and monitor the progress of production in this type of project, tools such as Gantt charts are used to show the different activities, their managers, and the timeline for each in a line graph such as this one:

Figure 3.26. Gantt Chart

	21-May	23-May	25-May	27-May	29-May	31-May	2-Jun	4-Jun
Task1								
Task2								
Task3								
Task4								
Task5								
Task6								
Task7								
Task8								

Source: Prepared by the author

Depending on the type of product and circumstances, you can use a more agile approach (implementing frameworks like Scrum) or a waterfall approach (like Gantt charts). In general, I suggest using agile approaches whenever the product is continuously evolving (as with software) and cascading approaches when manufacturing a product in mass production. Still, keep in mind that you can apply the agile mindset even if your plans are static, continually reviewing them and changing them as needed.

There are many tools to define and optimize the processes related to your organization's internal activity, such as Business Process Management Notation (BPMN), which offer you a series of graphic elements to describe a process simply and even automate it with compatible systems. In fact, BPMN was a great success because it allowed the business staff (in charge of defining and executing the processes) and the technical staff (in charge of automating the processes with computer systems) to speak a common language and align the business with the systems according to the defined processes focused on executing the operations.

In the example below, you see a diagram that synthesizes the process of buying a product on Amazon. I have used a version of BPMN that is very simple to understand and makes the task of designing, communicating, and improving the internal processes of an organization very easy.

Figure 3.27. Process of a Product Purchase on Amazon

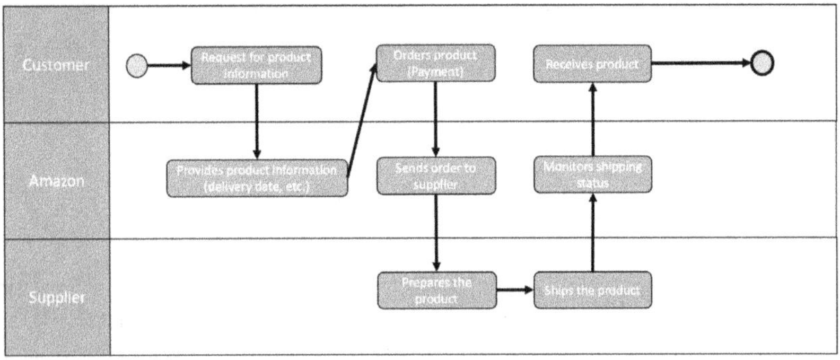

Customer
Amazon
Supplier
Request for product information
Orders product (Payment)
Receives product
Provides product information (delivery date, etc.)
Sends order to supplier
Monitors shipping status
Prepares the product
Ships the product

Source: Prepared by the author

Remember that it is not simply about executing our activity but about learning continuously. Therefore, I recommend that, whatever tool you use, you add learning-oriented actions. In this case, we may send a customer-satisfaction survey in which we ask if they liked the product and if they are satisfied with the process of buying and receiving the product. There are also other, more advanced methods, such as Lean Six Sigma, which can be very useful when it comes to continuously improving your processes.

Before I end this chapter, I would like to mention the OKR system, which became popular at the beginning of the 21st century after being used by companies such as Google or LinkedIn. This system allows you to manage and measure the progress of an organization towards the fulfillment of a series of objectives and key results in certain periods (usually between one and three months). If you decide to implement OKR in your project, remember to maintain an attitude of continuous learning and evolution. I recommend that you add exploration-oriented goals and key results to keep learning and continually evolve the organization.

Final Reflections on the Process Axis

There are different types of approaches when addressing the processes, as well as a multitude of tools that allow us to implement each of these approaches in a simpler and more orderly way. Throughout the chapter, we have seen several of these tools: Scrum, Kanban, Gantt charts, etc. As we saw in previous chapters, however, the key is not in the tools but in doing what makes sense in each phase of our project. Purpose Launchpad can help you a lot with that, because it constantly guides you on what kind of processes are necessary and how to put them into practice.

Nor should you forget another of the "mantras" that I have been repeating throughout the book: the most important thing is mindset. One of the principles we saw in the second part of the book says it clearly: "Act with the right mindset beyond processes and tools." If you apply the right mindset to each of the phases (becoming an "explorer," "validator," or "impactor"), you will naturally end up implementing the processes and tools that best suit you at all times.

Table 3.6. Summary of the Process Axis

PROCESS AXIS		
Exploration Focus all activity on discovering the most promising path	**Evaluation** Experiment with processes to learn how to best perform the activity	**Impact** Improve processes to optimize results

	Exploration	Evaluation	Impact
Construction	Discover by following the eight axes	Agility to develop	Agility to improve
Execution	The best process is no process	Learn while you execute	Execute while you learn

Source: Prepared by the author

Activity

Considering your own project (startup or new product), do the following activities (if you don't have a project, think of one that you're familiar with):

1. Determine what phase your project is in. Remember that, although a specific axis (such as people) might be at a more advanced stage, your initiative will be in whichever phase the least-evolved axis is in. Remember that you can use the Purpose Launchpad Assessment to determine this.

2. Depending on the phase in which your project is, perform the following actions:

   a. Exploration phase:
   - If you have defined processes, try to eliminate or simplify them as much as possible.
   - Create a list of actions to take to advance the axes that are still under exploration. You may need to do this once you finish the next two chapters, focused respectively on the Product axes and metrics.

   b. Evaluation phase:
   - Review how you are developing the project in general and try to improve it based on an agile approach. You can apply Scrum or Kanban for the product and Purpose Launchpad for the overall initiative.
   - Review how you are doing your day-to-day activities and try to implement agile modes that help you make your operations more flexible while adding elements to keep learning continuously.

> c. Impact phase:
> - Consider if you need to continue developing your startup or your product in an agile way. If you're mass producing, you may need to implement cascading processes. If so, keep in mind the principles of agility to act in the event of unforeseen events or to acquire new learning.
> - Define your processes with a visual tool that helps you. Add the elements that are necessary to guide them to learning and try to optimize them continuously.

Resources

- Agile Manifesto: *agilemanifesto.org*
- BPMN Template: *www.purposealliance.org/resources/plantilla-bpmn*

21
Make Something People Want

A couple of times throughout the book I've talked about Airbnb; it's a good example of many of the concepts I'm explaining regarding startups. Although its journey as a company began in San Francisco in 2008, the idea had been born earlier. Two of its founders, Brian Chesky and Joe Gebbia, had met at the Rhode Island School of Design. After graduating, Chesky got a job in Los Angeles and Gebbia in San Francisco. In 2007, Gebbia convinced Chesky to move to San Francisco, and they shared a flat with another young man, ultimately Airbnb's third founder: Nathan Blecharczyk, a Harvard computer science graduate. At the end of that year, their rent went up by 25 percent. Blecharczyk decided to move out and look for something cheaper, so Chesky and Gebbia began to think about ways to earn extra money to help pay the rent. One day, they heard about a Society of Industrial Designers of America convention to be held in San Francisco that would be attended by people from all over the country. Gebbia came up with an idea: buy a few inflatable mattresses and offer lodging, with access to Internet and breakfast, in Blecharczyk's empty room.

They soon had their first three customers, two men and a woman, who paid $80 each to stay one night with breakfast. During the convention, they earned about $1,000, enough to cover the rent. In addition, they met people from different states and made new friends. They had undoubtedly had a good idea! In fact, they thought that this idea could be the beginning of a big business, since there were many people like them who needed extra income and numerous visitors or tourists who were looking for low-cost lodging.

To take their idea to the next level, Chesky and Gebbia called on their former roommate, Blecharczyk, to develop a website to connect hosts with guests. They decided to name the project Air Bed and Breakfast, combining the first version of their product, an inflatable bed, with the phrase Bed & Breakfast. They soon simplified it to Airbnb.

Using their own experience, they developed the website with a focus on temporary lodging in locations where events were held. In fact, initially, users had to find an event when first entering the website, then search for an available room, and finally connected with the host to formalize the reservation.

Figure 3.28. AirBnB's Old Look

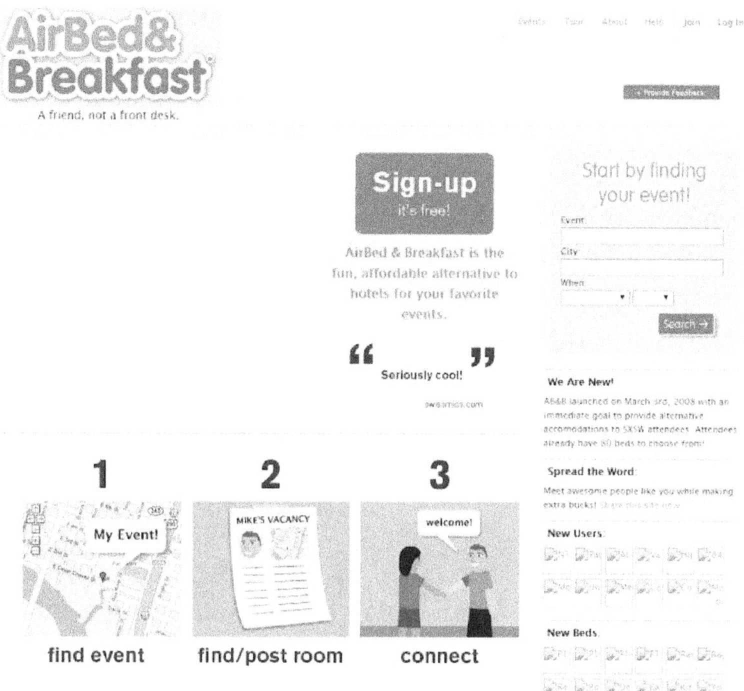

Fuente: web.archive.org

The model was simple: hosts ran ads with available rooms, event attendees chose budget accommodations with breakfast near their destination, and the website charged a commission for each booking. In addition, hosts could meet interesting people and guests felt at home, which gave it a community component that set it apart from other, more traditional types of rentals.

Yet, when they tried to get funding, they failed. They turned to fifteen investors; eight rejected them, and seven completely ignored them. These were difficult times. At the end of January 2009, the famous startup accelerator Y Combinator decided to support them with its initial financing program, consisting of $20,000 and three months of accompaniment to perfect the product and try to fit it into the market. They adopted Y Combinator's motto, "Make something people want," and they learned from the experience. Today, as everyone knows, Airbnb is the largest lodging chain in the world, with more than four million hosts who have already hosted over a billion guests in their homes, apartments, and bedrooms in almost every country in the world.

The case of Airbnb, like others like it, shows us that the path is almost never simple (much less linear) but also that, if we take the right steps, we can achieve our vision and our purpose. For that, it is essential that you define and develop your product, which should be a consequence of what you have defined and learned about the rest of your initiative's elements.

Traditional product development techniques follow a cascading process. They work well when you have complete certainty of the problem you are solving and that the solution you have in mind is going to be accepted by the market. The problem is known, and so is the solution. We can represent it with the following graph:

Figure 3.29. Waterfall process

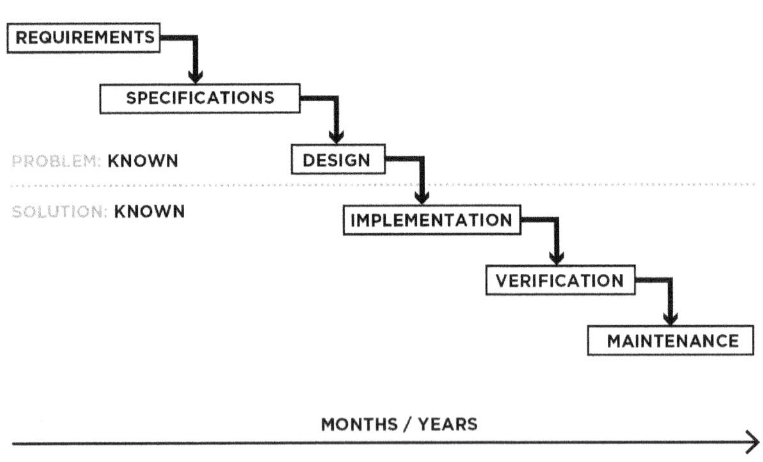

Source: Prepared by the author

However, when we haven't fully validated the problem that we're going to solve, we need to integrate other types of techniques, such as Customer Development. In the case of Airbnb, for example, they initially focused on people's need to find lodging when they were traveling to attend an event, but they finally understood (after talking to real customers) that they could satisfy the need to find lodging for all types of travelers.

On the other hand, even if you know the problem you are trying to solve, the most normal thing is that you do not have complete certainty that the solution you have devised will work. This is where agile development techniques combined with Customer Development are useful, as they allow the product to evolve gradually as you learn from real customers' feedback.

Figure 3.30. Customer Development Combined with Agile Development

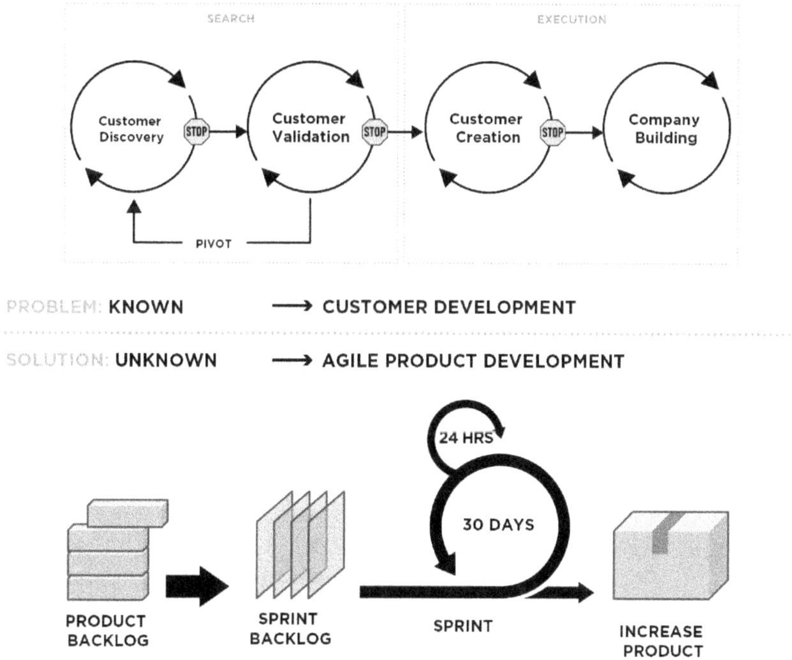

Source: Prepared by the author

Eric Ries, who I've mentioned in previous chapters, encourages us to let go of waterfall approaches when developing a product. Instead, he proposes a three-step loop to follow: build, measure, and learn. The idea is to take these steps iteratively, in a loop, as quickly as possible to maximize learning from data and real experience. To do this, Ries takes his model a step further, integrating the scientific method into the innovation process. Since innovative ideas are only hypotheses, Lean Startup tells us that, to evaluate them, we must carry out experiments, analyze the results, and, based on the data obtained, make decisions. This will be the loop that we repeat to evolve our product.

Figure 3.31. Lean Startup Process

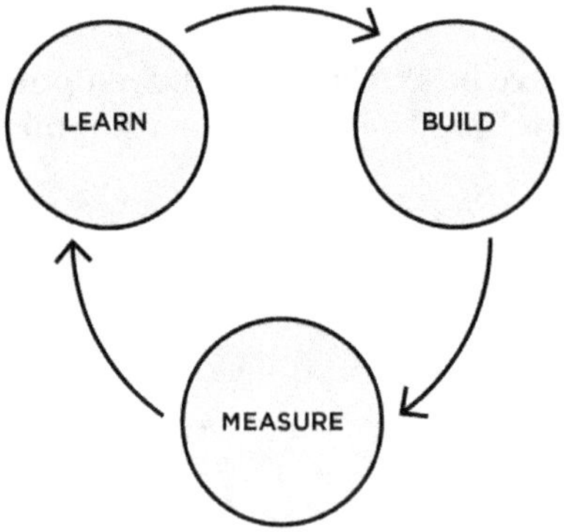

Source: Eric Ries, *The Lean Startup*

Imagine that you have $100,000 to develop a product, and each month you have fixed expenses of $10,000. If you follow a cascading approach, analyzing and designing the product for a month, developing it in detail over the next eight, and concentrating the launch on one month, you're betting it all on just one card, and reality tells you it's highly unlikely you'll get it right.

Now imagine doing it following the Lean Startup approach. First, you spend three weeks developing a simple version of the product, and, during the following week, you conduct experiments with real customers. This way, in a single month, you will obtain data and conclusions that will allow you to learn how to improve the product. Then you repeat this loop during the following months, and, with your customers' feedback, you improve the product. Instead of playing it all on one card, you have ten chances to get it right. By the way, this was exactly what the founders of Airbnb did by following Y Combinator instructions. And, because of that, they ended up making something people wanted.

Lean Startup was influenced by another very successful technique in product manufacturing and distribution called Lean Manufacturing. It consists of manufacturing and distributing the number of products that the market truly demands to avoid waste. Before the existence of Lean Manufacturing, product manufacturers made quantities based on their sales forecasts, which were rarely accurate. Then they "pushed" their products into the market to try to sell them all. Thanks to Lean Manufacturing, producers can know the market demand in real time based on actual sales and manufacture and distribute accordingly. In this way, it is the demand that "pulls" the product.

Imagine that you have a shoe factory and that, based on your sales history, you estimate that, during the next year, you will sell 10,000 pairs of shoes. You get down to work, and you manufacture them and distribute them in the right stores. This is what is called a push approach.

Figure 3.32. Push Approach

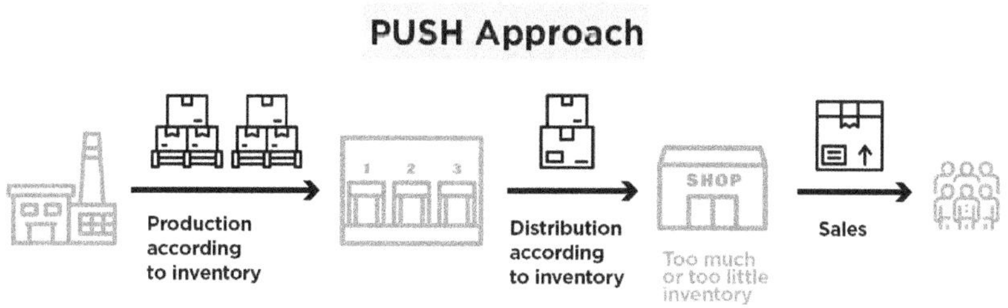

PUSH Approach

Source: Prepared by the author

Maybe the market demands more, and, since you have already closed production, you lose a good business opportunity. It could also happen that the market demands less, which will generate a significant loss for your business.

With a Lean Manufacturing approach, you'll manufacture a first batch of shoes and distribute them to the establishments, but you will not rest there; you will continuously measure sales to detect when your distributors are about to run out of stock. When that happens, you'll be making more units of your product to restock. This way you manufacture as the market "pulls" your product, and you manage to eliminate waste and take advantage of all the opportunities that may arise. This is what is known as a pull approach.

Figure 3.33. Pull Approach
Lean Manufacturing

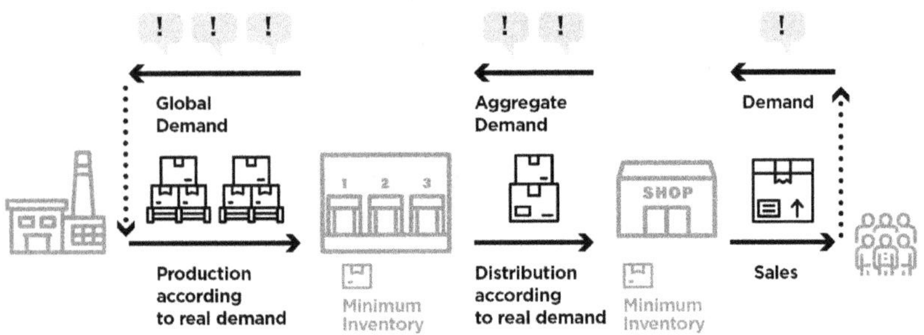

Source: Prepared by the author

Just as Lean Manufacturing helps you avoid waste when it comes to manufacturing and distributing the wrong number of products on the market, the Lean Startup approach helps us not develop the wrong product and helps us make something that people really want.

The Product in the Exploration Phase

In this phase, the objective is to discover the right value proposition to solve the needs of our customers and translate it into a product concept. In other words, it's about finding the fit between the problem and the solution. Remember that the value proposition is the promise we make to our customers (e.g., "We'll take you from place to place") and that the product is how we'll deliver on that promise (e.g., air travel). Having discovered the right value proposition through interactions with real customers (as I described in the chapter on the Customer axis), now is the time to start thinking about how to transform the promise into a tangible reality. We will do this following the loop I mentioned earlier: building, measuring, and learning.

First, we build a "low-fidelity prototype" that will help you communicate your product: a presentation, a mockup, a video, or a website (now, I mean a descriptive website, not an application on the web that does what your product intends to do). This will allow you to not only have something tangible to teach your potential customers but to start thinking about how best to transform your value proposition into something real. Remember that your ideas are still hypotheses, so avoid falling in love with your prototype.

I have often met people, mainly software developers, who have told me that it costs them very little to create a prototype that really works and thus have something more to show their customers. Although it may seem like a good idea, it isn't. Because of our psychology, when we create something, we get emotionally attached to our creation, and it will be that much more difficult to invalidate the hypothesis in the future. Instead, you'll likely end up trying to sell and justify your creation instead of listening to your customers.

Next, perform a very simple experiment: show your low-fidelity prototype to real customers and get their feedback. The key is that you be open to making changes to your approach; don't make changes just because one or two people suggest it—do so because you find patterns that continuously repeat themselves.

From that, define a minimum viable product (MVP)—that is, an elementary version of a product that can be used by your customers and allows you to maximize learning with a minimum investment of time and money on your part. This is what the founders of Airbnb did, without being aware of it yet, when they bought inflatable mattresses to accommodate guests.

Important: you should not develop the MVP now; you should merely define it based on what potential customers tell you when you show them your low-fidelity prototype.

Figure 3.34. Lean Startup in the Exploration Phase

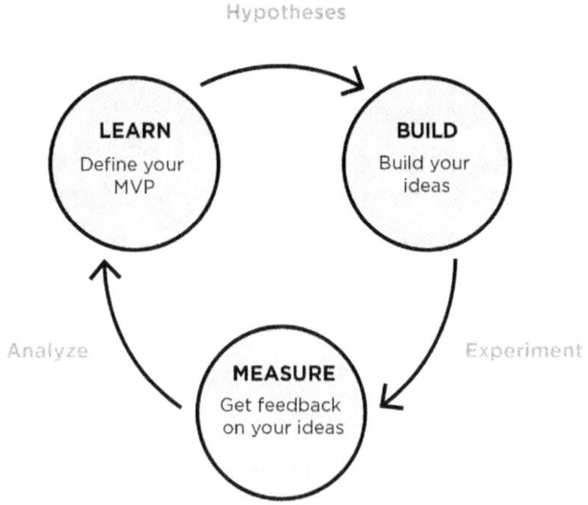

Source: Prepared by the author

The Product in the Evaluation Phase

Once you're here, you already have a verbal validation of your project or product by some potential customers who have confirmed that they like the idea. You also have a definition of what a first version of the startup or product might look like. Now it's time to build your first MVP, learn from real experience, iterate the product properly, and find the fit with the market.

Although it might seem strange to you, to do that, before creating it, you must sell it. You must show that there are customers willing to invest their time or money in your MVP. You can use the low-resolution prototype you created to show it to potential customers, with the difference that now you must get the first real customers or users (if necessary, clarify that the first version of your MVP may not be as complete as the first low-resolution prototype you made). As we saw in the Customer axis, you must focus on early adopters, because they will understand that what they have in their hands is not a finished product but an MVP.

Only when you have sold it will you get down to work and build it. To do this, you must be creative (remember the example of Airbnb and the inflatable mattress) and keep in mind that the goal is still to learn, not sell. In other words, don't try to justify every aspect of your MVP to try to sell it at all costs to your users, because the point is not to increase sales but to learn. In its initial stages, the unit that measures a startup's or a new product's progress is validated learning, not the number of sales or customers.

When communicating with your customers, I suggest that you be as personal as possible. We often think that sending them a satisfaction survey will be enough, but normally it isn't. I recommend that you have real conversations with them so that you can hear their tone of voice, even see the expression on their faces, either in person or by video call. Body language can give you a lot of information.

This is the time when you should remember the Purpose Launchpad principle of "Validate what you learn before building." Even when we have real metrics about product usage, the most important thing is still to talk to users to find out what's behind the numbers. The conversations are what will really allow you to understand your customers and learn from them.

Airbnb decided to change its name (the original was Air Bed and Breakfast) after conversations they had with users, who told them that the name was very long and that sometimes they didn't even know how to write it. They also discovered that musician Barry Manilow had rented an entire house while on tour. Until that time, the platform required the host to be present to provide breakfast to the guest, which meant not being able to offer the entire house. This self-imposed limitation had prevented them from exploring other hosting options. So, after getting in touch with him and other travelers, they decided to adjust their product and open the platform to other types of reservations, including complete lodgings.

Remember that a good MVP is not designed or made to become the final product. Normally, you make it, throw it away, and do it again until your users are satisfied. So, don't look at your MVP as a first version of your product but as part of the process to figure out what your product should look like. Engineers are usually trained to build something that works and is durable, and that's part of the reason why it's not always easy to find people with the right mindset. At this time, you must be willing to discard what you build, since, in a short time, it will possibly become obsolete and you will have to start from scratch, leveraging now the valuable learnings that real customers and users will have given you.

To complete the evaluation phase regarding the product, you will have to get paying customers or users who invest real time in your service, as well as having most of your customers or users satisfied with your product or service. In other words, you will have to get the product-market fit. To do this, I recommend that you continue with the Lean Startup loop (build, measure, and learn) constantly and rigorously. There are complementary tools as well, such as the Product-Market Fit Canvas (among many others), that can help you sort your ideas, raise different hypotheses related to the product, and iterate it according to what you are learning.

Figure 3.35. Lean Startup in the Evaluation Phase

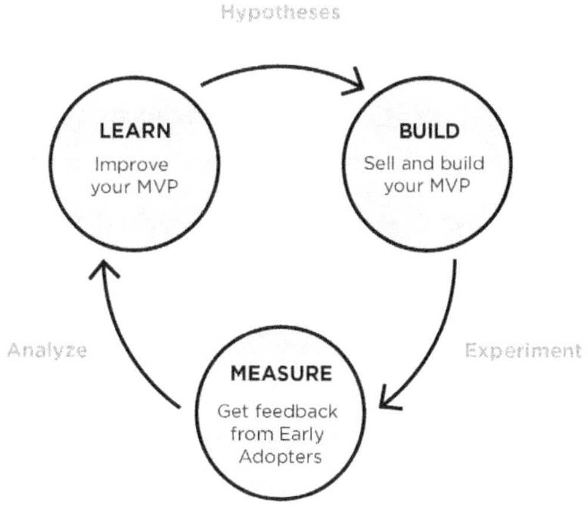

Source: Prepared by the author

The Product in the Impact Phase

The goal now is to move from an MVP to a massively saleable product (MSP) and maximize sales opportunities. Keep in mind that, although your proposal has had an excellent reception among early adopters, you don't know whether the rest of your potential customers will accept it. Therefore, you must think about what features it might lack and what improvements you can make (this is usually the key point).

Again, you must raise a series of hypotheses, in this case related to the characteristics that will optimize the user experience. For that, you must think not only about the product but about what comes before and what comes after—that is, how you offer and sell the product experience and how you give after-sales support and customer service.

Everything must be perfect, but we will not achieve perfection from the very beginning; we will do this iteratively, as we continue to learn. I recommend that you always see your product as a living experiment, whether it is an MVP or an MSP, and that you never stop gathering customer feedback. In this phase, you can already consider conducting mass surveys to obtain the maximum possible amount of market information, but never stop talking directly with certain customers and real users. Only they can explain to you what's behind the numbers.

Returning to the example of Airbnb, in 2009, they decided to expand their operations to New York, but the number of bookings did not grow as expected. So, they packed their bags and went to New York to share the experience with their clients (both with travelers and hosts), with whom they had multiple conversations. They finally spotted the problem: the photographs of the lodgings in the platform's ads weren't attractive enough for people looking to stay in New York. The mass market in this area was much more demanding than the early adopters of San Francisco. With this information in hand, they established the policy of including professional photographs in all advertisements. The results were immediate: the platform's monthly revenue doubled!

Figure 3.36. Number of nights booked on Airbnb

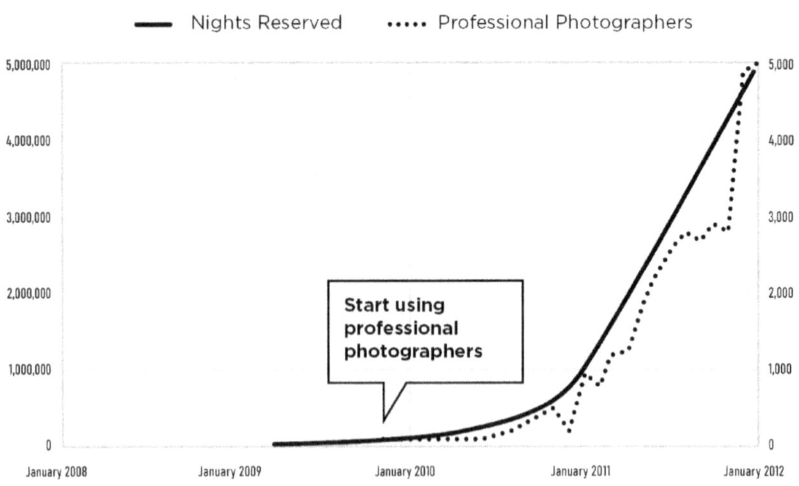

Source: Prepared by the author

Therefore, in this phase, you must continue to improve not only the product but the sales process and after-sales service. If you manage to do this continuously and with discipline, your product will have many more options to conquer the mass market, and you will have the opportunity to create a positive impact on a large scale.

Figure 3.37. Lean Startup in the Impact Phase

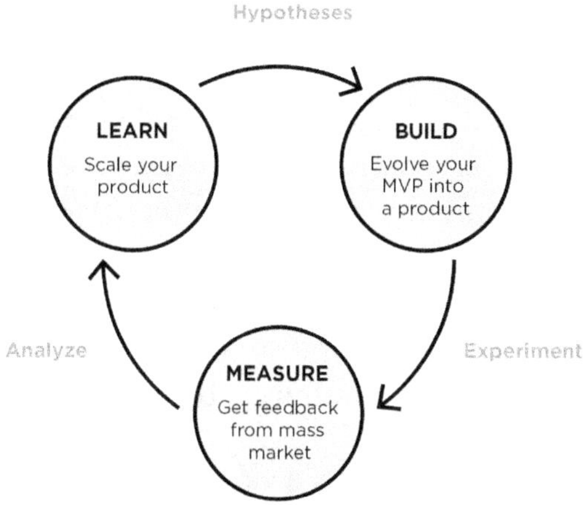

Hypotheses

LEARN
Scale your product

BUILD
Evolve your MVP into a product

Analyze

Experiment

MEASURE
Get feedback from mass market

Source: Prepared by the author

Final Thoughts on the Product Axis

A traditional mindset can lead us to hurry to build a product, since we all like to materialize our ideas into something tangible, especially when we think they are good ideas (and we all think so!). But, as we have seen throughout the book, every idea is at first a simple hypothesis that can be validated or discarded. This is what one of the Purpose Launchpad values refers to when it says, "Customer data over intuition." It leads to one of the principles that you should never forget: "Validate what you learn before building."

Therefore, remember that, in the Exploration phase, all you must do is talk to potential customers to find real problems (as we saw in the chapter focused on the Customer axis) and possible value propositions that verbally validate your idea. Only when you've found the fit between the problem and the solution will you be ready to move on to the Evaluation phase, where, having found real customers who pay for your product, you will develop an initial MVP to continue learning from the experience and iterate it until you find the fit with the market. From a product perspective, at this point, you'll be ready to move into the Impact phase and focus on optimizing the product, improving the user experience, and scaling it.

To walk this path, I suggest that you look for inspiration in the Lean Startup model. It is not necessarily cheaper or faster, but it helps you minimize wasted resources. And let me add here that the key, as always, is in the mindset, in acting while remembering that, whether it is in an idea phase, an MVP, or an MSP, our product is an experiment from which we must continuously learn in order to make something people want.

Table 3.7. Product Axis Summary

PRODUCT AXIS		
Exploration Translate your value proposal into a product concept	**Evaluation** Develop a Minimum Viable Product (MVP) and satisfy your early adopters	**Impact** Evolve your MVP into a product and optimize the user experience
Build	Build your ideas	Sell and build your Minimum Viable Product	Evolve your MVP into a product
Measure	Get feedback on your ideas	Get feedback from your early adopters	Get feedback from the mass market
Learn	Define your Minimum Viable Product	Improve your MVP	Scale your product

Source: Prepared by the author

Activity

Considering your own project (startup or new product), do the following activities (if you don't have a project, think of one that you're familiar with):

1. Determine what phase your project is in. Remember that, although a specific axis (such as the product axis) might be at a more advanced stage, your initiative will be in whichever phase the least-evolved axis is in. Remember that you can use the Purpose Launchpad Assessment to determine this.

2. Depending on which phase your project is in, do the following:

   a. Exploration phase:
   - If you have in mind the value proposition to offer but do not have a product yet, create a low-fidelity prototype and show it to potential customers to obtain their feedback (remember to combine these actions with what we saw in the Customer axis chapter).
   - If you already have a product, try defining what its reduced version could be as a minimum viable product.

   b. Evaluation phase: Adapt your low-fidelity prototype (or create it if you don't have it) to describe what your MVP could look like and try to get your first early adopters. If you already have customers, try to focus on early adopters and get direct and continuous feedback to continuously improve your product.

   c. Impact phase: Analyze your sales process and your product to try to find what changes you need to make to achieve the desired growth. And don't forget to talk to users to get key input.

Resources

- Value Proposition Canvas: *www.purposealliance.org/re-sources/value-proposition-canvas/*
- Product/Market Fit Canvas: *www.purposealliance.org/resources/product-market-fit-canvas/*

22
Measure Your Progress
and Your Impact on the World

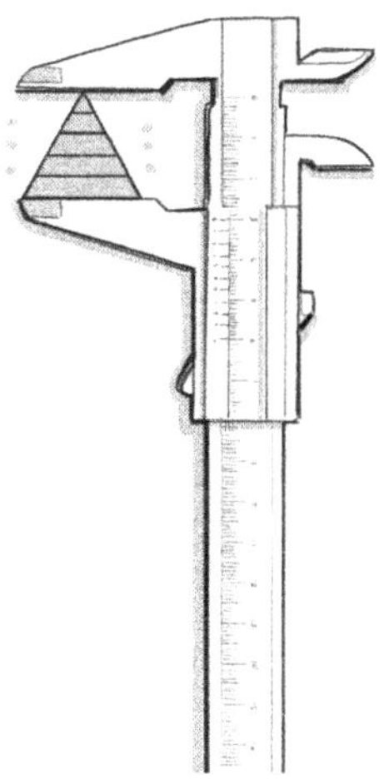

One of Peter Drucker's best-known phrases is that "what is not measured cannot be improved" and that, consequently, it can end up disappearing. In your case, if you create a startup or launch a product and do not have minimum financial control, it is very possible that you will go bankrupt at some point, because you won't know how much you can spend according to your income.

I would like to paraphrase this famous maxim: that which is not standardized cannot be compared. Financial accounting has evolved towards standards that allow us to compare different organizations on financial issues. For example, if we take two organizations, we can know which of them has a greater volume of business or which one makes the largest investment to manufacture their products. However, there are still no standards for some types of metrics that we will see throughout this chapter. We find a clear example when measuring impact, since there is currently no standardized system to measure it. This means that we cannot compare between two organizations and determine which one generates a greater positive impact.

The goal of this chapter is not to propose a model that helps us standardize impact but to define certain mechanisms that will help you know if your initiative is generating a positive impact on the world or not and to have a reference for continuous improvement. Finally, I will also venture to give my own view on how I think impact measurement might evolve in the future.

To begin with, as we saw in a previous chapter when discussing the Impact Pyramid, you need a basis to create a positive impact—a product that generates value for your customers or users—so that you can obtain income that allows you to be sustainable at a financial level, and you must also prevent your activity from generating a negative impact at a social and environmental level. Only by balancing these circumstances will you be able to say that you are creating a positive impact on the world. To measure each of these issues, you will need different types of related accounting.

Figure 3.38. Metrics Applied to the Impact Pyramid

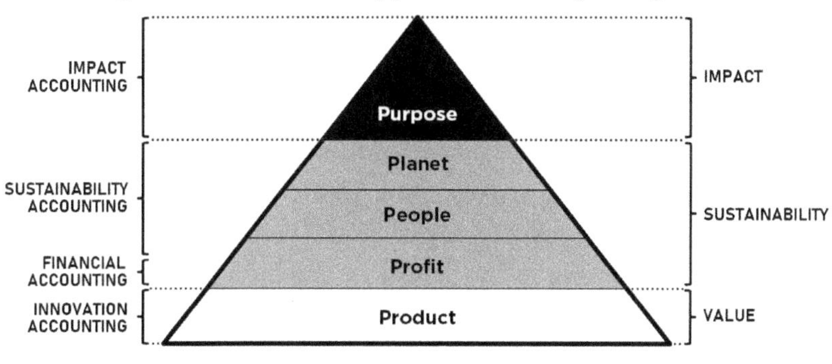

Source: Prepared by the author

At the base, we find innovation accounting and financial accounting. In most startups and innovative projects, financial accounting metrics do not provide relevant information in the initial phases, since the income is zero then. Innovation metrics are more useful there. In fact, techniques based on financial accounting are not applicable to calculating the value of a project in its early stages of development. A clear example is Instagram. When Facebook decided to buy it for $1 billion, the startup did not have revenue yet, although it already had great value and enormous potential, as evidenced by its subsequent results: in 2020, it earned $24 billion dollars, more than 35 percent of Facebook's total revenue. When Facebook decided to buy Instagram, it did so based on other data, such as the percentage of active users and the time they spent using the app. These metrics, among many others, form "innovation accounting," a concept coined by Eric Ries in his book *Lean Startup* to refer to the way to evaluate progress when financial metrics are zero or do not give us any useful information.

On the other hand, if we move up the Impact Pyramid, we find sustainability accounting. As we saw in the axis related to triple sustainability, it is not enough to be sustainable economically; we must also be sustainable socially and environmentally.

This accounting measures the footprint we leave on the environment, society, and the economy. It is important to clarify that the economic component of sustainability not only looks at our initiative's economic viability but also at whether we carry out the activity sustainably in our economic environment (generating employment, paying taxes, etc.). That's why sustainability accounting also partly covers the pyramid level related to economic benefit, as you can see in the graph.

Sustainability accounting does not have globally adopted standards, but there are certain models that are getting a lot of traction. One is ESG reporting, which I mentioned in the Sustainability axis chapter (closely linked to metrics) and which is used by many organizations. We must use it, however, only as a reference, because it is not yet a completely reliable measure and does not provide a standard for organizations' sustainability and impact.

Finally, there's impact accounting. The line between sustainability and impact is very thin, since, once an organization operates sustainably and avoids generating a negative footprint, any contribution it is making to the world will be part of its positive impact. Impact accounting measures just that: our positive contribution to the world, including our customers and our own organization. It is precisely at the top of the pyramid because all the other metrics mentioned above (the value provided to customers and the organization's economic, social, and environmental sustainability) contribute in one way or another to its positive impact.

Impact metrics are especially relevant as the initiative moves forward in fulfilling its purpose. A good example is Tesla, which I have mentioned at length. Tesla publishes an annual impact report showing metrics aligned with its purpose and providing data such as that, in 2020, its vehicles contributed to avoiding over 5 million metric tons of CO_2 emissions, for example.

Any new product, startup, or even an established organization needs these four types of accounting (innovation, financial, sustainability, and impact) to be considered a valuable, viable, sustainable, and purpose-oriented organization. These four accounting systems are also intimately connected. Generating value to our customers through our products will provide us with the economic resources that will make us financially viable, and economic stability will allow us to carry out our activity in a sustainable way with society and the environment. This will put us in a position to create a positive impact on the world.

Metrics in the Exploration Phase

At this phase, you still don't have to measure anything in relation to your finances, so we'll leave the financial accounting for later. In fact, if your initiative is a new startup, I advise you not to yet form a company or invest any resources other than your own time (and that of your potential team) to explore the opportunity. As we saw in the Sustainability axis, you can create financial projections to analyze possible scenarios, but remember that it is not a financial plan to be followed but just simple hypotheses that you will have to evaluate.

Now the most important thing is innovation accounting. Here, the only type of metrics you need are qualitative—that is, the insight you obtain from conversations with potential clients or even books you read as part of your exploratory work. In fact, one of the values of Purpose Launchpad, as we saw in that chapter, states: "Customer data over intuition." This is true not only at the beginning but at any stage of the project, as any one finding can change everything. Remember the experience of the Airbnb founders, who, after having open conversations with their customers, decided to change their brand name and even their photo policy, which was the basis of their subsequent exponential growth.

In relation to sustainability accounting, in the Exploration phase, you must begin to make an initial approach to your future corporate social responsibility and corporate environmental responsibility plans, as well as the type of metrics needed to manage your path towards triple sustainability. Since there is no standard, each initiative must have a set of metrics that measure its own sustainability model comprehensively according to the type of activity and the effects that its activities and products generate. In addition to the ESG reports I've mentioned, you could be inspired by the B Impact Assessment (which is the mechanism used to give the B Corp seal) and the 17 Sustainable Development Goals and their 169 associated goals.

Taking into consideration any possible indicators related to social sustainability (employee conditions, fair trade, etc.), environmental sustainability (emissions, waste management, etc.), and economic sustainability (external contracting, payment of taxes, etc.), I suggest that you stay with a subset applicable to your activity. You can use the sustainability chain tool for this, an evolution of Michael Porter's value chain, with which you can measure and manage the margin (income minus expenses) of an established business and its footprint in terms of sustainability.

Figure 3.39. Sustainability Chain

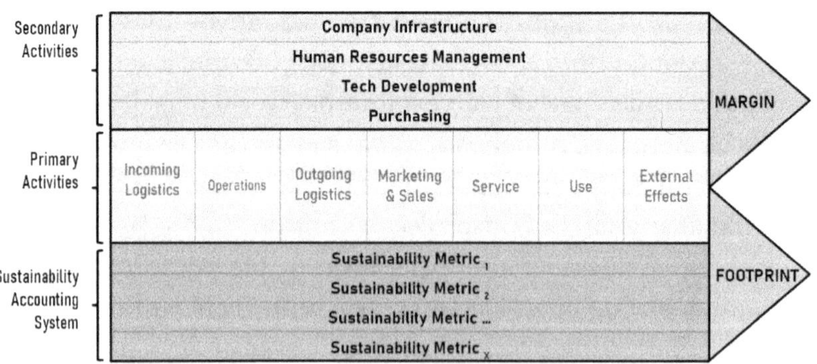

Source: Prepared by the author

The sustainability chain has the original elements of the value chain (primary activities, secondary activities, and margin) along with two new elements (sustainability and footprint accounting systems). Let's take a brief look at what each of these elements consists of:

- Primary activities: those with which you create value for the end customer, from the coordination of suppliers (if necessary) to production and sales. For startups and disruptive products, the type of primary activities may be slightly different from what Porter suggests in his standard value chain. In addition, in order to measure the impact beyond our activity, you should add two new elements to the primary activities: the use of your product or service and the side effects to the external environment. We'll look at all this in greater detail later.
- Secondary Activities: what the initiative needs to support its primary activities that doesn't necessarily generate direct value for the end customer, such as human resource management, finance, etc.
- Margin: the difference between the income obtained (which may be greater as we maximize the value generated in the client by the primary activities and the number of sales) and the expenses generated by the primary and secondary activities.
- Sustainability Accounting System: a series of sustainability metrics that will have a positive or negative value depending on the initiative's primary or secondary activities. For example, imagine that one of the primary activities is to travel around the world to conduct workshops for different organizations. This would mean creating a sustainability metric for CO_2 emissions, which would be negatively affected with each trip we make. If we change

the focus of our service and carry out these workshops in a virtual format, the effect on the sustainability metric of CO_2 emissions would be considerable. In addition, if we take any kind of action to generate clean energy, we will significantly contribute to making this metric positive.

- Footprint: the result of the final values of the different sustainability metrics. The goal is to have a neutral footprint so that we can say that our activity is totally sustainable through the chain. If the footprint is positive, this will be part of the positive impact we will begin to generate.

Ultimately, the goal is for our footprint to be neutral or positive. Suppose one of our system's metrics is the amount of CO_2 emissions saved per year. If we generate 10 tons but save 15 by using renewable energy, the result is that we saved 5 tons of CO_2, so our impact is positive. This is precisely what Google achieved in 2007, the year in which it became an emissions-neutral company (it saves the same amount of CO_2 it consumes).

When defining your sustainability accounting system, I recommend that you create a first version of your sustainability chain, since, by analyzing your initiative's different primary and secondary activities, you will be able to visualize in greater detail which sustainability metrics you have to include.

Figure 3.40. Sustainability Accounting System

Sustainability Accounting System
Sustainability Metric_1
Sustainability Metric_2
Sustainability Metric_3
Sustainability $\text{Metric}_{...}$
Sustainability Metric_x

Source: Prepared by the author

In the Exploration phase, impact metrics begin to be important. You've probably already defined your purpose, but it's not definite enough and is more an inspiring message that gives us a direction, not helping us measure whether we have made progress or not. Here the main impact metric comes into play, known as starshot, a quantifiable and time-bound objective that makes our purpose a reality, translating it into something measurable beyond the inspiring phrase. Remember that the reason we call this metric starshot is because, after all, reaching our purpose means we're heading towards our North Star. Tesla's starshot is very clear: "To produce 20 million electric vehicles a year and generate 1,500 GWh by 2030." In practical terms, this would mean that, by 2030, Tesla would sell 20 percent of the world's vehicles, which of course would be electric. In addition, it would generate 1 percent of the energy consumed globally from clean energy sources, such as the sun. There is no doubt that, once Tesla reaches its starshot, they will have notoriously helped accelerate the transition to a sustainable energy model.

Starshot, however, does not always offer the possibility of measuring progress in the short term—that is, when we are in the early stages of the initiative. Let's look at another of Elon Musk's companies, SpaceX, as a reference. Its purpose is "to make humans a multiplanetary species," and its starshot is "to send a million humans to Mars by 2050." To date, SpaceX has not made any progress on its starshot, as it has not yet sent any humans to Mars, but it has generated a positive impact along the way thanks to the reusable rockets it has created, which have successfully made a total of 73 launches and landings between 2017 and 2021.

Each initiative must have its own set of impact metrics according to its type of activity and the positive effects that its actions and products intend to generate in the world. Therefore, impact metrics will usually be specific to each initiative depending on its activity, which means that you will have to define your specific and fully customized impact accounting system for your project. Remember SpaceX's starshot (sending a million humans to Mars by 2050), which serves as its main impact metric. You can also imagine other types of initiatives, such as the development of a platform to help people find a stable partner, such as my first startup, BuscarAmigos.com, which I talked about in the Introduction. A good impact metric could be the number of long-lasting and happy couples generated. None of these impact metrics will be found in a standard system such as that established by the United Nations SDGs or the ESG model. However, if you need inspiration when defining your starshot or your system of impact metrics, you can also take those well-known systems as a reference, since, after all, these models foster a sustainable world.

In short, each initiative requires its own impact accounting system whose main metric will be the starshot, but remember that we are only in the Exploration phase, so it is important to keep in mind that impact and sustainability accounting systems are nothing more than hypotheses. At the beginning, it is practically impossible to specifically know the real activities that we will carry out in the future and to be sure that the starshot we defined is the correct one.

Metrics in the Evaluation Phase

Remember that, in the Evaluation phase, you are already in full action, using resources to build your initiative, trying to add value for your customers, and starting to generate a positive impact. In addition, you have already considered how you will measure the evolution of all these aspects, so the time has come to start monitoring and analyzing your initiative's development.

The goal is to measure to improve your initiative until it is ready to scale its impact. Following Purpose Launchpad's natural flow, the results and learnings obtained in this axis will be the key to continue developing the remaining axes, with as many iterations as necessary of our initiative's approach until we can fit it into the market and lay the foundations to scale it later.

It's important at this juncture to monitor cash flow. According to a study by US Bank, 82 percent of startups fail due to a lack of cash. Obviously, it is very possible that this is only the symptom and not the root cause, which could well be lack of market, a bad product, an overstaffed team, etc. In any case, the truth is that the key metric you should focus on right now is your cash flow. Later you will perform a more complex financial analysis and get other types of metrics, but now make sure you do not run out of money in your bank account. You can make your own spreadsheet that you update weekly, tracking the money you have in the bank account, the expenses and income you expect in the coming weeks or months. It will be much easier for you to get the expenses right than the income, which are always hypotheses. And you should be prepared to manage your cash and your project if you do not get the income you expect. In fact, I recommend that you somehow separate your secured income forecasts (such as sales that you have already closed and are receivable) from the income that you have not secured (such as projected sales or even sales that you have set as a goal and that you have not yet made.) Properly managing your bookkeeping as another metric will keep you safe while you learn to realistically manage the financial aspect of your project and your expectations.

Regarding your innovation accounting system metrics, in the Evaluation, phase you should start defining and measuring quantitative metrics to know if you are adding real value to your customers or if you must make an adjustment. There are multiple metrics that can be very useful when it comes to understanding the status of your project and making decisions. Maybe you know or have heard of some of them: CPC, CAC, LTV, CHURN,

NPS, etc. The key is to know which one you should focus on at any given moment and how to define an innovation accounting system that evolves alongside your initiative.

It's also very important to know which metrics we should never focus on. Eric Ries calls them "vanity metrics" because they make us feel good but don't give us useful insights into the value of what we're doing. The risk is that they can also confuse us. An example can be the number of new users registered on a platform. Initially, it may seem like a very relevant metric, but what happens if, through paid advertising or any other promotion mechanism, we manage to increase our platform by thousands of new users but none of them actively use it? Instead of the number of users, it would be much more convenient to measure the percentage of active users we have on the platform, which would give us much more relevant information about our innovation process, since it would tell us if users are finding value in it or not. Normally, metrics consisting of an absolute number (number of registrations, number of visits, number of products, etc.) are vanity metrics that, while giving us relevant information, should not be our focus—and much less a part of our strategy.

Another important point to keep in mind regarding innovation metrics in the Evaluation phase is the type of elements we want to measure and those we don't. Remember that your product has not yet fit into the market and that you still need to evaluate certain hypotheses and continue iterating your MVP until it becomes a product that satisfies most customers and allows you to grow. Therefore, it is time to focus on metrics that help you evaluate whether the product is providing real value or not. Some examples of these "value metrics" are:

- NPS (Net Promoter Score): This measures customer loyalty based on their recommendations, which it does by asking the customer or user for a rating of 0 to 10 on whether they would recommend the product to someone else, 0 being not at all and 10 being definitely. The final NPS calculation gives us a figure between -100 and +100, calculated with the percentage of customers considered promoters (those who have answered the question with either 9 or 10) minus those considered detractors (who have answered the question with a number between 0 and 6). There is no absolute good or bad NPS number, but there is an average for every industry.

- Churn Ratio: This is the rate of customer cancellation and measures the percentage of customers who have stopped using or buying our service. This ratio is especially useful in recurring services.
- Percentage of Active Users: As we saw before, this is the percentage of active users of a platform, application, or such. It is calculated by dividing the total number of users by the number of active users.

Define the metrics that make sense for your initiative without forgetting that now is the time to evaluate the value of products and services, not to measure if you are growing. That will come in the next phase. At this time, it is normal to make some investment in marketing, but the goal is not to grow in sales yet but rather to attract a minimum number of customers that allows us to continue learning about the value generated and make the necessary changes to move from the MVP to the real product.

In this Evaluation phase, you must also begin to measure everything related to the sustainability metrics that you defined in the Exploration phase to evaluate how close or far you are from achieving triple sustainability. Once your initiative has started rolling, you must also review the overall sustainability accounting system to assess whether you should add or remove any metrics based on actual activity. Remember that everything you defined in the Exploration phase was nothing more than hypothesis and that it is normal for there to be changes in your approach over time. Finally, depending on the actual results you are obtaining, continue to review and improve your corporate social responsibility and corporate environmental responsibility plans, as it is essential for your footprint to be neutral before you create a real positive impact.

When it comes to your impact metrics, you may need to remove or add some, even if the main impact metric, your starshot, has changed. Without a doubt, the most exciting thing about this phase is when you start measuring your progress on your starshot in whole numbers. Your efforts are finally being rewarded. You are officially creating a real positive impact!

Metrics in the Impact Phase

At this point, you will have managed to fit your initiative into the market, and you will have income. You may not yet be economically sustainable, but you have already validated that you bring real value to your customers. You've also started to make progress on your external sustainability and are making progress on your starshot. Now you need to focus on the key metrics to optimize your initiative's performance, scale your impact, and realize your purpose.

Since you need to be profitable (or at least economically sustainable) to be able to scale, the key metric you need to focus on from a financial accounting standpoint is the business margin, which is calculated by subtracting expenses from revenue. You can play around with values such as the price of your product or service, the volume of customers, or the sales margin of each product, among others, to optimize your approach and achieve the desired profitability. The sustainability chain, which I have mentioned before, will help you visualize a way to increase the value of your primary activities and minimize the cost of your primary and secondary activities to maximize the business margin. You will have to adapt the sustainability chain to your initiative's current focus, since the type of primary and secondary activities could have varied considerably after possible changes and pivots of your business model. Your margin will not only be able to positively impact your business, but it will also have a positive impact on shareholders and other groups with whom you may share your profits.

As far as the innovation accounting system is concerned, at this stage, you should focus on growth metrics. To do that, you must continue to complete your system with metrics that help you boost the growth of your business. Take the sales funnel as a base, which could have a series of customized phases depending on the type of activity, and define the metrics that give you key information to analyze the performance in each phase.

Figure 3.41. Innovation Accounting System Based on the Sales Funnel

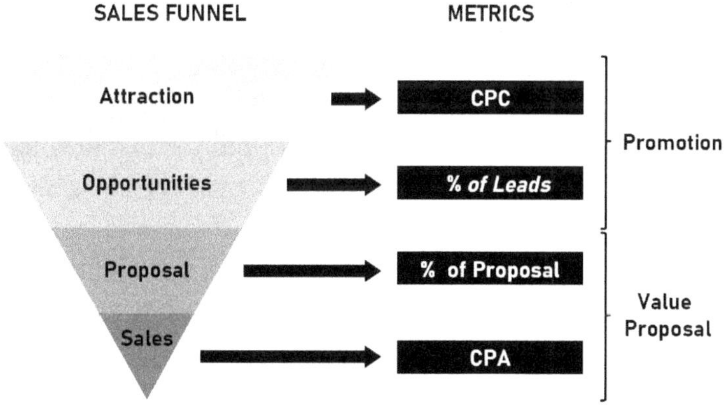

Source: Prepared by the author

As you can see in the figure above, a sales funnel usually has a first stage focused on attracting potential customers, another on detecting real opportunities, and another focused on presenting the value proposition to close the sale. You optimize the sales funnel from the bottom up, first focusing on the metrics for presenting and selling the value proposition, since, if this part is not optimized, no matter how many potential customers you attract with promotion tactics, your sales will not grow proportionally and you will be wasting your resources.

To improve the different stages of the funnel, we will obviously have to measure and improve certain metrics. Below are some of the most common related to the presentation and sale of the value proposition:

- Customer acquisition cost (CAC) tells us how much money we spend on average to attract a new paying customer to our business. This metric will tell us how the value proposition fits in with the price and the shopping experience.
- Percentage of customers who request our proposal, either physically through a direct channel or online by visiting our website and arriving at the screen where they can purchase the product or service, indicates the level of customers' real interest in our value proposition.

Once the sales mechanism is optimized, you can now focus on quantitative metrics focused on promoting your product, including:

- Percentage of leads indicates the percentage of people who have been actively interested in our value proposition with respect to the total number of people who have visited our website or to whom we have shown our value proposition. This metric will tell us if we are promoting our value proposition in the right market.
- Cost per click (CPC) tells us how much money we spend on average on paid promotions to generate a click that

automatically leads to our website. The metric could also be adapted for physical environments, although it is always easier to measure this initial phase of the funnel in digital ones. This metric will tell us if the messages and promotion tactics are capturing the interest of potential customers.

You may need a different set of metrics for each type of startup or product. The key here is to define a group of metrics that will help you learn how to sell and scale your business. In any case, always remember that qualitative metrics are above quantitative metrics, so, if you don't know why you are getting a series of results and values, I recommend that you talk to people who are going through the different stages of the funnel to understand the numbers.

Throughout this phase, if you have not achieved it before, you should take your initiative towards triple sustainability. Social and environmental sustainability is already imperative, so, if you have not yet achieved them, you should analyze the metrics and criteria that are stopping you and implement actions and changes. Only then will your initiative be ready to move on to the next step and start creating a real impact.

Just as you've optimized your business funnel to drive and scale sales, you'll need to analyze and make the necessary adjustments to your operations, the way you connect to and manage abundance, and your overall initiative to accelerate your contribution to the world. Once you manage to reach your starshot, you can say that you have made your purpose a reality.

Final Reflections on the Metrics Axis

This chapter may have seemed a bit complex, as I have introduced many new concepts. I suggest that you consult it as many times as necessary when putting it into practice. I also recommend that you reread it together with the Sustainability axis chapter, since both axes are intricately linked.

To facilitate the understanding and application of this chapter, I have summarized below the type of metrics that you should define and use in each of the phases for the different types of accounting systems.

Table 3.8. Summary of the Key Metrics for Each Phase of Purpose Launchpad

	KEY METRICS		
	Exploration	**Evaluation**	**Impact**
Impact accounting	• Impact-specific metrics: • Define starshot • Define impact-specific metrics	• Impact-specific metrics: • *Starshot* • Impact-specific metrics	• Impact-specific metrics: • *Starshot* • Impact-specific metrics
Sustainability accounting	• Common sustainability metrics • Social (employment, community, etc.) • Environmental (emissions, etc.)	• Common sustainability metrics • Social (employment, community, etc.) • Environmental (emissions, etc.)	• Common sustainability metrics • Social (employment, community, etc.) • Environmental (emissions, etc.)
Financial accounting	**Mockup** • Cash management scenarios • Funding needs scenarios	**Cashflow** • Forecast for cash management • Forecast income • Forecast expenses	**Profit** • Margin • Logical business parameters
Innovation accounting	• Qualitative discovery metrics • Capture findings on problems • Capture findings on solutions	• Qualitative value metrics • NPS • *Churn Rate* • % of active users	• Qualitative growth metrics • CAC • CAC • LTV

Source: Prepared by the author

As you can see, it is about crossing the three phases (Exploration, Evaluation, and Impact) with the different types of accounting systems (innovation, financial, sustainability, and impact). From this matrix, you can define the different types of metrics you need when measuring your initiative's progress and impact so that you can improve it, as Peter Drucker suggests.

It will not be as easy to compare initiatives in some of these areas, because, as we have seen throughout the chapter, not all of them have universal systems. Only financial accounting is based on a set of accepted standard metrics applied to all types of initiatives in the same way, and it is required by most public administrations. However, innovation and sustainability accounting, although based on standard and known metrics, is not always applied in the same way. Sustainability accounting, as I stated earlier in this book, could become a standard as long as we limit ourselves to measuring the project's social and environmental sustainability (since those parameters can be standardized) without trying to measure the project's impact.

It is precisely impact accounting itself that generates differences and makes it impossible to create a standardized system, since each initiative tries to contribute to the world in a totally different way according to its purpose and its starshot. Therefore, we will have to assume that the way to measure impact and compare it between different initiatives cannot be achieved with the usual standard measurement systems.

If we separate impact from sustainability, as I propose, a sustainability accounting system could be fully standardized and evolve towards models that measure and verify comprehensive sustainability in a similar way for all organizations and activities. In this way, we would help reduce impact-washing and green-washing (practices which many corporations follow to show the metrics that place them as sustainable or impact-oriented when they really aren't), since the set of metrics would be the same for all organizations and could be verified objectively, leaving the metrics that differ for each type of organization in the impact accounting system, which would be dealt with separately.

That is why there is currently no universal measurement system that allows comparing the level of impact of different initiatives. Such a hypothetical system should be able to translate any impact accounting system into its own unique measure, which is very difficult, as each of us interprets impact subjectively. For example, was the extinction of the dinosaurs a positive or negative impact? If we could ask them, they would certainly tell us that the impact was very negative, but for us it was positive, since, if they had not become extinct, perhaps our species would never have existed.

In my opinion, the day there is a universal impact measurement system it won't be an equation-based metric; it will be based on an evaluation with a social component. In other words, it will have to be society that evaluates an initiative's impact on the world. Perhaps one day there will be a universal impact system, but I won't go into that here, because we'd need another book.

I would like to end this chapter with something practical that you can apply to your projects. As one of the Purpose Launchpad principles states, we must "measure progress through validated positive impact," and, to do that, we must combine all types of accounting. This implies taking into consideration and appropriately verifying the value delivered to our customers, the economic value generated for our organization, the degree of sustainability with which we carry out our activity, and the positive contribution we make to the world, as shown in the following table.

Table 3.9. Set of Metrics to Measure Total Impact

IMPACT	
Impact-specific metrics: • Starshot • Impact-specific metrics	**Specific Impact Accounting** +
Common sustainability metrics: • Social (employment, community, etc.) • Environmental (emissions, etc.)	**Sustainability Accounting** +
Economic profit: • Organization net margin • Shareholder dividends • Other allocations	**Financial Accounting** +
Value and growth metrics: • NPA, Churn Rate, % of active users • CAC, CAC, LTV	**Innovation Accounting** =
TOTAL IMPACT	

Source: Prepared by the author

Remember that only by measuring validated positive impact will we know for sure if we are developing our initiatives correctly and if we are carrying out the right initiatives.

The different accounting systems and metrics presented in this chapter are not only applicable to startups and new products but also to corporations and established organizations, as we will see in the next part of the book. In addition, at the end of the book, you will find, among other resources, a tool called "Tester for Purpose-Oriented Organizations" that will help you verify if an organization is truly purpose-oriented or if, instead, it's only a communication strategy. I encourage you to apply this tool to your project to make sure you're on the right track.

In the past, we understood that a millionaire was a person who earned more than a million euros or dollars. Today, it is no longer enough to generate economic income. In fact, we may not get the money if we focus only on that. Millionaires are now the ones who positively impact the lives of more than a million people, which is usually accompanied by proportional economic income thanks to the positive contribution they generate in the world. This is where I encourage you to become a millionaire, even a billionaire. It will be good for you; it will be good for everyone.

Table 3.10. Metrics Axis Summary

	METRICS AXIS		
	Exploration Discover what you should measure (and what you shouldn't)	**Evaluation** Begin measuring to improve	**Impact** Continue measuring and improving to reach your purpose
Impact accounting	Define your impact metrics	Measure your way towards impact	Reach your starshot and your purpose!
Sustainability accounting	Define your sustainability metrics	Measure your way towards sustainability	Reach triple sustainability!
Financial accounting	Don't measure financial metrics	Monitor your cash flow	Manage your profitability for growth
Innovation accounting	Focus on qualitative metrics	Focus on value metrics	Focus on growth metrics

Source: Prepared by the author

Activity

Considering your own project (startup or new product), do the following activities (if you don't have a project, think of one that you're familiar with):

1. Determine what phase your project is in. Remember that, although a specific axis (such as the product axis) might be at a more advanced stage, your initiative will be in whichever phase the least-evolved axis is in. Remember that you can use the Purpose Launchpad Assessment to determine this.
2. Depending on which phase your project is in, do the following:
   a. Exploration phase:
   - Define what kind of information you need from your customers to evaluate the problems and the solution you are thinking of developing. Create a document (share it if you're part of a team) where you begin gathering that information.
   - Define a first version of your sustainability accounting system from your sustainability chain.
   - Define a first version of your impact accounting system, including the starshot and a first set of impact metrics from your impact chain.
   b. Evaluation phase:
   - Create a simple tool that allows you to monitor your cash position and make forecasts for two to three months.

- Create a first group of metrics that make up your innovation accounting system and that are focused on the value you generate to your customers.
- If you don't have it yet, create a sustainability accounting system or improve the one you have and start taking real action on the various metrics.
- If you don't have it yet, create an impact accounting system and start taking real action on the starshot and other possible metrics you include in the system.

c. Impact phase:

- Turn your cash-flow projection into a financial plan in which you can monitor and update your income and expenses to know your margin. Add a series of parameters depending on the business model of your initiative and play with them to analyze different approaches until you reach the break-even point.
- Expand your innovation accounting system with a second group of metrics associated with the sales funnel to begin improving your sales.
- If you don't have it yet, create a sustainability accounting system or improve the one you have and start taking real action on the various metrics.
- If you don't have it yet, create an impact accounting system and start taking real action on the starshot and other possible metrics you include in the system.

Resources

- Lean Canvas: *www.purposealliance.org/resources/lean-canvas*
- Impact Accounting Canvas: *www.purposealliance.org/resources/impact-accounting-canvas*

Part Four

Evolution of
Established Organizations

23
Industries Create Scarcity, Purpose-Driven Ecosystems Generate Abundance

Healthy competition can be very positive. There are many examples of this in the world of sports as well as in business, like the competition between Ferruccio Lamborghini and Enzo Ferrari, founders of the car companies that bear their names, that went on for years. Lamborghini, whose family were grape growers, initially benefited from his knowledge of mechanics to become an important manufacturer of agricultural machinery in Italy. After this success, he began to use part of his wealth to follow one of his passions: sports cars. He owned an important collection that included several Ferraris. At one point, Ferruccio publicly criticized Ferrari's mechanics for the low quality of its components, to which Enzo replied that "a tractor manufacturer cannot understand the complexity of a Ferrari." Stepping boldly up to the challenge, Ferruccio decided to create his own brand of sports cars to compete with Ferrari, first on the racing circuits and then in dealerships. Lamborghini soon took over a good part of the market and forced Ferrari to improve the design of its vehicles and raise its quality standards.

Rivalry and competition, however, can also be very damaging. This is what happens when several companies fight to the death in a limited market—that is, in what Chan Kim and Renée Mauborgne call "a red ocean" in their well-known book *The Blue Ocean Strategy*. The main problem of traditional companies focused on one industry is that, sooner or later, the markets in which they operate become saturated, generating a rivalry based on scarcity that ends up harming all competitors.

That's not the case with purpose-oriented organizations, which have an unlimited playing field. To make their purpose a reality, they must solve a multitude of challenges in different areas, which, in the end, becomes an abundance of opportunities, especially when they connect with an ecosystem linked to their purpose or generate their own. This is what has happened with Apple, for example. It was dedicated to manufacturing and selling computers until multiple competitors emerged and the market became saturated. Then Steve Jobs recalled why the company existed: "We believe that people with passion can improve the world." From then on, Apple became what it is today: an ecosystem focused on a purpose of empowering people's creative exploration and self-expression. Apple continues to design and sell computers, but it also offers several products and services in line with its purpose: smartphones, watches, apps, music, online content, cloud storage, and more. When it was an industry-focused company, its customers would buy one of their computers every two to three years; after becoming a purpose-driven ecosystem, their customers use their products and services, which are also interconnected, daily.

Figure 4.1. Apple's Purpose-Oriented Ecosystem

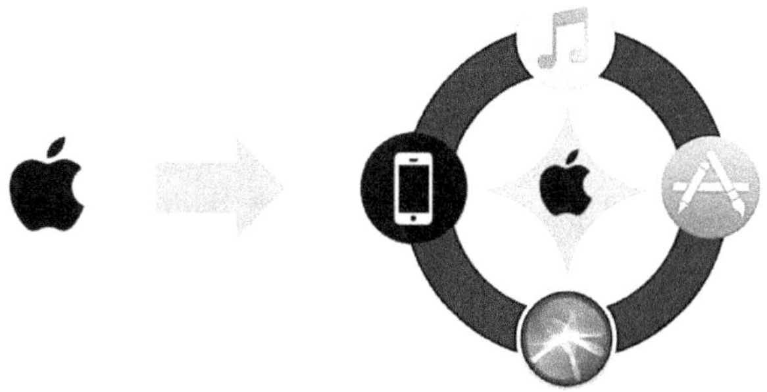

Source: Prepared by the author

As I've mentioned before, Tesla is another clear example: not only does it manufacture and sell cars, but it has generated an entire ecosystem around its purpose to accelerate the world's transition to a sustainable energy model. In addition to cars, it sells solar panels for homes, high-capacity batteries, or even applications for its devices. This allows it to access an abundance of opportunities and penetrate a myriad of markets, something that is rcflcctcd in its skyrocketing market value.

The same is true for Google. Which industry does Google belong to? The answer is none of them and many of them at the same time. At first it was an industry-focused organization (web search engines), but later it became a purpose-oriented ecosystem, creating multiple products, services, and even new organizations. In fact, its evolution led the parent company to change its name to Alphabet, which, in addition to Google, covers other products and services such as Gmail, Adwords, or YouTube. By operating with an abundance approach around its purpose, it continually connects with new markets and new opportunities.

Like Apple, Tesla, or Alphabet, every day there are more organizations that decide to evolve towards models of abundance and move away from those red oceans in which many sharks compete for the same school of fish. Instead of fighting over one fish more or one fewer, they work to generate their own ecosystem and stop competing in a single league.

By the way, I refer to organizational ecosystems because of the great similarity that exists with biological ecosystems. Like in the latter, in purpose-oriented organizational ecosystems, there are a multitude of organisms (initiatives of all kinds, products, services, and organizations) that interact with their environment and one another through cycles of nutrients and energy in which some generate what others need. Each purpose-oriented ecosystem is different from the others, but all have at least these three elements:

- The **purpose**, which is the raison d'être of the ecosystem and everything that happens within it. It is at the center of the ecosystem and shapes everything else with the aim of generating a positive impact.
- The **initiatives**, which are the set of businesses, products, and services that the ecosystem offers to solve the main challenges and market needs linked to the purpose.
- The **community**, which is the people and organizations aligned with the purpose that help in one way or another to make it a reality. It is the ecosystem's membrane; the greater it is, the greater its impact.

Figure 4.2. Purpose-Oriented Ecosystem

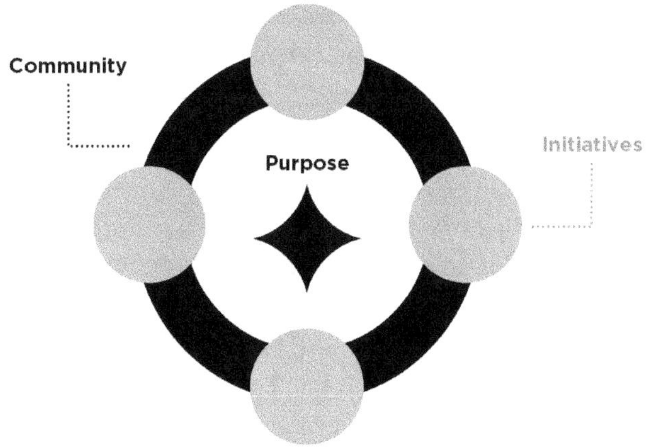

Source: Prepared by the author

Regarding the business model or income generation of the different initiatives of an ecosystem, it is important to understand that not all should be oriented to obtain an economic benefit, not even income. Some initiatives will generate revenue and resources, while others will only consume them, as with Siri on Apple or WhatsApp on Facebook. Although they do not generate business for the ecosystem, these initiatives have a very important function for the balance of the ecosystem (providing complementary value to users in the case of Siri and capturing data in the case of WhatsApp).

One of the most relevant effects generated by purpose-oriented ecosystems is that members of their community have much more power than previous consumers did. In fact, when we find two ecosystems with similar purposes, direct competition disappears thanks to the interaction that is generated at the community level. The competition generated by scarcity-based markets is a thing of the past. Members of communities that live their purpose in a real way collaborate and belong to different communities simultaneously without the need for different companies or ecosystems to have to make specific collaboration agreements. Users use products and services from different ecosystems, putting what really matters at the center: purpose.

Google's community, for example, uses its products and services in combination with those of other similar purpose-oriented ecosystems. Google Docs users also use Microsoft products (Word, Excel, etc.) when organizing their information into different types of documents. Google Calendar users combine its functionality with that of other applications, such as Windows Calendar or Apple Calendar. And the list goes on.

Figure 4.3. Connection Between Purpose-Oriented Ecosystems

Google TED WikipediA Microsoft

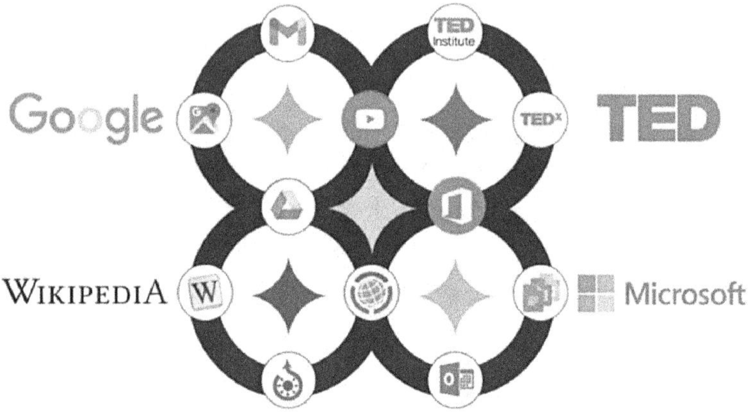

Source: Prepared by the author

Purpose-oriented ecosystems aren't just for large corporations. This trend is also completely changing the way organizations of all kinds are beginning to interact with the environment. I remember the case of Casa Cantillano's, a Honduran coffee company that was concerned because its production was limited by agricultural land owned by the company. Lionel Carrillo, a Purpose Launchpad mentor, helped the organization define a new playing field, starting with its purpose: "to unite all the families of the world through a cup of coffee." This allowed them to start changing its owners' and employees' mindset to evolve towards an ecosystem that currently integrates the abundance of coffee growers and offers the world a series of new products and services in collaboration with their local environment. At the same time, they generate a positive impact on the country's families by contributing to the socioeconomic development of rural workers from the city of Lluvia de Peces.

The case of Casa Cantillano's is just one example. Every day, more local ecosystems emerge that generate abundance for their members and positive impact on their immediate environment. We also find purpose-oriented ecosystems that are not driven by an organization but emerge from communities whose members have very similar purposes. CGAP, for example, is an ecosystem in which more than thirty organizations from around the world came together with the purpose of improving the lives of people without resources, especially women, through financial inclusion. Keeping purpose at their center, the organizations that make up the ecosystem collaborate to put new inclusive and accountable financial systems in place to help lift people out of poverty. These actions have a positive impact on those less fortunate and generate opportunities for collaboration and new horizons for the organizations that make up the ecosystem.

The power of purpose and the ecosystems created around them are driving new areas of abundance, both for the organizations that generate these ecosystems, which can leverage multiple business opportunities, and for people, who can enjoy the many resources offered by ecosystems and combine them as they prefer.

The organizational model as we have known it has become obsolete. The time has come to avoid the lethal rivalry generated by industries and their corresponding markets, which, sooner or later, become saturated, leading us to scarcity. It's time to act with an abundance mindset and focus on a purpose to take advantage of the multitude of opportunities that emerge around you.

In this new paradigm, there are no losers and winners. The important thing is no longer to be the market leader but a reference for the community linked to our purpose so that we can be the gateway to an ecosystem that allows its members to meet their needs and fulfill their own individual purpose. In this way, everyone wins: companies, their customers, and the whole world.

Key Points

- Traditional organizations focused on one industry end up operating in saturated markets that generate scarcity and hurt all competitors.
- Purpose-focused organizations benefit from the abundance of existing possibilities related to that purpose and can take advantage of them if they evolve into an ecosystem model.
- The concept of an industry-oriented organization becomes obsolete in the face of purpose-oriented ecosystems, which have three fundamental elements: purpose (located in the center), initiatives, and community.
- We can further leverage the ecosystem model by connecting with other ecosystems related to our purpose.

24
Implementing Purpose Launchpad in Established Organizations

Purpose Launchpad is not limited to guiding the evolution of startups and new products; it is also very useful for facilitating the evolution of established organizations to create a positive impact on the world and on their own results. It can be of great help when it comes to defining and activating your purpose, evolving your team's mindset, and generating your own purpose-oriented ecosystem or connecting it with existing ecosystems.

Figure 4.4. Purpose Launchpad Aimed at Organizations

Source: Prepared by the author

It's true that startups and established organizations are totally different worlds, so the way we will apply Purpose Launchpad to each of them will be very different. In the case of established organizations, the objective will be to evolve them towards new models, as we will see throughout this fourth part of the book. The main key will, however, be the same as for startups: change the mindset of the people in the organization regardless of their position in it.

It should be clear that, when I speak of established organizations, I mean all kinds of companies, for profit or not, that have a validated business model and whose income makes them economically viable. Obviously, this is a very generic definition and covers many profiles. For example, it can be a startup that has evolved properly and has become a consolidated business, a company of any size that has a solid position in its market, a company with a validated business model that is currently going through temporary difficulties due to issues outside the organization, such as a change in market trends, or even a group of companies with a traditional approach that wants to evolve towards a more current model and become a purpose-oriented ecosystem.

Although their profile and circumstances differ, all of them are forced to evolve to remain relevant in their current environment.

If they don't evolve, the rapid and continuous changes in the environment can leave them out of the game at any time. Even leading established organizations, for which the shift to new models might not seem like an urgent life-and-death matter, require continuous adaptation to their environment to maintain their privileged position.

Evolving an established organization is not an easy task. Just as the number of successful startups is small, the percentage of established organizations that successfully evolve to new models is very low. This is due to the myriad of challenges they face. The main one is internal resistance, which blocks new initiatives and innovation. An established organization is designed to execute a predetermined plan under a known business model, not to seek new business models within an environment of high uncertainty. Therefore, to properly evolve an organization, it isn't enough for it to be aware of the need to evolve or even to launch initiatives with the participation of a small group of people. It will be necessary to promote a massive cultural change of the mindset of every person in the organization, guided by a common purpose.

So far, we have seen how to apply the Purpose Launchpad framework in a startup or for a new product or service. As you can imagine, it is more complex when dealing with a large organization or a company with a very wide portfolio of products and services. All the axes we have seen are more difficult to apply, because we can have multiple products, multiple teams, multiple groups of metrics, etc. That is why the implementation is carried out through Purpose Launchpad Applications, specific processes that use different elements of the framework to respond to specific needs of the organization: to inspire and awaken leaders and different teams, to define the organization's purpose, to attract communities associated with the purpose, to generate different initiatives to develop an ecosystem, and to massively update the organization's mindset to facilitate the process of evolution, among others. In the same way that Purpose Launchpad relies on a multitude of innovation tools and methodologies, Purpose Launchpad Applications rely on the general framework to define specific processes that solve specific needs.

Figure 4.5. Purpose Launchpad Apps and Tools

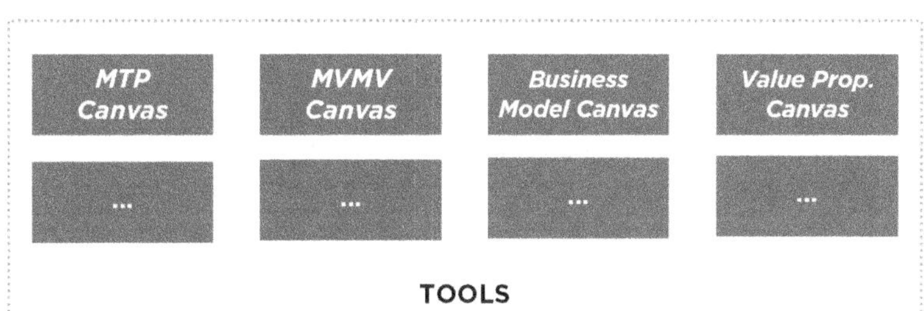

Source: Prepared by the author

In the next chapters, we will analyze in greater detail the different challenges that established organizations face when evolving their business models and creating a positive impact. We will look at how to deal with them by implementing some of the Purpose Launchpad Applications. In addition, I'll offer you a link to download a more detailed implementation guide for each of the apps if you wish to help you take your organization and your teams' mindset to the next level. Let's get started!

Key Points

- Purpose Launchpad is very useful for established organizations when it comes to guiding them in the evolution of their business model to become purpose-oriented ecosystems or to connect with existing ecosystems.
- Established organizations can be anything from start-ups that have evolved properly to companies of all sizes or even business groups.
- Established organizations need to evolve into new models on an ongoing basis, even if they have a privileged position in their market.
- To do this, they must face different challenges, the main one being their own internal resistance to innovation.
- Purpose Launchpad Applications are specific processes that use different elements of the framework to respond to these challenges.
- The best way to evolve an organization is to evolve people's mindsets.

25
Defining an Established Organization's Purpose

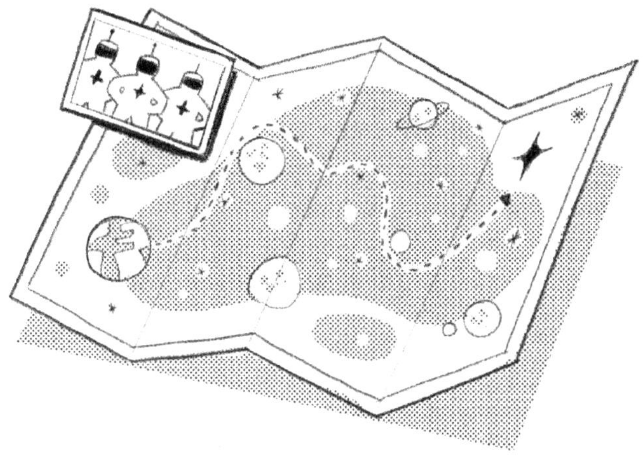

In 1963, US President John F. Kennedy visited NASA facilities as part of his support for the Apollo 11 project, the one that landed the first men on the moon. In each department, he greeted the staff and took an interest in their functions. At one point during the visit, as the entourage walked down a hallway, President Kennedy stood next to a person on the cleaning staff and asked, "What do you do?" The man proudly replied, "Mr. President, I am helping mankind get to the moon."

That great milestone did not occur until a few years later, on July 20, 1969. And it was in part made possible by that cleaning man working at NASA, who clearly understood the importance of his contribution and felt part of that greater purpose. In fact, if the organization had not been so clear about its purpose and had not adequately communicated it to all its staff, that employee would never have responded as he did to the President of the United States.

Organizations able to properly communicate their purpose make it an important asset, firstly because it gives everyone a common direction and they all contribute to making it happen, giving meaning to every action, and, secondly, because they attract quality talent and people who are very committed to the organization. This makes the organization achieve results that would not be possible otherwise. When John F. Kennedy announced in 1961 that man would set foot on the Moon before the end of that decade, he attracted over 400,000 very highly motivated people who collaborated in one way or another to make that extraordinary purpose a reality.

Defining and integrating a purpose into an established organization is usually not an easy task. It is important to do this correctly and involve the necessary people. One of the applications offered by Purpose Launchpad is the Purpose Discovery process consisting of three steps, each one with a series of guidelines.

1) Step 1: Configure the Process

Before defining the purpose, it is necessary to consider who should participate in the process and how to carry it out. Depending on the history of the organization and the current state of the team, three different scenarios can occur. The first is to define the purpose with a very small group of people, including the founders (if they are still alive) and the group of leaders in charge of proposing the vision and strategy. The second is to open the process so that everyone in the organization can have their say, even if the final decision is made by the leaders. And the third is to let the people of the organization define the purpose of the organization under the supervision of their leaders. These last two approaches will help us integrate the organization and reinforce the sense of belonging to it.

2) Step 2: Define and Integrate the Purpose

Once the people who should participate in the process have decided, we act. I recommend that you use a tool that allows you to ask the key questions to properly discover and define the purpose, such as MTP Canvas, which I have talked about earlier.

This step is not only to define the purpose but to integrate it and align it with the rest of the strategic elements of the organization: its vision, mission, and values. At the end of the process, you should have an all-inclusive approach so that the entire strategy makes sense.

Finally, keep in mind that the way to substantiate a purpose, which is usually expressed very generically, is to complement it with the starshot, a concept that we introduced in the axes chapter in the second part. This way, we can translate the purpose into concrete figures and set a time limit for the objective.

3) Step 3: Activate the Purpose

Once the purpose is defined, it is essential to communicate it and put it into practice continuously. I recommend creating a communication plan to make the purpose known to both internal teams and society. Internally, it is essential that the organization's highest authority communicates the purpose so that its importance is clear. Externally, it is important that the purpose goes beyond words and is accompanied by actions that demonstrate that it is not a mere slogan but a way of presenting the identity of the organization.

Purpose must become the compass that guides the organization to create the impact it truly seeks. It is essential that the people who form the organization internalize the purpose and take it into account in everything they do. It is also very important to connect with external communities linked to the purpose and generate new initiatives, as well as to leverage the purpose to evolve the organization towards the ecosystem model or to connect it with existing ones. We will see more about how to do all this in upcoming chapters.

I personally experienced the case of Coteminas, one of the world's most important textile companies. We decided to begin their modernization process by defining their purpose and immediately saw that we had to go back to the company's origins. Founded in 1967 by Don José Alencar Gomes, the transformation process of the organization was led by his son, Josué Gomes da Silva, the current CEO, and his grandson, Josué Alencar, and involved the entire management team. Always keeping the figure and thoughts of the founder in mind, they finally defined their purpose as "to promote wellbeing." This inspired the organization to create new textile-based products (such as smart pillows that measure and improve sleep) and to initiate a series of strategic investments and new health initiatives.

Final Thoughts on Defining the Purpose

Discovering and defining the purpose is critical to properly guiding a company in its process of constant transformation, as well as to establish the role it should have in society and its impact on it. Without this clearly defined element, everything we do will lack the right energy and direction.

Every day, it becomes more important that organizations and people are aware of the reason why we exist. The well-known English writer and keynote speaker Simon Sinek stated it this way: "Money is like fuel. Vehicles need fuel, but the purpose of a vehicle is not to buy more fuel. Business is the same. The purpose of business is not to make money but to advance a greater cause or purpose." Even for those organizations and individuals who think the main goal is to generate profits, creating a positive impact on the world makes sense. As Marcus Aurelius' famous quote reminds us: "Have I done something for the common good? Then, I too have benefited."

I experienced one of the most beautiful processes of purpose discovery at Total, a company in Spain, whose 350 employees were joined by a group of eighteen Purpose Launchpad mentors. Together, we co-created a purpose for the company: to provide the best, affordable, clean, sustainable energy as possible and make it accessible to as many people as possible. A few months after this process, the company decided to change its name to TotalEnergies, and today they are more focused than ever on clean energy. In the words of its vice president, Tom Van de Cruys, the new purpose is "a great foundation for developing our company and everything we do. We will keep the result close to our hearts and in everything we do in the future."

All organizations with purpose have the potential to achieve such extraordinary advances as the one that took man to the moon. Purpose-oriented organizations and ecosystems have the ability to attract highly talented people looking for meaningful projects, as well as generate enormous motivation in its teams and its people, who become ambassadors of purpose because they feel they are contributing to something bigger than themselves by creating a positive impact on their lives and the world.

Key Points

- The great challenge of today's companies is not only to generate economic benefits but also a positive impact on the world.
- The starting point for expanding an organization's impact is to properly define and communicate its purpose.
- To define an organization's purpose, you must follow three steps: decide which people will participate in the process, define and integrate the purpose, and communicate and activate the purpose on an ongoing basis.
- Purposeful organizations that implement their purpose properly generate benefits for the world and for themselves.

Resources

- MTP Canvas: *www.purposealliance.org/resources/mtp-canvas*
- *Purpose Discovery Application*: *www.purposealliance. org/purpose-launchpad/applications/purpose-discovery*
- "Definition of Massive Transformative Purpose (MTP) for TotalEnergies" Impact Case: *www.purposealliance.org/ impact-cases/purpose-discovery*

26
Align The Organization's Culture with Its Purpose

Walmart is the company with the most employees in the world: more than two million people spread over twenty-eight countries. Founded by Sam Walton in 1962, it has a clear purpose: "to improve the world by helping people live better, renewing the planet, and building thriving and resilient communities anytime, anywhere."

However, in the past, Walmart has found itself in a complicated position, mired in numerous challenges that it finally managed to overcome by evolving, thanks to the strength and direction of its own purpose. One of the most important challenges Walmart faced was waste management. In October 2005, the company's CEO, Lee Scott, committed to pushing a sustainability plan and set a goal of "zero waste."

In the years that followed, Walmart went from being one of the world's largest waste producers to leading the shift toward recyclable packaging and sustainability. How did they do it? On the one hand, they accomplished this by launching new initiatives, such as the one aimed at its suppliers called Gigaton, since its objective was to avoid contributing one billion metric tons (one gigaton) of greenhouse gases from the global value chain by 2030. More than three thousand suppliers joined. On the other hand, it drove a cultural shift among its two million employees (whom it calls "associates") thanks to the company's strong purpose, example-based leadership, and empowerment, something that was already in the genes of the organization. In fact, Sam Walton is often quoted for a famous phrase: "Listen to your associates; they are your best idea generators."

Much of the initiatives that have made Walmart one of the world's leaders in environmental sustainability, maximizing energy efficiency and reducing waste, were ideas generated by its associates in line with the organization's purpose. One example is Darrell Meyers, an associate from North Carolina. While in the break room one day, he noticed that there was a light bulb on twenty-four hours a day in every vending machine. Meyers thought about how much electricity was wasted and wondered how much money the company could save if it removed the lights from all the vending machines. His idea was very well received, and the company decided to remove those bulbs from all its stores, saving more than a million dollars in energy costs and reducing their environmental impact.

An organization's culture is not something that must be changed at specific times but requires continuous evolution. In my opinion, there are four keys that have allowed Walmart to evolve its culture. The first is having a clear and strong purpose, which has kept the organization's direction steady despite multiple changes in the environment.

The second is communicating the required organizational changes to make the purpose a reality, which includes new perspectives of the world. In this sense, Walmart has managed to make all its employees understand the importance of being a sustainable organization and positioning itself as such worldwide. In addition to internal communication, Walmart also publicly shares its results in terms of sustainability using the ESG model, which I described in detail in the last chapter of the third part, titled "Measure Your Progress and Your Impact on the World." If you haven't read it yet, I recommend that you do, as it will help you understand how to measure your organization's sustainability and impact on the world.

The third key is to actively involve teams, listening to them and allowing them to generate ideas that not only add value in the right direction for change but also create a sense of belonging to the organization and allows them to be a part of the change, which is key when going through the complications arising during any transition. As we saw in the example above, Walmart has continuously empowered its employees to be engines and generators of ideas throughout the evolution process.

Finally, the fourth element is to constantly maintain the actions of cultural change, just like the environment's constant changes.

Some organizations emerge with a clear purpose from the beginning and strengthen it as they move forward. This is the case of Universal DX, founded by Juan Martínez Barea and his partner Marko Bitenc in 2012 with the purpose of creating a future in which cancer is curable. Thanks to the clear direction of the company's leadership and its strong culture of innovation and collaboration, the organization is generating exceptional results. Their tests for detecting certain types of cancer have already achieved a sensitivity above 90 percent.

Organizations that can continuously evolve their culture while keeping purpose at the center reap multiple benefits. If they also manage to spread their purpose beyond their own teams, such as to their suppliers and even to external communities (as we will see in the next chapter), they connect with a source of abundance (talent, energy, opportunities) that takes them to the next level.

Cultural changes are not easy, however. In fact, they have traditionally been one of the most complicated issues for organizations. As explained by Paolo Sacchi, CEO of Ransa (a leading logistics operator in Latin America), "It is not enough to make a change at the top of the organization, but we must promote change at all levels to turn all the people in the organization into ambassadors of purpose."

To achieve cultural change in a traditional organization, we can rely on the purpose following a simple—but very powerful—virtuous cycle consisting of communicating the purpose internally in the organization and creating a space so that teams can put it into practice in an experimental environment, which will motivate them to do so later in real business situations. One of the Purpose Launchpad applications is called the Purpose Launchpad workshop and consists of a dynamic enabling an organization's teams to generate initiatives oriented to the organization's purpose (and even to define possible purposes should the organization not have one yet) to promote a cultural change that helps the organization adapt to their circumstances and generate a positive impact, both in its business and in the world.

**Figure 4.6. Cyclical Process to Drive
Cultural Change Through Purpose**

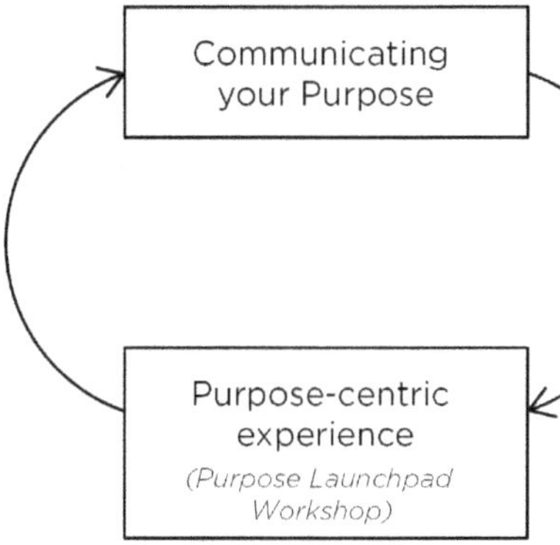

Communicating
your Purpose

Purpose-centric
experience
(Purpose Launchpad
Workshop)

Source: Prepared by the author

Let's take a closer look at how to implement these two steps within an established organization.

There are multiple ways to implement the first step. I always recommend making an open presentation to the different teams of the organization to communicate or remember the purpose, which, of course, must be previously defined. This communication action has a top-down approach, so the highest authority of the organization must participate in some way, being responsible for recalling the purpose as a basis for driving change. The organization might not have a purpose, in which case we can communicate to inspire change and eventually launch a process of purpose discovery. In both cases, this can be a keynote lecture supported by external speakers, since sometimes our message is better heard from someone outside the organization.

One of the companies where I have been fortunate to implement this process is Siemens Colombia, which subsequently replicated it throughout Latin America. Reinaldo García, president of Siemens Colombia, addressed hundreds of people in an initial speech, recalling the organization's purpose and speaking of the importance of promoting transformation in the organization.

My subsequent keynote provided an outside perspective on how the world is evolving toward purpose-oriented ecosystems. Thanks to this communication, we were able to inspire the different teams and prepare them for cultural change.

In this step of the process, it is advisable to focus on describing the changes in the environment and being clear about why it is necessary to continuously evolve not only the organization but the mindset of its people. It is about inspiring (explaining why) and not about defining specific processes or specific methodologies (which would be the how).

The second step in the process is to facilitate the purpose-focused experience. It's about moving from words to actions and giving people space to find the right direction themselves. There is no better way to engage people than by co-creating the path with them. Therefore, what I recommend at this stage is to give the teams the opportunity to suggest their own initiatives and the mechanisms to put them in place and evaluate them (bottom-up approach). A Purpose Launchpad workshop was held at Siemens Colombia with a group of fifty people from the organization. Based on the purpose, they generated new initiatives using the Purpose Launchpad and its different axes.

Remember that workshops do not work magically; it is usually not possible to launch the proposed initiatives. The reality is that workshops are actions focused more on providing people with an experience that helps them transform and are not aimed as much at generating long-lasting initiatives (for that to happen, we will look at other alternatives in the following chapters). The workshops allow teams to imagine new possibilities and, above all, internalize the force of purpose and the need for change. They help participants evolve in the way they view the organization and the world to change their mindset and accompany the organization in its process of continuous cultural change.

Final Thoughts

As my good friend Jorge Zenteno, whom I met when he held the position of Deputy General Director of Specialized Business at Banco Santander in Mexico, once told me, "The only way to change the culture of an organization is to change the way in which its people behave." To achieve a change in people, it is not enough to implement a process; you must act at the value level, evolving their belief system and giving real meaning to a mindset change. Just like a basketball coach must make decisions thinking about the entire team and not the specific needs or interests of a single player, the different people in an organization need to understand that there are times when they must change the way they see things and act for the general good of the organization. It is not about optimizing the collective, not the individual, good.

There are people who prefer to stay in a comfort zone without being forced to change. They do not see that, although it may be an effort to do things differently in the short term, if they act from generosity, they will facilitate an overall change that will benefit the organization and therefore themselves. When people in the organization come to understand the importance of values like generosity and are empowered with elements like the purpose of the organization, cultural change happens with an energy as strong as the energy generating the purpose itself.

Key Points

- Cultural change is key to adapting the organization to the continuous changes of its environment.
- Some basic elements for cultural change are having a clear purpose, communicating it, and empowering teams to generate ideas and initiatives that activate the purpose in a real way.
- The organization must align not only their employees with its culture but also their suppliers and external collaborators.
- Cultural evolution actions must be maintained constantly to adapt the organization and the mindset of its teams to the continuous change of the environment.

Resources

- *Keynotes*: *www.franciscopalao.com/keynotes*
- *Purpose Launchpad Application Workshop*: *www.purposealliance.org/purpose-launchpad/applications/purpose-launchpad-workshop*
- "Inspiring Siemens to Transform the Organization and the World" Impact Case: *www.purposealliance.org/impact-cases/purpose-launchpad-workshop*

27
Generating Community
and New Initiatives

I will always remember how I discovered the extraordinary power of community and, most importantly, how to connect with
this fascinating treasure. After twenty years of entrepreneurship,
I had set out to spend a slightly quieter season lecturing. It was
March 12, 2020, and my next keynote was scheduled for the following week in Asunción, Paraguay. However, that day I received

an email informing me that, due to the emerging pandemic caused by the COVID-19 virus, the event had been canceled. In a few hours, the world panicked, many countries closed their borders and declared a state of national emergency, most international flights were suspended, and billions of people locked themselves in their homes of their own free will or at the request of their governments.

Faced with that situation, I felt that I could not sit idly by. That same day, March 12, I decided to launch a challenge to the world to help stop the pandemic. The challenge was to generate new initiatives that solved problems related to the pandemic. Participants could register on a website where, in addition to the form, they would find some of the innovation tools that we have been seeing throughout this book. In just one week, which was the proposed time for the challenge, more than 350 people from all continents signed up!

A few days later, seeing the success of the initiative, my friend Paul Epping told me he wanted to replicate it in the United Arab Emirates. I immediately offered my help, and we launched a new event. Again, hundreds of people signed up for the challenge! Later, this type of challenge was replicated in other countries, such as Argentina, Mexico, Colombia, Peru, Ecuador, and Spain. Curiously, even though I live in Spain, it was Soledad Llorente, professor of transformation and intrapreneurship at IE University and a certified Purpose Launchpad mentor, who led the challenge there through her own initiative. Thanks to the power of the community, the movement had gone beyond me. In just a few weeks, thousands of people were involved, and more than a hundred initiatives had emerged, many of which are still actively generating a positive impact on the world.

The extraordinary energy of that movement looked like magic, but it wasn't: the secret was in how the right purpose was able to unlock the power of the community. Thousands of people around the world decided to collaborate selflessly and join other people they didn't even know, investing their time and energy toward a common cause. The two key elements that awakened and activated the community were the purpose and possibility of co-creating. On the one hand, we shared a common purpose: to curb the pandemic. And, on the other, we decided to move from being observers to main actors. Together, both made the community come together in a common project.

During one of the challenges, a person I hadn't known previously called me and said, "Thank you for launching all this. Now I'm aware that I too can create positive change in the world." At that very moment, I decided to launch Purpose Alliance, initially a community and now also an ecosystem dedicated to empowering extraordinary people and organizations to help them create a better world. At the time of writing (March 2022), we have already carried out more than thirty-five challenges, giving people from all over the world the opportunity to actively participate. I have been able to see firsthand how the power of people multiplies exponentially when we collaborate.

An established organization that can connect with the community has access to a treasure. The benefits are enormous. It connects the organization to an abundance of people who, when moved by a purpose that inspires them, have a very high level of commitment and energy. It also connects the organization with an abundance of ideas and initiatives, as well as with new talent (the new generations are more purpose-oriented than ever), even with new customers and partners who share its purpose. If all this were not enough, it gains positioning in the market and in the world.

However, established organizations must face multiple challenges when it comes to connecting with communities and harnessing their full potential. The first is recognizing the need to look outside for new knowledge and talent. The second is having a purpose really geared towards improving the world so that you can attract the right people. The third is putting purpose into action and creating a space for communities to come together and interact with them appropriately. Finally, in many cases, it will also be necessary to internally manage the organization's immune system's reaction, since some people or areas may feel threatened by including outsiders in creative processes.

The first of the applications developed on Purpose Launchpad was Purpose Challenge, which consists of a process to attract and generate communities and new initiatives around an organization and its purpose. This application has been used to implement all the challenges I mentioned earlier. Like all the applications I mention developed within the Purpose Alliance community, it can be downloaded using the link at the end of the chapter.

Purpose Challenge contemplates four phases:

Figure 4.7. Purpose Challenge Phases

Define the Challenge	→	Promote the Challenge	→	Prepare the Community	→	Co-create with the Community

Source: Prepared by the author

1) *Define the Challenge*

The first step in launching a Purpose Challenge is to define a challenge linked to the organization's purpose that attracts people, entities, and communities we have an interest in connecting with. During this phase, we must think about the results we expect: improving the visibility of the organization, generating innovative ideas, finding new talent, getting new clients, or even a combination of all of these. We must also define what kind of participants we would like to include in the challenge, the dates the different activities will be held, and the necessary logistical aspects for everything to work optimally.

One of the most impactful challenges I have experienced was the one launched by Boston Scientific, a leading manufacturer of medical devices, and the Clínica Bíblica Hospital, the largest and most complete in Costa Rica. Boston Scientific's purpose focuses on transforming people's lives through innovative solutions that improve patients' health. It is making a significant effort to develop digital and other solutions that help them take their purpose to another level. The Clínica Bíblica Hospital has the purpose of saving lives and bringing quality health to all people. After several conversations to align their purposes and the interests of the community, they launched a Purpose Challenge open to individuals and entities that would like to contribute to the next challenge: creating a better future for health in Costa Rica.

2) Promote the Challenge

With the purpose as a flag, there is a series of communication actions to attract people and entities willing to participate in the challenge. Let's look at an example. Spain and other surrounding countries suffered a significant rise in the cost of electricity at the end of 2021, which caused great discomfort in society and the closure of many businesses that couldn't cope with the increase. Cuerva, a small electricity company founded in Granada (Spain) in 1939 by José Cuerva Cobo, and which is currently headed by his two grandsons, Gerardo and Ignacio Cuerva, did not sit idly by. In accordance with its purpose, focused on giving access to energy to transform the world, they created and promoted a Purpose Challenge to design the future of energy in Spain, a challenge that was immediately joined by a large number of people. They promoted it both externally to communities of people motivated by this problem and internally to the people within the organization. In the words of the company's CEO, Ignacio Cuerva, "The challenge is to combine people with a more traditional mentality, who are very good at what they do on a technical level, with people with a fresher approach to create the future of the energy industry."

3) Prepare the Community

Before acting, it is essential to prepare the pitch. We must communicate the reason why the Purpose Challenge is launched, explain how it will work and, above all, provide a common framework for everyone participating to speak the same language. During this phase, open training is offered to all participants so that they have a minimum understanding of innovation methodologies and about the most relevant elements that need to be defined (the eight axes) to generate new initiatives to create a real impact. In addition, it is very important to continue to inspire the participants, often by organizing conferences with relevant people linked in some way to the challenge's purpose and who can offer new perspectives.

Finally, before going to the next phase of the Purpose Challenge, all participants must be welcomed with an inspirational keynote that underlines the purpose's direction and guides all participants towards the next steps.

4) Co-create with the Community

The best way to build long-term relationships with the community is to co-create projects that permanently connect us through initiatives that can have a positive impact on the world and our organization.

To do this, people who have joined the challenge and are prepared to participate will be grouped into teams. Each team will have a multi-hour work session during which they will carry out an ideation process with the mentor's guidance and develop the initiative as far as possible. When defining the initiative, it is advisable to use the eight axes of Purpose Launchpad so as not to leave any important issues in the pipeline. Obviously, it is not possible to fully develop an initiative or evaluate it in the market in just a few hours, so these will be hypotheses awaiting evaluation.

Once the teams have finished defining their initiatives, the ideal would be to hold a general session in which all the proposed initiatives are presented and a group of area experts can provide their input, allowing the teams to begin improving and developing the approach for those initiatives.

From my experience, it is incredible how several initiatives of great value can be generated in a few hours, but the connection that is created with the community, and the people's energy and enthusiasm, is even more surprising. Returning to the example I mentioned earlier, Michael Alvarez, head of Digital Health at Boston Scientific, declared, "We have come together and have established key areas to improve health in Costa Rica. The truth is that I am very inspired to see how people from different backgrounds have come together around this purpose. It has been an honor to be a part of this experience."

Final Thoughts

Ignacio Cuerva once told me that one of the most important challenges when it comes to promoting organizations' impact in the world is communicating it. In life, there are things that cannot be explained in words; it is necessary to experience them. That's why taking action with a challenge based on a common purpose and openly launching it to the world is the best way to make the organization and the community understand that they can work together, not only to generate more business but to create a positive impact on the world that benefits everyone. Remember, the power of community is a treasure within the reach of any organization that has a good purpose.

Key Points

- Communities connect us with an abundance of talent and initiatives that we can't find internally in any organization.
- The power of purpose can attract communities and connect them with an organization to take it to the next level.
- Creating projects in common with the community will generate a strong long-term connection.
- Purpose Launchpad has an application called Purpose Challenge that allows organizations to connect and generate communities linked to their purpose, position themselves in the market, generate synergies with potential customers and partners, and generate initiatives together with the community to create a positive impact.

Resources

- *Purpose Challenge Application*: *www.purposealliance. org/purpose-launchpad/applications/purpose-challenge*
- "The Future of Health in Costa Rica" Impact Case: *www. purposealliance.org/impact-cases/purpose-challenge*

28
Adapting the Habitat
to New Initiatives

The term *personal computer* appeared for the first time in 1975 in an article in *Popular Electronics* magazine. The first of these devices, the Altair 8800, surprised even its creators when it generated thousands of orders in its first month. In fact, the Altair launch generated a new industry for the home computer, which new players soon joined. Among them was the giant IBM, which had already marketed its first desktop microcomputer, the IBM

5100, whose design and price of about $20,000 did not make it accessible as a personal device. The company made several attempts to create a competitive product, bu0,t due to its complex bureaucratic procedures and its slow and expensive production processes (new products normally required between four and five years for development), it always arrived on the market late and poorly. One market analyst, referring to these difficulties, went so far as to say that "getting IBM to launch a personal computer is as difficult as getting an elephant to tap dance."

In 1980, IBM President John Opel, aware of these problems and of the importance of entering this new growth market, decided to do something different. He created an initiative called Project Chess, assigning twelve people with special permissions to bypass IBM's self-imposed protocols and restrictions (which were common at the time). The team, led by Don Estridge, was installed in offices in Boca Raton (Florida), far away from the company's headquarters in New York State. They operated with complete autonomy, sometimes even going completely against IBM's internal policies, such as using components from other manufacturers. The result was the IBM PC introduced on August 12, 1981, which became a bestseller, to the point that *Time* magazine named it "person" of the year in 1982.

The bottom line is that the IBM PC had to be developed in a different environment than the core business because the organization's heavy machinery left no room for exploration. When you try to launch an innovative initiative within an organization, it is common for a kind of immune system to be triggered that attacks innovators and their ideas as if they were a virus. This is not always a negative thing. The system is doing its function, which is to protect the current business, which works well and generates the revenue needed to make the organization viable today. However, parallel exploration is necessary to find the business that will allow the organization's future viability. In fact, properly managing the immune system is not only helpful for finding new sources of income but also new initiatives needed to achieve the organization's purpose.

One of the most important elements we must consider when starting to define the environment of any type of initiative is whether it is an innovative or disruptive project, which are very different concepts. Innovation is about improving something that already exists, while disruption is about doing something totally different from what existed previously. When IBM started working on its first personal computer in the 80s, it was undoubtedly a company that was very good at innovating, as it worked continuously on improving all its products. However, to successfully disrupt, they had to move away from their usual processes. This is one of the keys: innovative initiatives can be carried out within the organization, but disruptive ones need a different perspective, one distant from the organization's core activity.

In any case, whether it is innovation or disruption, it is not enough to develop it correctly; it must also have the right habitat. This is like planting a seed: it will only grow if you plant it in a favorable environment and provide the nutrients it needs, which, in our case, are the external factors that accompany each of the initiative's axes. This is what we call the habitat.

Figure 4.8. Habitat for Innovative/Disruptive Initiatives

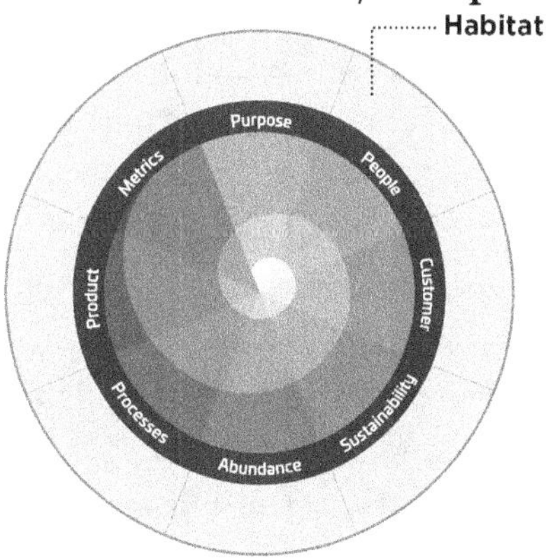

Source: Prepared by the author

The key element in creating a suitable environment for innovation and disruption to emerge within an established organization is leadership. Let's look at an example, that of Guayente Sanmartín, one of HP's main directors, appointed in June 2018 as Global General Manager of Large Format Printing (she is currently the director of their 3D-printing business). Until that time, this type of printer was only available to certain professionals (such as architecture studios) due to their large size and high price. Guayente defined a new purpose focused on "democratizing large-format printing" and began to create the right circumstances for this to happen, placing special emphasis on cultural change and collaboration with external experts (including Corina Almagro, a certified Purpose Launchpad mentor). This led to the launch of a new printer model that cost almost 50 percent less than previous models, making it more accessible. According to Sanmartín herself, "In order for the new initiatives of the organization to be developed correctly, the leader must define a clear purpose, provide the necessary rigor, and generate the right environment."

The rigor when developing an innovative or disruptive initiative can be provided by the Purpose Launchpad framework itself. The right environment will depend on how we manage everything related to the initiative's eight axes within the development context. Purpose Launchpad has its own tool called Purpose Launchpad Habitat Canvas that makes it easier for an organization's leaders to ask key questions when defining a particular initiative's proper environment. This tool can be downloaded using the link at the end of the chapter.

In case the new initiatives have an external origin, as happens when an organization acquires a startup, it will also be essential to consider what the appropriate habitat is for this type of project, which usually already arrives with a very marked culture of its own. In fact, in most cases, the ideal is to connect them with the ecosystem without changing or altering their conditions or the way they function. This is what Facebook did when acquiring WhatsApp: maintain the startup's autonomy and simply connect the necessary elements with the general ecosystem to favor synergies and enhance their common purpose.

Below are some indications on how to adapt the habitat for each of an initiative's eight axes developed by an established organization (remember: Purpose, People, Customers, Sustainability, Abundance, Product, Processes, and Metrics).

Habitat for the Purpose Axis

The main organization's purpose must be maintained. Otherwise, we run the risk of evolving in a different direction. However, initiatives must be free to define their vision and mission, which will give them their own identity. In fact, in purpose-oriented ecosystems driven by an organization, we typically find a purpose common to all initiatives and a specific vision and mission for each one.

Let's look at the example of Decathlon. This is a company strongly oriented to the purpose of making the benefits of practicing sports sustainably accessible to as many people as possible. Decathlon Spain's disruption team's initiatives uphold this purpose, even though some have been incubated away from the core business (as IBM did with its personal computer). José María Santos, responsible for new business models at Decathlon Spain, sums it up as follows: "When creating new initiatives, it is necessary to build a team aligned with the organization's purpose and isolate it from the rest of the company so that it can move forward properly." Proof that the purpose is indeed very clear to the whole team is evident in the words of Francisco Martínez, his right-hand man: "Since its birth, Decathlon has always had a very strong purpose, and the leaders of the company have always been the first to preach it so that the rest of the company and the initiatives are mobilized in the same direction".

Habitat for the People Axis

Ideally, all initiatives within the organization and the ecosystem should share the same community so that it grows with new contributions and generates synergies among its members. Therefore, the organization's job in creating the right environment for initiatives will be to provide them with mechanisms that allow it to access the general community, albeit progressively—that is, first on an experimental basis in the Exploration and Evaluation phases and then completely in the Impact phase.

Another key related to the People Axis will be to provide the initiative with the right team. They must have an exploratory mindset during the early phases, which is not easy, because execution-oriented people predominate in established organizations. The team must have the necessary dedication and focus to develop the new initiative. When this is disruptive, it must have total dedication, since it is very difficult to be part of the organization's main business's normal workday, which tends to usually be in execution mode and at times be focused on developing a new initiative, which is usually in search mode. Having a good team with complete availability is precisely one of the most critical elements when it comes to guaranteeing or maximizing an initiative's chances of success.

It will be essential to review issues such as each team member's type of contract or employment, even if they must have some participation in these initiatives' ownership, since they are still intrapreneurs (entrepreneurs within the environment of an organization). If we want the initiative to move forward in the best possible way, we will have to take care of the team and give it the space and conditions it really needs. After all, as José María Santos said, "Business alone is nothing. What's important is the people who work on it."

Habitat for the Customer Axis

Ideally, the initiative should develop its own customers from the start and not focus on the current customer base, as it could find itself misdirected towards the wrong market segment. As the general director of large printers at HP, Guayente Sanmartín points out, "Understanding who your new customers are now and what they really want, as well as knowing who your new competitors are, is key to fitting a new initiative into the market."

Sometimes, it is recommended that the main organization provide the new initiative with access to its customer base to evaluate hypotheses and assess which customer segments interest it, which may be similar or totally different from the organization's. To do this, it is possible that the resistance of the commercial team to share its customers with the new initiative may have to be overcome. That is why it is advisable to do it in phases: if the initiative is in the Exploration phase, allow only the team of the new initiative to have conversations but without going further or trying to sell. It is also advisable to create appropriate incentive systems that align the organization's business teams with those of the new initiative. This is what some large retail chains did, for example, when they began to launch their own platforms, which were seen internally as competition for the physical stores. In the end, they agreed that, if a customer located in a physical store's geographical area placed an online order, the sale would go to that establishment.

Habitat for the Sustainability Axis

In 2014, Facebook decided to buy WhatsApp for a whopping $19 billion and include it in its ecosystem. It was, and in most countries continues to be, a free app, so its very limited income is nowhere near enough to support itself. However, the value it generates in terms of data and users for the Facebook ecosystem is invaluable. Its acquisition, along with that of other companies such as Instagram, was key to Facebook's and its entire ecosystem's further development.

Most traditional organizations don't make this type of investment because they don't understand that the ecosystem model implies that not all its elements provide the same type of value. As in biological ecosystems, in which not all living beings generate oxygen, in an ecosystem of organizations, not all entities generate income or are self-sustaining. Now, that does not mean that they are not fundamental to the balance of the ecosystem. They may be needed to generate data, interconnect community members, etc. Therefore, regarding the economic sustainability of certain initiatives, the organization may have to provide the necessary resources for their operation, even if they're not profitable economically, if they provide necessary value for the overall ecosystem.

From the point of view of the Sustainability axis, it is also important to remember that any initiative must bring positive value to society and its environment. In fact, there are more and more organizations that understand the importance of sustainably carrying out their activity. An example of this is Sener, the first engineering company registered in Spain and currently a world leader in areas such as infrastructure, energy, naval, and aerospace. Aware of the importance of carrying out its activity sustainably, it has not only internally promoted sustainability but also with all its clients, with special emphasis on the circular economy and sustainability projects. Sener has its own methodology called S^3 through which it comes to providing its clients with comprehensive sustainability solutions, either within the framework of its own organization or by connecting them with its network of clients within its own ecosystem, whose purpose is focused on creating a sustainable world.

In terms of social and environmental sustainability, it will be essential not only to evaluate the initiative on its own but to see it as a whole and find ways to generate circular sustainability models within the ecosystem of the organization itself or even by connecting with external ecosystems. If our main organization or any of our initiatives are not environmentally sustainable, we could evaluate the possibility of launching a new initiative that uses its waste as raw material. A possibility in line with the above is that the organization promotes initiatives that are not sustainable at an economic level but that have a positive impact in environmental terms. In this case, the objective would be to ensure the overall sustainability of the entire organization, since the initiative would translate into a better social positioning that could generate greater income for the organization.

In short, we must seek balance for the entire ecosystem, understanding that not all initiatives and elements of our ecosystem must necessarily be sustainable at all three levels (economic, social, and environmental) on their own. In relation to how to achieve and measure triple sustainability and the impact of organizations in the world, I recommend that, if you have not already done so, read the chapters from the third part entitled "Achieve Triple Sustainability" and "Measure Your Progress and Your Impact on the World."

Habitat for the Abundance Axis

One of the main reasons we launch new initiatives is precisely to find new sources of abundance. It is therefore obvious that initiatives must find their own sources of abundance. However, sometimes some of the established organization's resources can be very beneficial for the new initiative. In the words of Guayente Sanmartín, "The main organization's internal technological infrastructure can be a great driver of new business." The key is to act with an abundance mindset and not merely provide access to those internal resources but help the initiative connect with external sources, because, no matter how large the organization is, they will always be limited. If we do so, we will be able to access new spaces and markets where we do not have a presence, which will expand the horizons of our ecosystem. In fact, as Sanmartín points out again, "The ultimate reason why new initiatives are launched around an established organization and its purpose is to expand the business and the impact we are already generating."

Habitat for the Process Axis

In terms of processes, the way in which the organization must generate the right environment for new initiatives comes down to one concept: autonomy. Especially during the early phases, focused on exploration, it will be critical that the people in charge of the new project can do things their own way, even if it seems like they're trying to break the rules of the main organization. As Sener's director of innovation, Oscar Julia, comments, "The company needs entrepreneurs when it comes to launching innovative and disruptive initiatives, and the organization must give them the right space so that they can do things their way." And Elvira Garcia, director of engineering and energy at Sener, adds, "We must help the organization's people to lose their fear of properly transforming themselves, and so it is necessary to give them the necessary autonomy."

The level of autonomy will depend on the initiative's stage and the exact place in its development. If the initiative is in a phase of Exploration or Evaluation, it must have a very high level of autonomy, not only to achieve the necessary speed and agility but also to face failure and learning as part of the team's day-to-day work.

On the other hand, if the initiative has a strong disruptive character and is far from the main organization, it will be essential that you develop your own processes from the beginning and make them evolve independently, since it will most likely end up becoming a new organization. Josu Aramburu, responsible for Sener's sustainability line, says, "The key is to give initiatives the degree of autonomy they need, which does not mean that they are totally independent."

Habitat for the Product Axis

Remember that, in new initiatives, we must develop the customer before the product. It's not about putting in existing technology or products but developing something new that people really want. Elvira Garcia comments that, "in new initiatives, it is necessary to develop the value propositions and products that the new generations want."

In addition to developing the right product, you must do it the right way. To do this, the initiative team is ideally responsible for understanding the customer and making the first versions of the product and then, over time, create a product development team of their own. In this way, the development of both the customer and the product will be truly aligned, and everything will be carried out with the required agility.

It is possible that there will come a time when the initiative is ready to scale. This is when the main organization can offer you processes and infrastructures that allow you to improve your production and your arrival to market, but this will depend on each case. However, in general, it is preferable to keep the creation of new products and lines of business outside the more traditional areas of the organization, since the "immune system" could always be lurking, and the established processes of the main organization may not be agile enough to accompany the development of innovative or disruptive products.

Habitat for the Metrics Axis

The key to metrics is for the lead organization to understand the initiative's stage. If it is at a very early stage, for example, it makes no sense to ask for economic returns—or even a forecast for the future. The important thing is not the data but that the initiative team shares its learnings with the organization to verify that it is advancing properly. In fact, if the initiative is successfully developed, it is very possible that the objectives achieved will be totally unexpected.

As we saw in part three in the metrics chapter, beyond financial metrics, which indicate the initiative's economic performance, and the innovation metrics, which show us if we are advancing in terms of generating value to the market, it will be essential to connect the sustainability and impact metrics with the whole organization and the ecosystem in general to see the initiative's contribution to the organization's starshot. As we have already seen, this impact metric, like the purpose, is shared by all the initiatives that make up the ecosystem.

In the chapters dedicated to the generation and evolution of initiatives (such as startups and new products), we saw a tool called Purpose Launchpad Canvas that makes it easier for innovation teams to define and work on the eight axes, and here we will similarly look at a tool called Purpose Launchpad Habitat Canvas that helps organizations' leaders define and create the right environment for innovative initiatives by following the guidelines we have seen throughout this chapter.

Figure 4.9. Purpose Launchpad Habitat Canvas

Axis	Initiatives	Habitat
◈ Purpose		
People		
Customers		
Sustainability		
Abundance		
Processes		
Product		
Metrics		

Source: Prepared by the author

The Purpose Launchpad Habitat Canvas tool will help us ask ourselves the key questions to create the right environment for our initiatives. However, it is essential to keep in mind that the key is not the tool we use but our mindset, and, in this sense, the important thing will be to always remember the importance of creating the environment that the different initiatives need for their correct development.

Final Thoughts

In an established organization, leaders are the ones who must drive change—not necessarily by directly leading and managing new initiatives but by generating the right environment so that they can evolve appropriately.

In the same way that new initiatives arise with an innovative or disruptive character to achieve results that had not been achieved before, the organization and its leaders will have to ensure these initiatives can be developed in a totally different way than the rest of the organization operates.

In this regard, leaders must be courageous. On one occasion, years ago, I heard Ignacio Cuerva, who I mentioned in the previous chapter, say with great certainty, "I think that, in the future, energy will be free." This was said by the head of a company whose main source of income is the commercialization of energy, which shows that he was very brave in turning a traditional family-owned energy company into an ecosystem with global ambition. As Abraham Lincoln said, the only way to predict the future is to create it. That is why we will dedicate the last chapter of this part to explaining how to create an organization's future.

Key Points

- The leaders of organizations are responsible for providing the right environment for the correct development of initiatives.
- Depending on the degree of the initiative's innovation and disruption, they must be developed nearer or further away from the traditional business.
- New initiatives must maintain the purpose of the organization but with their own vision and mission.
- The new initiatives team must have the right space, availability, and focus.
- Customers of new initiatives may belong to a new market or to the organization's current customer base. In the second case, it will be necessary to manage the possible reluctance of commercial teams to share their contacts.
- All of an ecosystem's initiatives may not be self-sustainable at the financial level, but the entire ecosystem must be not only economically but also socially and environmentally sustainable.
- The initiative must enjoy autonomy in its processes.
- The product of the initiative does not have to use the current assets and products of the organization and should be developed by the new team.
- The metrics reported by the initiative to the organization will depend on its status, although all initiatives in an ecosystem must contribute to the entire ecosystem's purpose and therefore to its starshot.

Resources

- Purpose Launchpad Habitat Canvas: *www.purposealli-ance.org/resources/purpose-launchpad-habitat-canvas*
- "The Evolution of Cuerva from a Traditional Company to an Ecosystem Managed with Purpose Launchpad" Impact Case: *www.purposealliance.org/impact-cases/ecosystem-management-with-purpose-launchpad*

29
Creating the Future
of the Organization

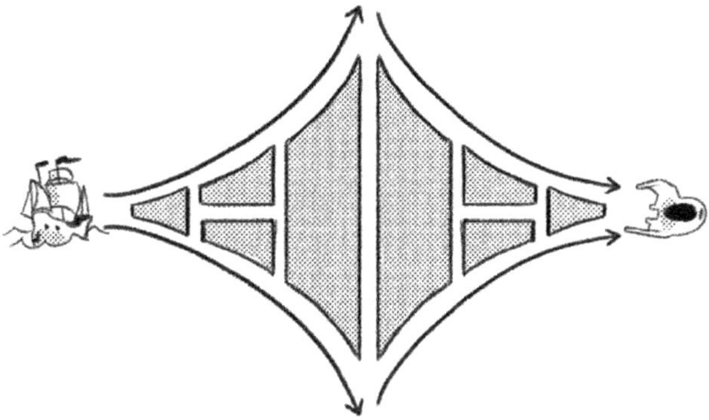

On April 1, 1976, Steve Jobs, Steve Wozniak, and Ronald Wayne founded Apple. That same year, they presented their first personal computer, the Apple I, which was later followed by new models. In 1980, the company ranked among the three largest personal computer companies in the world. As we saw earlier, IBM entered that business in 1981, and the market became increasingly competitive. The difficult situation generated great tensions between Steve Jobs and the company's top executive, which caused the former to leave Apple in 1985. Over the next few years, the Apple brand performed mediocrely and even nearly went bankrupt in the early 1990s. Fortunately, Jobs returned to Apple in 1997, and the company soon recovered the essence that had made it so popular and successful in its beginnings. That same year, he gave us a magnificent speech in which he explained how he planned to change Apple's decline, as, at the time, it did not have a very good image. His proposal was to reposition and develop the organization around its "core value," which he described as the raison d'être of the organization—that is, its purpose. He explained that it was a mistake to position an organization based on its products and services or, worse, based on the characteristics that make those products and services better than those of the competition. The important thing is to communicate the place it occupies in the world and the reason why it exists.

In that speech, Jobs explained with great eloquence that Apple does not make computers for people to do their work (although they also know how to do that) but because they "believe that people with passion can change the world for the better." He added, "The market is a totally different place than it was a decade ago, and Apple is totally different. Apple's place in it is totally different. And, believe me, the products and the distribution strategy and the manufacturing are totally different, and we understand that. But our core values have not changed. The things Apple believed in in its early days are the same things it believes in today."

That speech was not just a marketing masterclass; it was a statement of intent. In the years that followed, Apple continued to evolve around its purpose. Along the way, it made important moves, such as the one that led it to ally with Microsoft. As Jobs himself explained, "If we want to move forward and see Apple healthy and prosperous again, we have to put aside some things, like the idea that, for Apple to win, Microsoft has to lose. For Apple to win, it must do a very good job. And, if others help us, great, because we need all the help we can get; and, if we screw up and don't do a good job, it's not the fault of others—it's our own fault. I think it's a very important change of perspective. If we want Microsoft Office on the Mac, we better treat the company that produces it with a little gratitude … It's about making Apple healthy."

Over the next few years, as is known, Apple launched all sorts of products and services around its "core value," moving further and further away from the concept of industry and becoming an ecosystem. It even changed its name from Apple Computer, Inc., to simply Apple, Inc. It reinvented itself and created its own future, becoming the first company to reach one trillion dollars of market capitalization in 2018.

Apple's story can help any organization evolve. Today's world is different from tomorrow's, and that forces us to create the future of our organizations to remain relevant. Organizations, and especially their leaders, need to be aware of how critical it is to evolve continuously and focus on creating positive impact. In the words of Paolo Sacchi, CEO of Ransa, "The great challenge of today's companies is not only to be an organization that generates a great profit but to help society improve."

However, as I mentioned in the previous chapter, when an established organization tries to renovate its immune system, it becomes activated and attacks. This is possibly one of the reasons why, in most industries, major disruptions usually come from outside. Many established organizations are aware of the need to transform, but they don't know where to go or how to do it. What they do begin to see is that it is not enough to focus on one or several particular groups of people; it is necessary to reach all the people in the organization and transform their mindset.

Another problem that organizations always face when launching change-oriented initiatives is that, sooner or later, they lose energy and often end up disappearing. The reasons are varied, but. in general terms. they are related to having or not having the right environment for initiatives to flourish, as we saw in the previous chapter.

In my first book, *Exponential Transformation*, I presented a ten-week process called ExO Sprint that has been adopted by thousands of companies around the world to modernize traditional organizations. The first company to adopt it was INTERprotección, a Mexican family-owned insurance business that was aware of the disruption that is taking place in the insurance industry. After implementing the methodology, the company launched new initiatives, some of them in new markets where they were not present, oriented to the final consumer (B2B), generating thousands of dollars of daily income in a few weeks. As Francisco Casanueva, CEO of INTERprotección, said, "We were in the perfect place to be disrupted, but we didn't even know where to start. ExO Sprint was the answer; it was our best investment to move forward. We managed to completely transform our culture, breaking down borders and opening a new world of innovation. Our entire mindset has changed. It pushed us to bring out the best in ourselves, and now our competitors are wondering what happened."

ExO Sprint evolved, like everything in life. After the experience of recent years and the changes that the environment has experienced, I decided to create an improved version of this type of process that gave rise to a new Purpose Launchpad application called Impact Sprint. Its goal is to help organizations create their own future, adapt to the changing environment, and generate a positive impact, both in their business and in the world. Throughout this chapter, I will present the core pillars of Impact Sprint so that you can implement it entirely, which is what I recommend, since no one can ensure its operation unless it's implemented comprehensively. You could also take those elements that interest you and integrate them into your current organizational transformation approaches.

Some of Impact Sprint's most relevant changes and contributions include the following:

- It helps organizations evolve into an ecosystem of their own or connect with existing ecosystems, always keeping purpose at the center to access real abundance. To some extent, the process emulates the one that Apple followed and that we saw earlier in this chapter.
- It manages the organization's immune system so that it can maintain and drive the current business while exploring new business and opportunities.
- It allows everyone in the organization to participate and get involved in some way, which generates a massive change of mindset.
- It involves the external community in the evolution process, allowing it to contribute ideas and generate a stronger connection with the environment.
- It allows you to incorporate both existing initiatives and those that are generated throughout the process.
- It customizes each initiative's evolution process according to your specific needs.
- It generates the right environment for each of the initiatives, thus creating the necessary structure to form its own balanced ecosystem or connect with the most appropriate external ecosystems.

Impact Sprint includes the applications we have seen in the previous chapters, making it the most complete application of the framework. In its early stages, it has a divergent approach to generating or identifying many initiatives; in its second half, on the other hand, it incorporates a convergent approach to favor the evolution of the most promising initiatives, create the right environment for them, and build the future of the organization. Conversely, it combines a top-down approach in which the organization's leaders must support the process with a bottom-up approach in which several teams of people in the organization are empowered to generate different initiatives; the rest of the people in the organization will be able to follow the development of the process in real time and provide feedback to the teams that are developing the initiatives.

Its implementation requires at least six weeks, although, as I will explain at the end of the chapter, it can also be executed continuously to achieve permanent results. At the end of the chapter, you will also find a link to download a document where it is described in detail. Meanwhile, we will review the main steps below, summarized as follows:

Figure 4.10. Top Steps of the Impact Sprint App

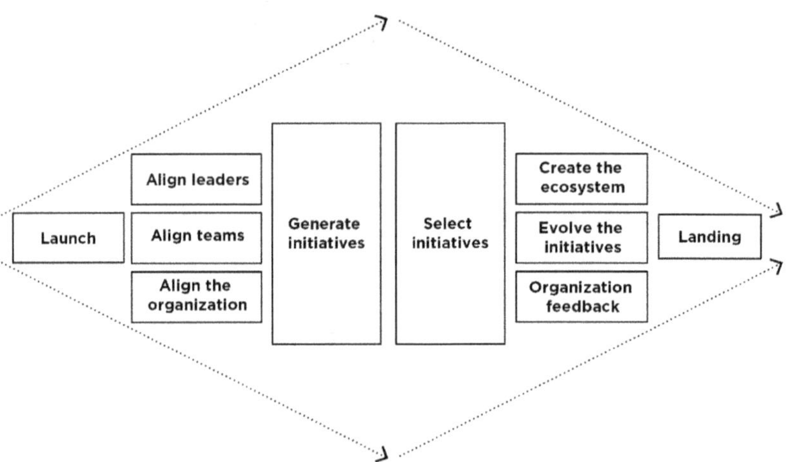

Source: Prepared by the author

Launch

Launch consists of waking the organization up, holding a conference for everyone in the company where we recall the reason for its existence—that is, its purpose (if it does not exist yet, the first thing to do is to define it). This conference, as with Steve Jobs's famous speech I referred to earlier, also aims to inspire everyone in the organization and encourage them to get involved in defining their future.

The session should be led by the head of the organization, who can be accompanied by an external person who explains in detail the Impact Sprint process. It is not only about informing but also about motivating. Francisco Casanueva, CEO of INTERprotección, explains it this way: "When we create something new, we generate the same adrenaline with which explorers and astronauts lived. As human beings, we are excited about what is not yet created, what does not yet exist. And, if you are able to live it and feel it, you will infect the people around you." This is precisely what the Impact Sprint launch is all about.

Align Leaders

The partial top-down approach Impact Sprint relies on is for organizational leaders to support the process. This will only be possible if they are aligned with the reason behind it and are familiar with the approach and the tools. To align them, a series of workshops will be held in which we make sure that they all understand the importance of the process and are on board with it.

It will be essential to explain the different phases of an innovative or disruptive initiative (Exploration, Evaluation, and Impact) so that they understand the type of environment that each requires. I also recommend that activities be carried out with tools such as the Habitats Initiatives Canvas.

In the second half of Impact Sprint, leaders will have to bring all these theory and preparatory dynamics into real practice to create the right environment for initiatives, so the sooner they understand the process, the better.

Align Teams

The partial bottom-up approach on which Impact Sprint is based is so that the people who wish to do so can actively participate in the process, generating and developing initiatives in its later stages. To do this, they must understand the reasons why continuous evolution is necessary and know the basic concepts and tools that will be used later.

During the initial conference, we will have already explained the process that will be followed in detail, giving all members of the organization or certain specific groups the opportunity to participate in it actively. It is essential that participation in this type of process is not imposed but rather that the people express their intention to participate in one way or another. From my experience, the energy experienced in the process and the results are totally different if the participants have been chosen by the organization's managers (push approach) from when they have participated on their own (pull approach).

Once we have the different groups of participants—who may be involved at different levels—we must ensure that they clearly understand the reasons we are putting this mechanism in place. The initial conference should have helped in this regard, but quick, timely actions do not usually have a lasting effect. The best way to achieve this is with practice. The ideal is to have basic content available so that the participants in the evolution process can know more about its basic elements and can be prepared to offer their opinions at any time.

The team members who will have an active role generating the innovative and disruptive initiatives during the next phase of the process will participate in a practical workshop where they will have the opportunity to learn about the eight axes and the three phases of Purpose Launchpad. In addition, they will simulate the process of generating initiatives and their evolution, which will allow them to begin seeing the extraordinary possibilities of the organization's evolution and begin to understand the great power they have in their hands as the main actors of that process.

Align the Organization

It is important that everyone in the organization is given the opportunity to be involved in the process. For different reasons, they won't all be able to be actively involved in generating and developing initiatives, but it will at least be important that they have the option to follow the initiatives' evolution and provide feedback, which will not only generate value for the initiatives but also the collective feeling of co-creation, which will facilitate the subsequent implementation of all initiatives and reduce the immune system's reaction to innovation. And, of course, this should be ensured so that everyone who wants to get involved in the process will be offered basic general training.

Generate Initiatives

It is time to act and begin considering the different initiatives to create a better future for the organization and for the world. We will do this by forming teams composed of people who have previously expressed their interest. A team can include people from all levels of the organization, and, within the team, they must participate regardless of their position. For everything to flow properly, it is advisable that they be guided by a certified Purpose Launchpad mentor, who will help them generate the appropriate initiatives for the organization's purpose and true objectives.

It is also possible to include people outside the organization. Opening the process to the community can bring enormous value, not only when it comes to generating ideas but also to connect with new talent that could eventually join the organization or any of the initiatives.

The generation of initiatives can be done in a single day, since it is not necessary to define and develop the details. The recommendation is that each team generate one or two initiatives with a minimum approach that explains how each of the eight axes would be applied.

In short, this part of the process consists of a collective brainstorming exercise aimed at obtaining as many ideas as possible. Some of these will end up being invalidated, and others will evolve to generate great value, but they will all be part of the organization's evolutionary path.

Select Initiatives

Astronauts who have gone out into space describe the moment they are able to view the entire Earth as one of the most transformative experiences of their lives, since, for the first time, they are truly aware of our planet's magnitude. They experience a deep sense of unity and common purpose. This is called an overview effect and is often experienced in the session where the results obtained in the previous stage are presented, which helps us understand the organization's immense potential.

It's time to start converging. Even if it is painful, we must discard some initiatives and select only the most promising ones. It is a task that must be performed by the team of organization leaders depending on what the goal is. You can also ask for the general opinion of everyone in the organization with a digital consultation system so that they can vote for their preferred initiatives. In this way, we will not only generate a feeling of collective co-creation, but we will really get very valuable feedback.

When making the selection, it is important to remember that not all initiatives have to be self-sustainable at an economic level or even generate income on their own. The important thing is that they play a role in ensuring the balance of the ecosystem and the evolution of the organization.

Following the process of selecting initiatives, we should hold a general session in which we communicate the results to the entire organization and offer those who wish to do so the possibility of participating in the next phase. In fact, it is very possible that, at that moment, we will discover new intrapreneurs in the organization, whom we must empower to achieve extraordinary results.

Creating the Ecosystem

It is important to generate the right initiatives that allows the organization to evolve to eventually become a purpose-oriented ecosystem or connect with other external ecosystems, such as generating the right environment and structure for initiatives to evolve correctly. To this end, we will hold a series of periodic sessions in parallel with the evolution of initiatives that I will explain below to ensure that they have the right environment. In this case, it is about directly applying everything we saw in the chapter "Adapting the Habitat to New Initiatives" by involving the leaders of the organization, since part of their responsibility is to generate the right context for these initiatives to flourish.

First, it will be important to start by defining how people will participate in the evolution process itself, since they could accrue over time (so as not to take them away from the business) or even dedicate themselves completely to the process for a few weeks. This was the case of an Impact Sprint for Rassini, a company which has always been aware of the importance of continuous evolution. In fact, it began as a mining company and ended up becoming a leader in the design and production of suspension and brake components in the automotive industry. Rassini's leaders decided that a group of people from the organization would exclusively dedicate themselves for a few weeks to evolve the initiatives, which allowed them to advance more in less time. Obviously, it is not necessary to reach this extreme, since a significant advancement can be achieved by dedicating only two or three hours per day and per person, but it is important that the rules of the game are defined during the process of evolution and, above all, that the team of leaders defines and implements the ecosystem model and the environment that the initiatives will follow during their evolution after Impact Sprint ends. This will be the key to achieving permanent results.

Evolution of Initiatives

People who have expressed interest in participating in this phase, grouped into teams focused on a single initiative, will work together with their mentors to develop the initiative by applying everything seen in the third part ("Evolution of Startups and New Products").

For each of the projects, a series of Sprint Purpose Launchpads will be set in motion in which the mentor will analyze the status of the initiative weekly as regards the eight axes and propose a series of actions to be carried out (backlog) so that the team members can continue to advance during the rest of the week. Throughout the process, team members will focus on exploring and evaluating the initiative to find the right path, invalidating certain hypotheses (or even the entire initiative) or solidifying the initiative in a new product or service (or even in a new startup) that generates great value and positive impact.

This phase is one of the most important of the whole process, because not only is there a profound evolution of the initiatives but also of the people who invest their time and energy. In fact, they tend to experience such a profound evolution that they become core assets of the organization.

Organizational Feedback

Together with the initiatives' evolution, it is important to enable the necessary mechanisms so that everyone in the organization who wishes to do so and has previously received the general training can give their opinion in a structured way and add value to the initiatives that are being developed by the different teams.

Landing

The end of the process is to integrate all the elements to create the future of the organization. After the generation and evolution of initiatives that have been carried out in the previous phases, now is the time to put our feet on the ground, analyze the advances, and continue making decisions about the structure of the ecosystem and about the initiatives that have evolved. The leaders, who have played a very active role throughout the process, observing weekly the evolution of the initiatives and designing the right environment based on their needs, will analyze in detail the overall picture, the continuous feedback received, and the circumstances of the company to decide which initiatives will continue. They will also make decisions about these initiatives' structures and environments, which may be internal for those with an innovative approach or external for the most disruptive.

The ideal is to hold another general closing session in which the results are shared and the decisions announced. This session can be quite transcendental, since it will show everyone in the organization that Impact Sprint was not just another process but has really marked a turning point in the organization, with tangible results and actions.

Final Thoughts

Creating the future of an organization requires an ongoing evolution process in order to adapt to the environment's circumstances. The key is to integrate it into the organization's DNA. And ,when I say integrate it, I don't mean integrating a process; I mean continuously evolving the culture and mindset of people at all levels of the organization. It is essential to always keep in mind the reason for the existence of the organization and keep that purpose front and center. You can change its activity, even all its products and services, but the reason it was born will always be the same.

So, if what we want is to grow the business of our organization, we must bear in mind that exponential growth is not sustainable (our planet is warning us about it). No industry supports continuous exponential growth, as there is a limit to the size of the market itself. As we have seen in the Impact Sprint approach, the right way to take our business to the next level is through regenerative growth, taking advantage of the abundance of opportunities that our purpose offers us and generating new initiatives around it to grow in a sustainable way and, at the same time, create a positive impact on the world.

Going back to where we started this last chapter, Apple was founded to support passionate people who want to change the world. Even their logo represents this essence. The famous bitten apple is a tribute to Alan Turing, considered one of the fathers of computer science and artificial intelligence, whose role during World War II was fundamental in creating a machine that deciphered Nazi codes. It is estimated that, thanks to his work, the war was shortened between two and four years, saving more than 21 million lives. His career ended suddenly in 1952 after being prosecuted for homosexuality, and two years later he died after biting into a poisoned apple.

Apple was born with the intention of supporting people like Alan Turing and encouraging them to continue changing the world. This was explained by Steve Jobs himself in his famous presentation of 1997, in which he marked the way for the future of Apple:

"Here's to the crazy ones, the misfits, the rebels,
the troublemakers, the round pegs in the square holes.
The ones who see things differently.
They're not fond of rules, and they have
no respect for the status quo.
You can quote them, disagree with them,
glorify, or vilify them. About the only thing you
can't do is ignore them, because they change things.
They push the human race forward.
And, while some see them as the crazy ones, we see genius.
Because the ones who are crazy enough to think
they can change the world are the ones who do."

Key Points

- The key to creating an organization's future is to put its purpose at the center and evolve its people's mindsets.
- Traditional organizational models are evolving into purpose-oriented ecosystems. Organizations can generate their own ecosystem or connect to existing ones.
- When it comes to creating the future of an organization, there are many challenges, such as managing the immune system's reaction to change, changing the mindset, identifying and developing the right initiatives, or creating the right environment for these initiatives to culminate successfully.
- Impact Sprint is a Purpose Launchpad application that presents important novelties and contributions with respect to previous processes. It helps organizations create their own future to adapt to the changing environment and create a positive impact, both in their business and in the world.
- When creating the future of an organization, we must think about how to positively impact the business and the world. Only organizations that do so will continue to be relevant.
- The evolution of an organization to create its future must be continuous.

Resources

- *Impact Sprint Application*: *www.purposealliance.org/purpose-launchpad/applications/impact-sprint*
- "Creating the future of MVS" Impact Case: *www.purpose-alliance.org/impact-cases/impact-sprint*

Afterword

Positive Impact: That is the Question

I started this book somewhat atypically for a text aimed at entrepreneurs, innovators, and organization leaders: asking you to think about yourself. My intention was for you to reflect on who you are, who you want to become, and on the reasons why you do what you do. I also intended that you become aware that nowadays you have access to tools that didn't exist until recently and to an enormous range of possibilities. Whatever your current occupation, your age, or where you live, you have more tools and resources to change the world than anyone has had in the past.

In the first chapters, I also asked you to ponder your personal purpose and to leverage it, to give the best of yourself and live a meaningful life. Purpose, however, is useless if it is not activated, if we do not move from words to action. Therefore, I have dedicated much of the book to explaining how to activate your internal purpose through the development of new initiatives or the evolution of established organizations, vehicles we can use to create a positive impact on the world.

I have dedicated the bulk of the book to explaining how to use the Purpose Launchpad framework to launch new initiatives (startups or new products) or to facilitate the evolution of an existing organization, always acting to create a positive impact. And I have insisted that the most important thing, beyond methodologies and tools, is to evolve your own mindset and the mindsets of those accompanying you in your projects. This goal is as simple to state as it is difficult to put into practice: not only to do things right but also to do the right things.

This is precisely the idea represented by the Impact Pyramid, which I would like to reiterate here in closing:

Figure A.1. Impact Pyramid

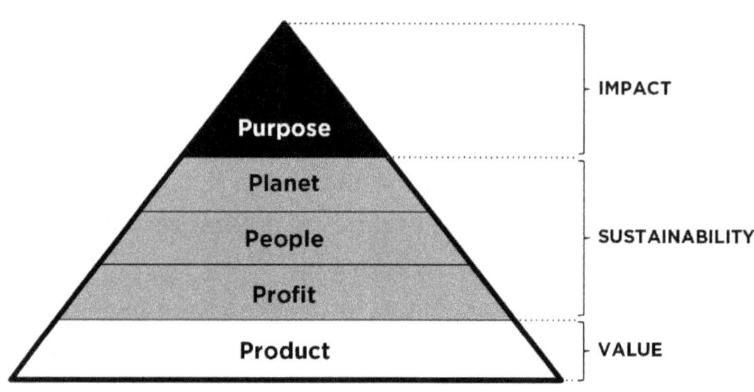

Source: prepared by the author

This pyramid presents a hierarchy that helps us comprehensively understand the concept of impact. At its base is the value we give to our customers through our products; this is basic for any initiative. Next comes the economic benefit we obtain, which enables us to be viable and operate sustainably at a social and environmental level. And, finally, when we have all these elements forming a solid foundation of triple sustainability, we have the positive contribution to the world, in line with our purpose.

Projects that rise to the top of the pyramid will not only create a positive impact on the world but also on themselves, since raising the level of the project will expand the magnitude of the benefits.

Impact is subjective, and it's not always possible to determine whether it is positive or not. My advice is that, to determine it, rely on your own perspective and the perspective of the people who will be directly or indirectly affected by your activity. You should also always be guided by the following maxim: "Treat others as you would like them to treat you."

Remember, you change the world. You do it every day as you interact with the world, directly or through initiatives or organizations that you are a part of. It is up to you to evolve constantly, just as the environment does. It's up to you to connect with abundance and leverage it. It's up to you to do things right and to do the right things. It is up to you to create positive impact—in your life, in your projects, and in the world.

Resources for Creating
a Positive Impact

The Purpose Alliance

On multiple occasions throughout the book, I have mentioned the Purpose Alliance, so by now you may well know that it is a community to empower extraordinary people and organizations to create a better world—people like you who try to develop projects that generate a positive impact on the world.

The Purpose Alliance community, made up of purpose-oriented people, provides access to different types of tools and content to facilitate your project development. It also helps you keep updating your mindset, because, as you know, the most important thing is not the tools or the technology but your mindset.

The Purpose Alliance has evolved into a purpose-oriented ecosystem. It began with the organization of a series of Purpose Challenges, in which the community generated initiatives responding to a series of global challenges. But since, it is not enough to have good ideas—they must be developed—the Purpose Alliance Evolver was launched to take the various initiatives to the next level. Then Purpose Alliance Services was created to empower, through the right mindset, established organizations seeking to have a positive impact on their business and the world.

The Purpose Alliance Academy also emerged from this ecosystem, offering Purpose-Launchpad-based high-quality training and certification to different types of profiles, basically purpose-oriented people who want to create a positive impact on the world.

Figure X.1. The Purpose Alliance Ecosystem

Source: prepared by the author

It is very possible that, by the time you read these lines, everything has continued to evolve and that there are new initiatives within the Purpose Alliance ecosystem. The only thing that is sure to prevail is its purpose, for it is what unites the community and drives it to create a positive impact through mutual collaboration and support. You can learn more about Purpose Alliance at the following link: www.purposealliance.org

Purpose Launchpad Certifications

Purpose Launchpad is, in short, a framework and a mindset to help you create a positive impact on the world and on your life. There is nothing more transcendent than living a life with purpose, and, to do this, it is essential to activate your purpose so that you can integrate it into your daily life.

If you are an entrepreneur, it will be essential to align your startups with your purpose. If you work for an organization, it will also be important to feel that your contribution is aligned with your purpose and that you help your organization to be purpose oriented. In fact, if you are a leader within an organization, it will also be critical that you understand how to manage cultural change, innovation, and the organization's own evolution by creating the right environment. If you are a consultant, it is crucial that you can bring the latest advances in innovation techniques to your clients and, above all, that you help them evolve their mindset. If you are an investor, through your, purpose you can find a way to invest your money to generate a positive impact on the world, which will undoubtedly help you considerably multiply your profitability. Remember that the greatest business opportunities are often related to humanity's greatest challenges. No matter who you are, at Purpose Alliance Academy, you will find a certification program that will allow you to gain a specific understanding of Purpose Launchpad and acquire the right mindset to create that positive impact in the world and in your life.

Keep in mind that these certification programs will not only help increase your knowledge, your experience, and your network of contacts but also will help you get in touch with other purpose-oriented professionals who can contribute positively to your projects, whether as entrepreneurs, innovators, leaders, mentors, or even investors.

Below, I'd like to briefly share these different programs, and I urge you to visit the Purpose Alliance Academy website for more information.

- **Purpose Launchpad Essentials** is a certification program aimed at anyone who wants to learn more about the fundamentals of Purpose Launchpad.

- **Purpose Launchpad Practitioner** is a certification program aimed at entrepreneurs who are working on their own startup and innovators who are possibly working on a project within an organization. The program offers in-depth knowledge about Purpose Launchpad and, above all, practical experience by way of a certified mentor to provide customized help for entrepreneurs and innovators to evolve their projects.

- **Purpose Launchpad Mentor** is a certification program aimed at experienced consultants and innovation leaders who help startups, other organizations, or their own organization with their continuous evolution. The program offers in-depth knowledge about Purpose Launchpad and, above all, an intense experience in project mentoring.

- **Purpose Launchpad Investor** is a certification program aimed at investors looking for purposeful projects to generate financial benefits while improving the world. The program focuses on how to leverage Purpose Launchpad to minimize investment risks and maximize positive impact.

- **Positive Impact Leader** is a program aimed at organization leaders trying to improve and evolve their business by changing their team's culture and through disruptive innovation. The program focuses on how to leverage Purpose Launchpad to create the right environment and bring the necessary rigor to organizations to translate purpose into positive impact within their business and the world.

If you are interested in any of these programs, I suggest you visit the Purpose Alliance Academy webpage, where you can learn much more about them:

www.purposealliance.org/academy

The Purpose Manifesto

As I explained in the chapter "Implement the Right Processes," a group of software development experts met in Utah in 2001 to create the *Agile Manifesto*. Their goal was to send an important message to the world to help develop software projects properly. Similarly, on March 18, 2022, a group of purpose-oriented people came together in Granada (Spain) to create the *Purpose Manifesto*. Our goal was to send an important message to the world to help individuals and organizations launch the right initiatives. The result was a document that includes a series of five principles and five values.

The *Purpose Manifesto* has a very broad scope of application, since it can be applied not only to startup-type undertakings or to established organizations but to any type of actions at a political level or to any daily action at a personal level. It provides a common framework for presenting different organizations and even new frameworks, as in the case of Purpose Launchpad, which takes the values and principles of the manifesto as a starting point for adapting its own values and principles to the framework's scope of action.

I recommend that you read it and think about how you can integrate or adapt some of its principles and values to your different initiatives. And, of course, I encourage you to sign the *Purpose Manifesto* if you feel it is aligned with you! You can find more information and download it in different languages at www.purposemanifesto.org.

Below is the text of the *Purpose Manifesto:*

Our purpose is inspiring everyday actions to make the world a better place.

We believe...

- *Everyone can make a positive impact.*
- *Purpose provides meaning to people and to organizations.*
- *Purpose-driven people and organizations who take action can transform the world for the better.*
- *All projects should be economically, socially, and environmentally sustainable.*
- *Profitability is compatible with positive impact in the world.*
- *Technology empowers purpose to scale positive impact.*

We value...

- *Purpose over problems and solutions.*
- *Lasting positive impact over short-term focus.*
- *Collaboration over competition.*
- *Collective & personal wellbeing over self-interest.*
- *Actions over intentions.*

We follow these principles in order to achieve what we value:

- *We promote a purpose-oriented mindset to create positive impact in the world.*
- *We imagine a better world, and we solve the challenges to achieve it.*
- *We measure, incentivize, and verify to ensure lasting positive impact on people and the planet.*
- *We increase profitability by maximizing positive, lasting impact.*

- *We can increase the total wealth of the ecosystem through reciprocity.*
- *We adopt and promote an abundance mindset.*
- *We increase access to new and existing opportunities by embracing technology.*
- *We take purpose-driven decisions while being conscious that we are accountable to the global ecosystem.*
- *We execute concrete actions to improve our environment.*
- *We foster and encourage others to act to improve the world.*

Lastly, below, we describe with greater detail the values and their principles in order to make everything more understandable.

Value 1: Purpose over problems and solutions.

- *To achieve purpose-driven goals, many problems need to be solved by implementing one or more solutions. If you can imagine it, you can do it.*
- *We promote a purpose-oriented mindset to create positive impact in the world.*
- *A purpose-driven mindset means becoming aware of and aligning our actions with the motive that inspires us to act. This invites us to identify problems and formulate potential solutions that generate a positive impact.*
- *We imagine a better world, and we solve the challenges to achieve it.*
- *Starting with what we want to achieve enables us to identify and understand the challenges that need to be solved along the way. We look for different solutions, and we embrace change to progress.*

Value 2: Lasting positive impact over short-term focus.

- *Short-term focus has become endemic in business, politics, and leadership. We value ensuring both immediate and lasting positive impact.*
- *We measure, incentivize, and verify to ensure lasting positive impact on people and the planet.*
- *The intent of positive impact needs to be accompanied by key metrics that measure and certify the impact on people and the planet. New forms of incentivization are required to drive a change in behavior towards delivering lasting positive impact.*
- *We increase profitability by maximizing lasting positive impact.*
- *The path to profitable and sustainable initiatives and organizations is through focusing on delivering lasting positive impact on people and the planet.*

Value 3: Collaboration over competition.

- *Competition leads to innovation; collaboration generates impact.*
- *We can increase the total wealth of the ecosystem through reciprocity.*
- *In this environment, all different stakeholders will generate actions and initiatives with a greater positive impact to achieve sustainability in social, environmental, and economic domains.*
- *We adopt and promote an abundance mindset.*
- *A mindset focused on detecting infinite opportunities—in other words, an abundance mindset—will give people and organizations freedom to collaborate.*

Value 4: Collective & personal wellbeing over self-interest.

- *We recognize that all life forms are interdependent. We recognize that contributing to the wellbeing beyond ourselves creates equilibrium.*

- *We increase access to new and existing opportunities by embracing technology.*
- *We use technology for connecting people and organizations to maximize positive impact and to unleash the potential of all human beings.*
- *We take purpose-driven decisions while being conscious that we are accountable to the global ecosystem.*
- *We hold ourselves accountable, and we act responsibly for the decisions we take today and their long-term consequences. After all, the future is in our hands.*

Value 5: Actions over intentions.
- *Go beyond a declaration of intentions. Make the decision to act and to mobilize to generate positive change.*
- *We execute concrete actions to improve our environment.*
- *Any positive action is valid, and every moment is a good one to implement it. It is time to take action. Let's activate change by example.*
- *We foster and encourage others to act to improve the world.*
- *All individuals, with our actions, can foster change in others.*

Tester for Purpose-Oriented Organizations

Throughout the book, we've seen the importance of startups and organizations being purpose oriented in order to create positive impact. However, we frequently see companies that try to position themselves as sustainable or impact oriented but which really aren't. We call this impact washing.

To help you identify this type of company—and even to help you on your own path towards evolving your organization to take it to the next level—I'd like to share a testing system for purpose-oriented organizations. It is essentially a chart that poses a series of questions about the organization you are analyzing and that helps you determine its true situation.

Figure X.2. Tester for Purpose-Driven Organizations

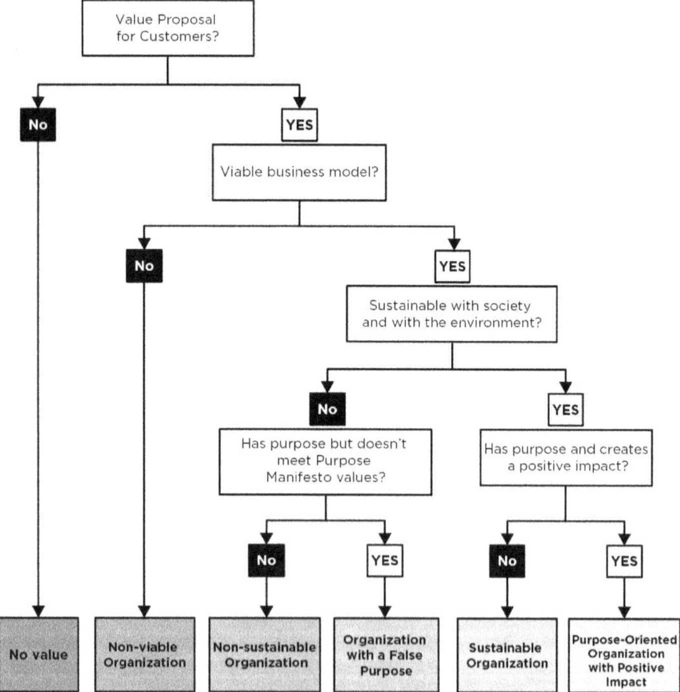

Source: prepared by the author

The chart is based on the Impact Pyramid, since it checks whether we meet the criteria of the lower layers until we reach purpose and positive impact. As you will recall, we can only consider ourselves a purpose-oriented organization that generates positive impact if we do so sustainably at an economic, social, and environmental level, for which we must have a viable business model based on the value we provide to our customers.

I encourage you to also use this chart as a guide when developing your own initiatives so that, even if initially you don't meet all the requirements to be a purpose-oriented organization with positive impact, you can set the foundation to do so in the near future.

Summary of Tools Integrated into Purpose Launchpad

Below is a list of various resources presented in this book. You'll find a more complete and updated list in the official Purpose Launchpad guide. Feel free to use other tools you know of, and remember that it's your mindset over tools.

FOR YOU	
Tool	**Link**
"Discover Your Personal Purpose" Program	
MTP Canvas	

FOR STARTUPS AND NEW PRODUCTS		
Tool	**Axis**	**Link**
Purpose Launchpad Guide	General	
Purpose Launchpad Canvas	General	
Purpose Launchpad Assessment	General	
MTP Canvas	Purpose	

Organization Identity Canvas	Purpose	
BOSI Test	People	
Community Canvas	People	
Team Canvas	People	
Value Proposition Canvas	Customers	
Business Model Canvas	Sustainability	
Sustainable Model Canvas	Sustainability	
ExO Canvas	Abundance	
Agile Manifesto	Processes	

BPMN Template	Processes	
Product/Market Fit Canvas	Product	
Lean Canvas	Product	
Impact Accounting Canvas	Metrics	

FOR ESTABLISHED ORGANIZATIONS		
Tool	**Application**	**Link**
Purpose Launchpad Guide	General	
Purpose Launchpad Canvas	General	
Purpose Launchpad Assessment	General	
MTP Canvas	Purpose Definition	

Purpose Discovery Application	Purpose Discovery	
"Definition of Massive Transformative Purpose (MTP) for TotalEnergies" Impact Case	Purpose Definition	
Keynotes	Culture Alignment	
Purpose Launchpad Workshop Application	Culture Alignment	
"Inspiring Siemens to Transform the Organization and the World" Impact Case	Culture Alignment	
Purpose Challenge Application	Generating Community	
"The Future of Health in Costa Rica" Impact Case	Generating Community	
Purpose Launchpad Habitat Canvas	Habitat for Initiatives	
"The Evolution of Cuerva from a Traditional Company to an Ecosystem Managed with Purpose Launchpad" Impact Case	Habitat for Initiatives	

Impact Sprint Application	Organization Evolution	
"Creating the Future of MVS" Impact Case	Organization Evolution	

Summary of Related Reading for Purpose Launchpad

Just as Purpose Launchpad suggests incorporating different innovation tools and techniques, it also suggests reading or consulting the following books:

Title	Authors	Area
Massive Transformative Purpose	Angel M. Herrera and Francisco Palao	Defining one's personal purpose and an organization's purpose
Entrepreneurial DNA	Joe Abraham	The entrepreneurial personality
Get Together	Kevin Huynh and Kai Elmer Sotto	Community management
The Art of Community	Charles Vogl	Community management
The Four Steps to the Epiphany	Steve Blank	Customer Development
The Startup Owner's Manual	Steve Blank and Bob Dorf	Customer Development
Business Model Generation	Alex Osterwalder	Business Model Canvas
Value Proposition Design	Alex Osterwalder	The customer
The Lean Startup	Eric Ries	Lean Startups
Blue Ocean Strategy	Chan Kim and Renée Mauborgne	Strategy
Lead and Disrupt	Charles A. O'Reilly and Michael L. Tushman	Strategy
The Innovator's Dilemma	Clayton M. Christensen	Strategy
Crossing the Chasm	Geoffrey Moore	Strategy

The Fourth Industrial Revolution	Klaus Schwab	Tech disruption
Abundance	Peter Diamandis	Abundance
Exponential Organizations	Salim Ismail, Yuri Van Geest, and Michael S. Malone	Exponential organizations
Exponential Transformation	Francisco Palao, Salim Ismail, and Michelle Lapierre	ExO Sprint
The Triple Bottom Line	John Elkington	Sustainability

Official Contributors

This book was written with input and support from the following group of extraordinary purpose-oriented people (entrepreneurs, innovators, investors, mentors, etc.):

- Andrea Llong (Peru)
- Asier Basterretxea Gómez (Spain)
- Beatriz Romanos Hernando (Spain)
- Carlos Prieto Carrasco (Spain)
- César Viera D. (Ecuador)
- Chakradhar Iyyunni (India)
- Clarence Tan (Australia)
- Corina Almagro (Spain)
- Cris Madureira (Brazil)
- Eduardo Labarca (Chile)
- Edwin Moreno (Mexico)
- Felipe Valdebenito Sandoval (Chile)
- Fernando de los Ríos (Peru)
- Hebert Pinto (Peru)
- José Marcelo Tam Málaga (Peru)
- Lionel Carrillo Chávez (Peru)
- Luis Alberto Marriott Chávez (Peru)
- Manel Fernández Jaria (Spain)
- Meryl Moritz (United States)
- Michael Friebe (Germany)
- Michael Rivers (United Kingdom)
- Miguel Ángel Rojas (Spain)
- Nancy Stortoni (Argentina)
- Oliver Morbach (Germany)
- Pablo Rodríguez Duarte (Mexico)
- Paco Briseño (Mexico)
- Paola Hurtado (Spain)
- Sanjay Ramanlal Gopal Bhana (South Africa)
- Simon Nopp (Austria)
- Soledad Llorente (Spain)
- Vittorio Sommella (Italy)

Acknowledgments

Many pieces of the universe, to whom I feel enormous gratitude, contributed to bringing this book to the light.

My thanks to my wife, Andrea, for her continuous and unconditional support during the writing of this book and in everything that has had to happen so it could come to light. Because of her, I believe more than ever that the woman (or man) accompanying you during your life must share the same values as you and have a purpose compatible with yours. You, Andrea, have shown me that compatibility using the most powerful force in the universe: love.

To my daughters Mar and Luna, because you fill each day with inspiration, joy, energy, and love, all things necessary for creating a better future. Mar, Luna, you deserve a better world, and I hope this book helps bring that about. In fact, with your very existence, you two are already creating positive impact in this world, and every day, through your actions, the impact will grow. I am fortunate to be your daddy.

To Francisco, my father, who instilled important values in me by example, like love of nature, the importance of sports, and responsibility and integrity. Without these key elements in my life, I would not have achieved as much as I have.

To my mother Emilia, who taught by example the importance of treating everyone kindly and being affectionate and generous. No matter how hard I try, I will never be as good as her.

To my brother Jorge, who has always reminded me of what is truly important, who has contributed to many of my projects, who has been patient and waited for me when I've been gone, and who has always been there whenever I needed anything.

To my sister-in-law, Carmen, who always brings joy to all family gatherings and has supported me whenever I needed it.

I thank my mother-in-law Leo and my sister-in-law Jessy for the support they have given Andrea and me during all the months it took to write this book.

To all my family—uncles, aunts, and cousins—for, although we live far from one another, I always think of you and know that you are always with me.

To my ancestors, who made it possible for me to enjoy today the goodness in this world—specifically my grandparents; from each of them I inherited something that has made me who I am. My grandmother Emilia passed down her joy and youthful spirit and my grandfather Amadeo his kindness and perseverance, my grandmother Carmen helped me believe in what we do, and my grandfather Juan gave me the entrepreneurial genes and attitude.

To all my good friends who have always been at my side, starting with Quesada, my first friend, and followed by José Carlos, my first best friend; Alfredo, who introduced me to technology and music; Toquero, my companion in countless adventures; Fernando, a great, authentic being; Adam, for his unconditional friendship and huge help preparing my application to Singularity University; Mari and Cori, the first girls to be my best friends; Sole, my "big sister"; Noel, my first and best friend in college (and beyond); Nachito, Paco, Adolfo, Sotillo, and Javi, my favorite freaks; and José Antonio, for his unconditional support and for always reminding me of fundamental values and that helping the people closest to you is a great purpose.

To Francisco Poyatos, a great artist and a great person, who has a special gift for interpreting the essence of what I want to say and illustrate it, who has not only accompanied me for this book but also many other projects in which I've been fortunate to have him by my side.

To Josep López, who has accompanied me along this book's writing process to make reading it much more enjoyable, friendly, and professional while continuously adapting to all my needs.

To Luke Palder and Denise Cikota for making magic with the great translation of the book into English in such a short period of time.

To all the extraordinary people who have made the Purpose Alliance community possible, especially Vittorio Sommella and Paco Briseño, who have been there with Andrea and me since the beginning as we built it. And to all the Purpose Launchpad mentors in general who have provided their opinions and experience to continuously improve everything we do, as well as to all the official framework contributors.

To all the good people who have supported me, inspired me, and boosted me during my forty years of life, starting very affectionately with Luis Castillo, who guided my dissertation and has always been an inspiration in my life; Juan Fernández, who also guided my dissertation and has always been supportive whenever I've needed it; Angel María Herrera, Andrés de Miguel, Concha del Amo, Loren Barranco, Mayte Puertas, Raúl Raya, Rafa Ruiz, Tomás Garzón, Oscar García, Eva Hidalgo, Manuel Vilar, Raúl Felip, Ignacio Cuerva, Luis Sánchez, David Montañés, Alfredo Rivela, Rafa Iborra, Álvaro Blanco, Luis Rey, Pablo Pérez, Jesús Candón, Tristan Kromer, Guayente Sanmartín, Jesús Chamorro, Michael Álvarez, Ginés Haro, and many more.

To my dogs Clarita and Manchita and my cats Sol and Tito, for bringing joy to innumerable moments of our days and constantly reminding me of the importance of all forms of life in this world.

To Paco de Lucía, for having composed and played so much of the music that has kept me company and inspired me as I wrote most of these pages.

In some way, you are all authors of this book, because you have been and continue to be essential people in my life. In your honor, and especially for those people I've mentioned who are no longer with us, I promise to continue to contribute to the creation of positive impact in the world so that your legacy will last forever.